In the Moment of Greatest
CALAMITY

In the Moment of Greatest

CALAMITY

TERRORISM, GRIEF, AND A VICTIM'S QUEST FOR JUSTICE

Susan F. Hirsch

PRINCETON UNIVERSITY PRESS

PRINCETON AND OXFORD

Requests for permission to reproduce material from this work should be sent
to Permissions, Princeton University Press

Published by Princeton University Press, 41 William Street,
Princeton, New Jersey 08540
In the United Kingdom: Princeton University Press, 3 Market Place,
Woodstock, Oxfordshire OX20 1SY
All Rights Reserved

Library of Congress Cataloging-in-Publication Data

Hirsch, Susan F.
In the moment of greatest calamity : terrorism, grief,
and a victim's quest for justice / Susan F. Hirsch.
p.   cm.
Includes bibliographical references and index.
ISBN-13: 978-0-691-12136-9 (alk. paper)
ISBN-10: 0-691-12136-2
1. Hirsch, Susan F. 2. Abdalla, Abdurahman Mohamed. 3. Victims of terrorism—
Africa, East—Biography. 4. Americans—Africa, East—Biography. 5. United States
Embassy Bombing, Dar es Salaam, Tanzania, 1998. 6. Trials (Terrorism)—
New York (State)—New York. I. Title.
HV6430.H46A3   2007
967.8'232042—dc22   2005037885

British Library Cataloging-in-Publication Data is available

This book has been composed in Palatino and Weidemann

Printed on acid-free paper. ∞

pup.princeton.edu

Printed in the United States of America

10 9 8 7 6 5 4 3 2 1

Portions of chapter 6 were published previously in the *Boston Review*.

DEDICATED TO THE MEMORY OF

My Beloved Husband
"Jamal" Abdurahman Mohamed Abdalla

Our Wise Fathers
Arnold Wayne Hirsch
Mohamed Abdurahman Mohamed Abdalla

And all those who lost their lives, their loves, and their dreams in the embassy bombings in Nairobi, Kenya, and Dar es Salaam, Tanzania

Contents

Preface

IN THIS BOOK I reflect on the 1998 East African embassy bombings and the prosecution several years later of four men accused of the bombings and related crimes. I write as an American survivor and the widow of an African victim. I write also from the perspective of a cultural anthropologist with years of experience conducting research and teaching in East Africa in predominantly Muslim communities. My perspective also bears the influence of my academic interest in legal systems, especially in the role of law as a reaction to violence. From an admittedly idiosyncratic position, the book describes my attempts to come to terms with a massive personal and public tragedy that demanded responses from me, from other victims, and from the governments of the societies affected. Above all, I wrote this book to convey my perspective as a victim who turned to law for a response to terrorism and found it as flawed as it was indispensable.

Writing about terrorism and its impact after having experienced its effects and while still living in fear of future attacks was challenging. Yet the implications of writing "as a victim" should not be assumed. When friends, colleagues, and strangers asked whether writing this book was "therapeutic" for me, I usually answered that other activities contributed more directly to my recovery from trauma and grief, namely, conventional counseling and time spent with trusted friends and family. This book does not chart the process and progress of my healing. That would have been a worthwhile (though daunting) project, and I admire brave scholars who have authored such works.

Other victims of the embassy bombings no doubt hold different impressions of the events I describe, and the text includes some of their perspectives. Representing a fuller range of victims' views, although the preferred approach in anthropology, would have required interviews with people still suffering from trauma, and as a trauma victim myself, I lacked the emotional stamina and training to accomplish such research. I especially regret my inability to tell the stories of those victims from Africa who felt that their interests were not well represented through the embassy bombings trial held in New York City in 2001. Thousands of East African victims were unable to attend the trial because of the distance and expense. Differences of "race," class, education, gender, age, political beliefs, employment status, and nationality also meant that many victims participated less fully than others.

Victims' perspectives on the bombings and the trial are shaped by the unique burdens we each carry, both consciously and unconsciously, as victims of violence. Among those burdens are fear, survivor guilt, the quest for justice, the desire for revenge, and the need to remember. Moreover, the burdens that haunt or motivate victims shift over time and through our participation in memorial events, legal proceedings, and therapeutic encounters. Two burdens I carried to the trial—the sense of responsibility for seeking justice for my deceased husband, myself, our families and communities after the bombings, and my lifelong commitment to fairness in the American judicial system—motivated my approach to the proceedings, particularly my attention to the death penalty, the experiences of victims, and the complexity of justice. The tendency in contemporary anthropology to focus on the power of governments and their institutions also influenced my approach. Another aspect of anthropology—the discipline's foundational concern with perceiving the world from the perspective of those whose lives may differ from one's own—also influenced my writing but at times has felt like a heavy burden. For instance, how could I push myself to "understand" why the men on trial, and others accused, would harm me and my husband? Because anthropologists pursue such questions, and sometimes situate our answers in the worldviews of others, we are accused by some of being "cultural relativists" in the negative sense of having no moral stance ourselves. In my view, the crucial task of explanation requires me to reach across differences yet in no way precludes me from judging the defendants and condemning their actions.

Inspired by anthropology's commitment to the pursuit of knowledge across differences, I conclude that justice sought through law must be combined with a parallel quest for deeper analyses of terrorist violence and its causes. Since the embassy bombings, the attacks of 9/11, and repeated instances of extremist violence around the world, we all have a stake in understanding the threat posed by terrorism, countering its destructive force, seeking justice for its victims, and building societies where such threats no longer arise. My hope is that this book will contribute to ongoing efforts to respond effectively to terrorism while upholding ideals of justice.

In the Moment of Greatest
CALAMITY

Figure 1. Map of East Africa. Credit: Tad Slawecki

INTRODUCTION

ON AUGUST 7, 1998, two truck bombs exploded almost simultaneously at U.S. embassies in Nairobi, Kenya, and Dar es Salaam, Tanzania. The blast in Dar threw me to the floor, scattering a wad of money the embassy's cashier had just handed me. I managed to stand and, with plaster and dust raining down, escaped out a nearby exit. Ignoring warnings to seek cover, I ran toward the embassy's main entrance. I was desperate to find my husband, Abdurahman Abdalla, who had been standing outside, waiting for me while I cashed a check. In one direction barbed wire blocked my path to him, in another crowds surged between us. A third route was a gauntlet of burning cars. Hysterical in my efforts to reach him, I eventually allowed a Tanzanian doctor to take me to a hospital where he insisted I would find my husband being treated for injuries and could receive care for my own abrasions and shock. After a day-long search of Dar's hospitals, I found my husband. He had been standing just yards from the truck bomb when it detonated. He was killed, along with eleven others nearby.

The embassy bombings in Kenya and Tanzania shattered the peace in East Africa. Together the blasts killed more than two hundred people and injured thousands. Most of the casualties were Kenyans, like my husband, and a few dozen shared his Muslim faith. Among the dead were twelve Americans, all U.S. government employees. Seen in hindsight, the bombings were early indications of al Qaeda's commitment to attack U.S. interests and forecast a new moment in American awareness of the threat of terrorism. Although only a few people realized it at the time, the embassy bombings were a wake-up call to the United States and to the world about the operations and goals of a new sort of enemy, and the distinctive and deadly tactics it would deploy in a long-planned war.

In the immediate aftermath of the embassy bombings, family and friends on two continents helped me to face the shock, grief, anger, confusion, and guilt that envelop and torment victims of violence. As the acute trauma abated, the urgency of questions grew about who had carried out these horrific acts and how. I found myself increasingly preoccupied by another question: Why? Why had the embassies been attacked? I began a quest to answer this and other related "why" questions, for myself, my husband, our families, and everyone else affected.

My search for an explanation was far outpaced by officials on several continents, who pursued the perpetrators and collected evidence of their crimes with the primary goal of bringing to justice those responsible for the bombings. The United States launched the largest criminal investigation ever undertaken abroad, and within months more than twenty men were indicted and several apprehended. Because the bombings targeted American citizens and embassies, which are considered U.S. federal property, four of those in custody faced trial in a federal court in Manhattan. The embassy bombings trial—held in the first six months of 2001—was an extraordinary public forum, where the U.S. government assumed the multiple responsibilities of acknowledging victims' losses and communicating to an inattentive public the threat posed by al Qaeda, as well as establishing the guilt or innocence of the four men on trial.

The U.S. legal system decisively shaped my quest to explain the bombings, as the trial drew me in with the promise of answers. Much of this book focuses on what I learned about the embassy bombings, and terrorism more generally, by participating in the embassy bombings trial and attempting to make sense of it as an anthropologist and a victim. Yet the book also focuses on what the trial failed to explain. As a response to the bombings, law ultimately left me unsatisfied, wanting—with even more intensity—an explanation, an answer to my question of why.

My husband and I met in the mid-1980s, when I arrived in Malindi, his coastal Kenyan town, to undertake a year-long study of contemporary Islamic law courts for my doctoral dissertation. His nickname was Jamal, which means beauty. His father, a respected elder in the Swahili Muslim community, was a key informant for my project, and his extended family welcomed me into their homes and lives. It was the anthropologist's ideal of intensive research, what we call "participant/observation." My relationship with Jamal developed over the next decade, as I worked toward my degree and Jamal built a small family business and gained stature as a community leader. With Jamal's assistance, my writing about life and law in Malindi highlighted the richness of Swahili culture, with its dual origins in Africa and the Middle East, and the uniqueness of coastal East African Islam, with its emphasis on piety, moderation, and pluralism. When my book was published a few weeks before the bombings, we celebrated its portrayal of Kenyan Muslims, which countered common misconceptions of Islam as hostile to the West, or inherently fundamentalist or sexist.

Ours was an unlikely but successful love, partnership, and understanding across continents, "races," religions, cultures, languages, and ways of life. Just two weeks before his death, Jamal and I had stopped in the U.S. Embassy in Dar es Salaam to pick up his immigrant visa for his first trip to the United States. After years of negotiating distance, we planned a fresh start together.

The embassy bombings destroyed our plans.

Just hours after the explosions, the unquestionable power of law to define the event became evident to me when Dar es Salaam's main hospital refused to release the victims' bodies, citing instructions from "American officials." We were caught between two legal systems: American criminal law, which required a thorough investigation, and the Islamic rules that mandate burial before sunset on the day of death. Waiting increased my anxiety, and Jamal's family in Kenya was understandably, though frantically, insistent to have him returned to Malindi for a proper burial as soon as possible.

Over the next two days my telephone rang constantly, and, pacing my apartment at the University of Dar es Salaam, I fielded dozens of sympathy calls and visits in a haze of shock and grief. Jamal's family called every couple of hours to check on the status of our return. As I negotiated logistical snafus with the numb efficiency that can be an aftereffect of trauma, CNN

International blared nonstop for the many friends and colleagues who came to pay respects. Over and over Osama bin Laden's picture appeared with statements explaining nothing: "A Saudi businessman linked to terrorism, he is suspected of involvement in the East African embassy bombings." Tanzanian friends, some Muslim, were confused. None of us had ever heard of bin Laden or al Qaeda. "If he did it," one asked, "why don't we know anything about him?" Another remarked, "He looks like an old man. How could he have done something like this?" "They say he did this all the way from Afghanistan. Where is that? It's not even in Africa."

Three days after the bombings, it seemed we would never leave for Kenya, and the growing tension brought on bouts of hysteria. In a rage born of frustration and grief, I called the official in charge at the U.S. Embassy, Deputy Ambassador John Lange, and demanded the release of Jamal's body. Taking on my anthropologist's role as an interpreter across cultures, I explained that Jamal's family was Muslim, which meant that an immediate burial was imperative. Ambassador Lange apologized for the delay. He said he had just gotten off the phone with President Bill Clinton, who had asked him to do two things. First, the president wanted his sympathies conveyed to the victims; and, second, he urged Lange to take every possible measure to preserve evidence from the crime scene. Hearing this, I resigned myself to wait until the autopsies were completed. Five days after the bombing, Jamal's body was released, and we left for Kenya where he would be buried and I would begin the long process of pulling together my shattered self.

Less than two weeks after the bombings, President Clinton ordered missile strikes on targets in Khartoum, Sudan, and Khost, Afghanistan. The strikes leveled both a Sudanese pharmaceutical plant alleged to be manufacturing chemical weapons and a military camp in Afghanistan where Osama bin Laden and his top military advisers were believed to be meeting. Although the U.S. government never released a report on the strikes (codenamed "Infinite Reach") at least two dozen al Qaeda personnel were presumed killed in Afghanistan (but not the intended high-ranking targets), and a Sudanese security guard died in Khartoum. The simultaneous timing of the strikes conveyed to the world, and especially to enemies, that within a matter of days the U.S. could mount an attack even more strategically complex than the dual embassy bombings.

At the same time as they demonstrated U.S. military prowess, the missile strikes pronounced a quick verdict on the question of who bore responsibility for the bombings: the mastermind was Osama bin Laden, a Saudi national who had once lived in Sudan, and they were carried out by his operatives, many of whom, having fought—with U.S. support—against the Soviets in Afghanistan, were still training there. Yet the clarity of the missile strikes as verdict and punishment blurred almost on impact. Cynics, especially political watchers in the United States, charged that the offensive was a version of "Wag the Dog" foreign policy designed to direct attention away from Clinton's scandalous involvement with a White House intern.[1] Even fairer-minded critics wondered about the wisdom of almost instantaneous retaliation with little evidence presented and no apparent military follow-up.[2] Responding to the flurry of criticism from friends and foes, U.S. officials justified the missile attacks as "self-defense" permitted by Article 51 of the U.N. Charter. As Secretary of State Madeleine Albright proclaimed, "When the United States is attacked, when our people are taken out, we will stand out unilaterally in self-defense and really let the world know what we believe in."[3]

So soon after the bombings, I had a hard time finding the words to express my opposition to the missile strikes. My gut feeling was that more violence could not possibly be productive. The missiles risked killing people uninvolved in terrorism, and, in my state of grief, I regretted the sorrow that would result from more deaths. I was also concerned that the U.S. government's swift resort to a display of force risked furthering the resolve of those determined to commit violence, and I felt scared for myself and for Jamal's family in East Africa. When some U.S. officials depicted the strikes as a justifiable means to avenge the suffering of "innocent victims,"[4] I became angry. Abhorrent to me was the reality that I, as a U.S. citizen, as well a victim of the bombings myself, would be forced to bear responsibility for the missiles' destruction.

As the controversy intensified, I grew increasingly skeptical of the U.S. government's quick attribution of responsibility. In my mind, determining who had accomplished these horrific acts would require some effort and take a long time, indeed *should* take a long time. I had the crushing feeling that if the U.S. government knew exactly who had harmed us, precisely where they lived, even their tactics and methods so certainly and so soon after the bombings, then it might have known enough to prevent them. In the swarm of my tangled thoughts and fears, a strong suspicion kept emerging: my own government might be guilty of failing to protect us.

The belief that the American government bore some responsibility for the destruction was a persistent, biting charge, especially in Kenya, where people expressed anger at the United States for, as they saw it, the embassy's vulnerable location in the busiest part of town and the U.S. government's rumored failure to heed warnings of an attack. Citing American callousness and racism, they also criticized the restrictions that U.S. personnel, particularly the Marines guarding the embassy, had placed on Kenyans who had tried to help after the bombings. An even harsher criticism charged that preserving documents—rather than people—was of primary concern to those who secured the embassy. Americans attached to the embassies in Nairobi and Dar es Salaam—many of whom had been injured in the attacks—were stunned by the acrimonious charges hurled at them and their government, and by what they believed were distortions that put the United States in the worst possible light. Such criticism led an American State Department employee, taxed beyond her ability to remain diplomatic, to insist hysterically, "How can they blame us? We wouldn't bomb our own people. *We* are hurt. *We* are the victims." But the image of America as a victim—so keenly felt by Americans staggered by the attack—was harder, or impossible, for others, also suffering, to accept. When a victim is powerful—in this case, the most powerful nation in the world—its very power can attract blame as much as sympathy after an attack. The other side of that truism is that the powerful endeavor to avoid blame, and, by virtue of their power, are well positioned to do so. Five months after the bombings, a specially convened Accountability Review Board issued a report dismissing charges of callousness and racism in the rescue effort as based on rumors, and, most important, exonerated U.S. officials from any specific wrongdoing in relation to the bombing.

Some victims persisted in raising the broadest questions, including, "Why have the enemies of your nation caused such destruction in ours?" Such questions risked rejection for reflecting the rage or irrationality of grief, but in my view the East Africans who asked them were sobered, not rendered irrational, by the bombings. They voiced a critique that centered on their own inextricable connection to a world power pursued by enemies that make diplomatic relations with the United States a dangerous business.

Blame's excess, deflected by the powerful, sadly can end up haunting the least powerful, who assume it. For victims who survived, the tendency to blame themselves was an overwhelming imperative, yet a trap to resist. In those early weeks after the bombing I realized that continuing to survive required a concerted, monumental effort to fight the irrational impetus to accept personal responsibility for the deaths of others, including Jamal. My mind played "what if" games: what if we had not stopped at the embassy? What if I hadn't visited the embassy ladies' room? What if I had insisted Jamal come inside with me? Such questions led nowhere; mercifully others convinced me that victims can get stuck in a maze of self-blame, and I tried hard to redirect my thinking.

The growing emphasis on a criminal justice approach to the bombings was, for some of us, a welcome alternative to accusations left unanswered by those in power and to our own self-blaming tendencies. I put my trust in the promise of an intensive investigation that would expose not only those responsible for detonating the bombs but also their reasons for doing so.

It is hard to convey what it was like to be an al-Qaeda victim in a pre-9/11 atmosphere. Not only was Osama bin Laden a name few people in America or East Africa recognized, but, when I returned to the United States several weeks after the bombings, the central tragedy in my life was simply not on the public radar. Almost no one appreciated what it meant to be a victim of terrorism. My desire to be counted as a deserving victim, and the sense that East Africans faced difficulties making their claims as victims, motivated me to become involved in the embassy bombings trial that began in January 2001. I believed that attending the trial might satisfy my quest for recognition of my suffering and loss, and would allow me to represent Jamal, his family, and the East Africans who had largely been forgotten despite their continued suffering. I was also looking for an explanation of what had happened, who had done it, and why. Until then, investigators and prosecutors had operated in relative secrecy, providing only partial accounts. Media reports were incomplete and sometimes ill-informed. The trial seemed my best option for obtaining answers. At the same time I sought a definitive response to the bombings from the U.S. government. When prosecutors and others asserted that the trial would bring justice, for me that meant paying tribute to victims' suffering, explaining the crime, and punishing those responsible. The government's promise that justice would be done was powerfully alluring, especially since the crime had received so little public attention.

Participating in the six-month-long case forced me to think hard about law's utility as a response to acts of terrorist violence and, relatedly, what sort of justice terror trials provide. I found, for instance, that a terror trial held in open court can be invaluable to victims of terror, simply by providing attention to the tragic event. Sitting together in court, we victims gained recognition for our suffering, as prosecutors exposed the threat of terrorism to the United States and the world. For the first time the trial presented a detailed and plausible account of how the embassy bombings were planned and executed. The public—both domestic and international—also benefited from the information openly disseminated through the trial.

The prosecutors' skill played a substantial role both in addressing the victims' desire to know more about the crime and in the trial's ultimate success. The federal prosecutors office in

New York's Southern District had previously dealt with terror cases, including the 1993 bombing of the World Trade Center (WTC). In a book about that trial, *Defending Mohammad*, Robert Precht confirms the expertise of the Southern District office on matters of terrorism. However, writing from the perspective of a defense attorney involved in the case, Precht raises important concerns about the prosecution's handling of terror suspects. He questions whether any of the defendants who were convicted of the 1993 WTC attack were treated fairly given the tremendous power of the prosecutors' office and the sense of threat to the United States that motivated its vigorous prosecution.

In the embassy bombings trial the government's power came down full force on the four defendants and, for me, raised similar questions about legal fairness. As a victim, the last thing I wanted was to observe a long trial only to find that distortions, lies, or railroading of the defendants or witnesses would invalidate the verdict, either officially or in my own mind. The trial had to be fair for me to be able to accept the findings as an accurate account of what happened. A hasty verdict of guilt was of less interest to me than a fair proceeding that would get to the bottom of the incident. To be called "justice," the verdict and punishment would have to emerge through fair procedures.

The 1993 WTC case and the embassy bombings case differed in one way that I came to believe had the most profound effect on whether the outcome of the latter could be called just: two of the four defendants in the embassy bombings trial faced the death penalty.[5] The prosecutors' pursuit of the death penalty and the defendants' attempts to avoid it, shaped the whole legal process: from the selection of the jury, to the use of victims' stories to sway jurors' emotions, to instances of desperate and disreputable courtroom tactics by lawyers on all sides. It also lengthened the legal process, not an insignificant point, especially for victims, and made it unlikely that any defendant would testify on his own behalf. I had gone into the trial thinking that, if the defendants were found guilty, then harsh punishment would be a just response. Yet the death penalty was unacceptable to me, a position I have held all my life. One reason is that the death penalty, as a form of state killing, is the supreme exercise of a government's power on an individual. If trials are prone to abuses of government power, and terror trials all the more because of the government's role as a "victim" of the attack, then wielding death as a possible outcome risks twisting justice beyond recognition.

The government's pursuit of the death penalty made participating in the embassy bombings trial especially difficult for those of us opposed to capital punishment. Had the trial not been a U.S. capital case, my experience would have been quite different and, as I came to believe, the public would have been better served in its need to learn what happened and to begin to acknowledge the reasons why. My experience at the trial has not led me to turn away from the law as a response to terrorism. Rather, it has encouraged me to ask whether a U.S. terror trial can satisfy all that a victim's quest for justice demands. For me, that quest must follow fair procedures and yield as full an accounting of the crime as possible. Because the political, religious, and cultural roots and repercussions of the bombings were never explored, the trial fell short of meeting my need for justice. This disappointment pushed me toward new understandings of justice and sparked my desire for something beyond the version of justice promised by law.

My experience of turning to the legal system, and letting it guide my response to the bombings, suggests that it can be a mistake for victims to let law, particularly an American capital prosecution, be the only means of making sense of a violent tragedy. Especially after 9/11, asking broader questions about terrorism is a necessary supplement to the pursuit of justice through law. I advocate pursuing justice through the legal process and also alongside it. That parallel effort may provide answers to the question of why the embassy bombings and other terrorist acts occur.

Mindful that the victims' rights movement, especially in the United States, has elevated law's role in victims' recovery from violence, I caution that law cannot provide all that victims deserve on their path toward healing and urge victims to look beyond law for recovery, whether turning to ritual or therapy or a productive social project. Moreover, other legal and quasi-legal procedures (e.g., non-capital trials, truth and reconciliation commissions, and international tribunals) might afford fairer and more satisfying responses to terrorism. Given the responses of the U.S. government to terrorism in the post–9/11 era, including war, incommunicado detention, summary execution of suspected operatives, and military tribunals shielded from public view, such arrangements are unlikely to be pursued officially; however, it is worthwhile to imagine whether such options might better serve victims and the public at a time when responding effectively to terrorist violence has become an acute concern.

Understanding why the embassy bombings occurred—specifically, what led the defendants and others to participate in terrorism—became for me a key component of pursuing justice. Drawing on my knowledge of East Africa, including familiarity with the communities where several defendants originated or settled, I began to develop an explanation of their participation in the bombings that considered political and economic features of the local context overlooked during the trial. Real and felt ethnic, religious, or political oppression operated together with on-the-ground despair caused by the effects of the global economy to foster an environment where terrorism could gain adherents. My explanation counters the tendency to attribute terrorist activity to globally circulating Islamic ideology, as if the ideology itself was capable of indoctrinating anyone who encountered it without other explanatory factors operating to influence choices or to encourage the leap from espousing an ideology to acting in its name. In East Africa—where a wide range of perspectives tied to ethnicity and religion have long been negotiated, mostly without violence—even very strong ideologies rarely possess that degree of power.

In building an explanation, one must examine how politicized extremist Islamic ideologies operate by gaining force and drawing adherents in specific contexts. At the same time one must unequivocally condemn the destructive force unleashed in their name. The pronouncements of Osama bin Laden, attacks by al Qaeda operatives, and a host of other violent acts, including some taken in reaction, are unacceptable religiously, morally, and politically, not least because they actively impede the positive and necessary project of working against the inequalities of current political and economic arrangements. At the time of the embassy bombings, ideology advocating violence in the name of Islam was limited, and in many places, East Africa, for example, such politicized ideas were vulnerable to local religious beliefs and political activities. The U.S.-led war on terror following 9/11 may have diminished al Qaeda's leadership and ranks; however, adherents to calls for violence in the name of radical political Islam appear to be growing. To everyone's peril, the forces mounting the war on terror may have forgotten (or ignored) the fact that responses to violence perceived as unjust go some measure toward encouraging more violence. As an American, I direct special attention to U.S. interests and foreign policies, especially America's leading role in the war on terror, in contributing to a growing sense of political oppression that may ultimately spark more violence.

Responding forcefully to terrorist acts is essential, and yet, as I argue, the response should, if at all possible, avoid escalating violent conflict. By telling the story of how law was used to respond to the embassy bombings, and assessing its positive and negative consequences, my hope is that this book will stimulate new approaches that foreground justice in the project of eliminating terrorism.

CHAPTER ONE
Becoming a Swahili Widow

The substance of grief is not imaginary. It's as real as rope or the absence of air, and like both these things it can kill. My body understood there was no safe place for me to be. . . . As long as I kept moving, my grief streamed out behind me like a swimmer's long hair in water. I knew the weight was there but it didn't touch me. Only when I stopped did the sick, dark stuff of it come floating around my face, catching my arms and throat till I began to drown
—Barbara Kingsolver, *The Poisonwood Bible*

Abu Huraira reported that Allah's Messenger (may peace be upon him) said: One who makes efforts (for earning to be spent) on a widow and the destitute is like a striver in the cause of Allah.
—Book 042, Number 7107

ONE NIGHT, a few months before the bombings, Jamal launched into a long story about his father's death, which had occurred several years before. Jamal had spent most of his adult life caring for his ailing father, who had outlived virtually everyone of his generation. When the doctor informed the family that Jamal's father was close to death, Jamal got behind him on his bed and, sitting with his legs straddled around the frail man's frame, held his father up against his chest to give him strength and help him breathe. Other relatives gathered around praying tearfully in the dimly lit room. Jamal was the first to realize that his father had stopped breathing and was finally, peacefully, no longer alive. He met the eyes of his older sister, Fauzia, and nodded to her that it was over. She gasped and started the high-pitched keening that announces a death in a Swahili family. He stopped her short by telling everyone loudly and sternly, "I don't want to hear any crying, any wailing, not even a tear, until we've prepared everything for the funeral." Sobs escaped, tears threatened to spill over, but his siblings and their children tried to obey him; the youngest of fourteen, and the closest to their father, Jamal commanded tremendous respect. His sisters hurried out to ready the four houses in the compound for the mourners and visitors who would soon arrive. Several male relatives soberly washed and dressed the body, wrapping it in the plain white shroud that accompanies all Muslims to their grave. Others went to the cemetery to arrange for the burial, which would have to happen before sundown that day. Just as everything was being completed, Jamal broke down, sobbing in grief.

On hearing this conclusion, I challenged him, "Why did you act like that? You knew they were suffering, they wanted to cry. Why be so harsh?" His answer betrayed no regrets, "Above all, the dead must be shown respect." He justified his behavior in another way by quoting a tradition attributed to the Prophet Mohamed, who advised mourners: "The real patience is at the moment of greatest calamity."[1] As Jamal explained, accepting every death as God's will was an act of faith for Muslims. Mourners who showed patience at the death of a loved one were revealing their faith at the very moment when maintaining it was hardest. His family's ability to show that faith in the sharply painful initial moments of grief would remain, for him, an abiding demonstration of respect for his father and of their deep reverence for Allah.

My phone calls after the bombing to embassy personnel, the hospital, and the undertaker demanding the release of Jamal's body probably failed to show the patience Jamal had counseled. But four days after the bombing, when the hospital finally let us take him, my whole being was focused on getting to his home town of Malindi. Jamal deserved the respect of a proper burial. Several sunsets having passed, his family had been patient long enough. Gathered at Mombasa's airport, Jamal's brothers and other male relatives and friends were disappointed that my planes had been delayed and the sun had already set. As I emerged on the runway, I ran straight for comfort to Mary Porter, a fellow anthropologist of the Swahili coast who had been my close friend for many years. On hearing about Jamal's death, Mary had arranged to come to Malindi to be with me for the funeral.[2]

Another tradition attributes to the Prophet Mohamed the saying often repeated about funeral processions: "If it's a good person, good things await (So it's best to arrive quickly). And if it's a bad person, there's reason to delay."[3] Saidi, husband to Jamal's niece, drove the borrowed sedan like lightning on the pitch-black road to Malindi. The pickup truck carried Jamal's casket; relatives and friends crowded around it, chanting prayers the whole way. The danger of our speed on a road littered with potholes failed to register with me; time was critical. Jamal had to be buried that night.

As we entered one of the four houses in the family compound, and I saw the pain on the faces of Jamal's sisters and our nieces, I became hysterical. Through their tears they thanked me repeatedly for bringing him back to them, for not burying him alone in Dar es Salaam. Jamal's older sister, Fauzia, his trusted compatriot in many family ventures, admonished us all to settle down until everything was ready for the burial, saying that Jamal would have wanted us to show control.

Not long after our arrival, the house where I would stay began to empty out. Everyone headed for the other side of the compound for the first part of the funeral. Confused and then frantic, I said, "I have to go there. I want to go." A young niece insisted that Swahili widows never appear at the funeral, because men might see them, which was forbidden. As I began to protest, another niece grabbed my hand and guided me quickly down a dark hallway to the other end of the long house. Mary followed, and we climbed onto a high stone stoop. I had trouble seeing across the courtyard until Mary told me to bend down a bit so the eaves would not block my view. Just at that moment, the bier holding Jamal's casket, borne by the men in his family, came into view across the courtyard. I remember vivid brightness, a brilliant cloth billowed, dozens of men shimmered in white robes. Lanterns, spotlights, and flashlights illuminated the path into the house where Jamal had grown up. The wails and keening of the women gathered in the back half of the house quieted once the body was brought through the doorway, and those gathered inside began the short, solemn ceremony to say good-bye.

After the procession entered the house, we were left staring at darkness. My knees buckled; I clutched at Mary. She helped me down from the stoop and back to the bedroom. Lying on the bed, I listened to the prayers and then to the sound trailing off as the men proceeded to the cemetery to bury Jamal near his father and his favorite uncle—who had also died young—in a grave facing the Indian Ocean.

When Jamal's sisters returned to the house, they found that all the rationality, calculation, and control I had drawn on to get myself and Jamal from Tanzania to Kenya had evaporated; I had finally fallen apart. My mind and body still reeling with trauma, and my heart breaking, I cried uncontrollably. I turned to those around me; I needed them to guide me, to help me handle the waves of crushing grief and the sick, empty feeling that gripped my stomach. At the same time I panicked, realizing that, quite simply, I had no idea how to mourn my husband.

Beginning right then, Jamal's family took charge. His sisters removed my jewelry and, while my head bobbed with each gasping sob, tied a silky scarf to cover my hair. They tried to calm me, saying over and over, "Subiri," which means "be patient," and another phrase: "Patience brings comfort in the future." When my agitation continued unabated, Jamal's brother brought me a tall herbal drink, the kind of tranquilizing potion that his father, and then Jamal, had specialized in preparing. I drank it down, and after a few minutes, became placid, and finally slept.

I spent almost every moment of the next three days sitting or lying on that bed, while every female who had known Jamal, and some who had not, came to the house to extend condolences. Many knew me as the American anthropologist who had lived in Malindi off and on for more than a decade. Mary and I were among the many scholars who found Swahili culture both a delight and a puzzle. The delight responds to the richness of coastal history. For at least a thousand years, Arab traders sailing from the present-day areas of Oman and Yemen stopped at the islands and mainland harbors along the Indian Ocean coast. Their wooden ships, called *dhows*, brought Islam, literacy, and trade goods to populations of fisher folk and farmers who tended groves of coconut, mango, and banana common in this tropical climate. Waiting for the seasonal winds that would carry them back home—laden with raw materials from the coast and the interior—some sailors married local women; others settled permanently. Scholars dispute the timing but agree that a distinctive Swahili population grew out of that mixture. Coastal people built mosques and houses of coral, creating towns all along the coast. Residents of these "stone towns" traded with their relatives in the "country towns" of nearby rural areas.[4] After a brief period of Portuguese colonization, sultans from Oman dominated the coastal region, governing from the island of Zanzibar to the south. The plantations they administered benefited from the slave trade they facilitated, which, on the Kenyan coast, ended in the early twentieth century during British colonization. As the Swahili population grew, Sunni Islam became firmly established and developed an East African character that bore the influences of migrating peoples and ideas from several parts of Arabia, North Africa, Persia, India, and the interior of the continent, as well as that of the coastal dwellers themselves. The diverse traditions melded into an identifiable cultural complex that includes profoundly beautiful poetry and songs, intricate religious scholarship and ritual practices, elaborate public ceremonies (especially weddings), and a tendency to be ethnically incorporative rather than exclusive, that is, to embrace differences of color and ethnicity. Alamin Mazrui and Ibrahim Noor, scholars who trace their own roots to the Kenyan coast, write of the "Swahilicizing" process through which immigrants and people from surrounding populations are accepted into Swahili culture.[5] Early on, slaves became Swahili through emancipation, and both marriage and conversion to Islam have provided significant avenues for expanding the Swahili population. The illustration on the cover of Mazrui and Shariff's book about Swahili culture—a photographic collage of people's heads and shoulders—portrays the physical diversity of Swahili people whose skin tones range from very light to very dark. Belief in Islam and Kiswahili as everyone's first language unite the Swahili population.

Scholars' puzzlement comes because, even in the midst of Swahilicization, the lines demarcating who is Swahili, and who is not, can at times be starkly drawn. Over the years the ethnic group has been configured in different ways by legal rules, especially in colonial times—sometimes including "Arabs," sometimes putting them in a separate category—and by personal preferences. Depending on whom you are talking to, anyone on the coast who is Muslim and speaks Kiswahili, can be Swahili or, alternatively, the term can refer only to a narrow group with undisputable ties to both coastal Africa and the Middle East. Internal divisions can also be sharp, especially among prominent families, who attempt to retain prestige over newcomers and anyone with slave origins. The people with whom I lived and worked most closely—in the towns of Mombasa and Malindi—traced long roots as Swahili. But until I became accustomed to their flexible notion of identity, they puzzled me by speaking of themselves at any given moment as Kenyan, African, Arab, Bajuni (or another of the many clans), and most often as Muslim, which distinguished them from most other Kenyans.[6] The multilayered identities were not incompatible; they make the group an ethnicity always in process.

Only a few of those who came to give their condolences knew before his death that Jamal and I were married. Our friendship had begun surreptitiously. We were all too aware that, unless married or closely related, a man and woman were not supposed to spend time alone together. Swahili families arranged most marriages; having a boyfriend or girlfriend, or even a friend of the opposite sex, was something to hide so as to avoid the speculation that would damage personal reputation and family honor. When Jamal's first marriage failed, our own romance blossomed. Mindful of shielding Jamal's three sons from gossip, and not knowing what the future held for us, we concealed our relationship as best we could. For personal and professional reasons, many years would pass before Jamal and I decided that a life together was possible. With support from Jamal's brothers and sisters, we married quietly and—a year before the bombings—left for Tanzania, where I would teach at the University of Dar es Salaam.

Figure 2. Jamal and I shortly after our wedding, July 1997. Credit: Sally Hirsch

The university proved a good place to begin married life. Negotiating our divergent nationalities, ethnicities, beliefs, gender, language, and class was probably easier where few people knew us than it would have been with friends and family eagerly watching our adjustment either in Kenya or the United States. Drawing from our contrasting pasts, we carefully laid the groundwork for a future lived in multiple places and talked frequently about the challenges we would eventually face. Even though I had lived in Malindi off and on, returning there as Jamal's wife would be a very different experience that would realign my personal and professional identities in the community. Men who had spoken openly with me in the past about my research might put more distance between us once they knew that I was married to one of their friends. Family and neighbors would have new expectations that I behave as a good Swahili wife by taking care of my husband, attending first and foremost to family matters, and perhaps dressing differently to reflect my new position in the community and in Jamal's family. Despite knowing that good-natured negotiation would resolve any conflicts, I was glad that our year in Dar es Salaam gave us a reprieve from confronting these changes. Never having traveled beyond East Africa, Jamal had concerns about what it would be like to live in a place with few Muslims and perhaps no one who appreciated the spiritual traditions of the Kenyan coast that so influenced his beliefs and practices. At the university Jamal adapted to living as an observant Muslim when only about a third of those around him shared his faith. At the same time he welcomed the experiences that awaited in the United States, believing that the unknown posed little threat to his deep sense of tradition and unshakeable faith.

We planned to leave for the United States on August 16, 1998. About a month before, a friend of Jamal's gave him a pocket-size American flag. More than a few times the mention of our upcoming trip led him to pull out the flag and wave it with such mock exuberance that we collapsed in laughter. As our departure neared, we became more apprehensive about the intricate challenges we might confront but also more excited about the next stage of our lives together. The explosion on August 7 shattered everything. Adjusting slowly into new roles and relationships was rendered irrelevant for Jamal, and impossible for me. In an instant, in the eyes of Jamal's community, I became a Swahili widow, having had but a short, sweet chance to be Jamal's wife.

As women and girls entered my bedroom in small groups, each first extended a hand for a ritual condolence handshake, clasping palms, then around the thumbs, then palms again, and saying "Pole," "Sorry." I had trouble getting out the conventional reply, "Ishapoa," which means, "It's already better." With those I knew well, we would grab shoulders and weep with abandon. After a few moments someone would pull us apart and try to calm us, especially me. Well-meaning souls sought to contain my desperation, pleading, "Stop crying, don't cry. It's okay. Enough, enough, now." Friends patted my shoulders, pried my handkerchief away to wipe tears from my cheeks, straightened the ever-present headscarf that marked me as a widow. But as soon as the next person came to pay respects, I was both free, and obligated, to cry again. Halfway through the first morning, as new arrivals continued, I was utterly exhausted.

Because Jamal was so young and his death so sudden, the tragedy so acute and the wait for the funeral so prolonged, his *matanga*—the term for the initial three days of mourning—was larger and more intense than those held for deaths that are sad but more expected.[7] Even so, the basic daily routine resembled the few I had previously attended. Women arrived early at the house; close relatives and friends stayed around the clock. Men tended to meet up at the mosque and come to the family compound for meals. Neighbors, friends, and more distant family came by in the late afternoon or early evening to hear groups of children from the Koranic schools recite prayers and be rewarded with donations. From my position in the bedroom, I never saw the little girls whose high-pitched chanting penetrated the bedroom door, but relatives reassured me that prayers offered for the dead ease their way to Paradise.

When did I realize that no one had uttered Jamal's name? He was simply *marehemu*, the blessed.

During the first afternoon of the matanga, Jamal's sister, Fauzia, sat beside me on the bed. Shaking her head sadly, she said, "After you lose your husband, you cry everyday." I had always thought of Fauzia as a dynamo in the family, stronger and more intimidating than the sisters closer to my own age. She and Jamal had collaborated on many family projects: building houses, setting up small businesses, and educating their children. After the death of Fauzia's husband about five years earlier, Jamal had assumed the obligation of helping his sister manage financially. Fauzia spoke to me quietly, relating how Jamal's death had compounded the already unbearable pain she still felt after losing her husband.

Though she walked with great difficulty, Hababa, an elderly relative who had adored Jamal, made the trip across the neighborhood to comfort me that first afternoon. She laid a necklace of glow-in-the-dark worry beads into my hands, and said, "Just count these when you can't bear it." She showed me what she had done after losing her husband years before. "Count each bead. Alhamdulilah. Alhamdulilah. Alhamdulilah."

Alhamdulilah. Praise be to God. Everyone was saying it. Jamal's sister, Sara, pulled herself out of a sobbing jag by repeating it loudly over and over, until she could breathe normally. Another sister gently explained, "You can't fight this. You must accept it. It's wrong to fight God's will." Sensing my inability to embrace Jamal's death as fate, our niece, Mariamu, tried to convince me: "Look at God's power, his plans. He brought you all the way from America to Kenya. Made the two of you fall in love. Took you both to Tanzania, just so that marehemu could meet the death intended for him. How could all that have happened without God's will?" My response was a chilling reality that I kept pushing back from consciousness, "But a few seconds—one way or the other—and it would have been me." Mariamu looked puzzled, "But it wasn't your time. It was his."

Accept Jamal's death as God's will? Praise God for his death? How could this sentiment be the right response to what appeared to be willful violence committed by humans? Islamic invocations of fate had always seemed to me to foreclose deeper inquiry into why tragic events occur. It crossed my mind that Jamal had made many attempts to address my misgivings about fate and criminal guilt. I remember the formidable questions I asked him and the Islamic judges I worked with: Doesn't belief in God's will let humans off the hook? Couldn't a person accused of committing a crime defend him- or herself by attributing the act to God's will? Patiently Jamal would quote Koranic verses that, each time, helped make belief in both a Divine plan and the agency of individual humans seem less an intractable contradiction. From our discussions I understood intellectually that submission to God's will, even in response to criminal violence, was primarily and most importantly an expression of deep faith that affirmed the unity and purpose of everything in God's universe. Allocating responsibility was a secondary concern, an important but qualitatively different act, because it dealt with relationships among humans, an area of lesser importance than one's own connection with God. Accepting God's will after a death implied acceptance of two stark beliefs. The first was the finality of death, death always being the end product of God's will. The second was that some meaning or purpose lay behind the death itself. After Jamal's death, both these notions were, at first, excruciatingly difficult for me to acknowledge. Yet rejecting death's finality could lead to a torturous game of denying what had happened, refusing to accept that Jamal was gone, and only postponing grief's return. Drawing on Jamal's own faith as a guide, I forced myself to acknowledge his death as God's will. The second idea, that some meaning or purpose lay behind his death, required belief beyond my capacity.

Late at night, as everyone else slept, confusion, terror, and guilt swarmed into the dark silence. I feared the flashbacks of noise and lights and crushing force that came without warning. I reached for the glowing beads hanging on the bedpost: "Alhamdulilah. Alhamdulilah." The relief of sleep.

On the morning of the matanga's second day, Mary and I found ourselves alone for a moment. Piercing through my haze of misery like a bolt of lightning, it hit me that I might find some solace in "Grief and a Headhunter's Rage," a famous anthropology essay written by Renato Rosaldo after the sudden death of his wife, Michelle, also an anthropologist.[8] I told Mary, "There's something in Rosaldo's essay that I think would help. Something important about grief." Neither of us could remember much of it, but one point popped into my head: Rosaldo wrote that during rituals, including rituals of mourning, people offer a "dose of platitudes," a phrase that captured the perfunctory quality of the condolence messages everyone kept repeating: "Alhamdulilah." "Subiri." "Pole." Knowing that the rich essay offered more, including an extended reflection on the interconnection of grief and rage—the latter an emotion I had yet to feel—my frustration increased. Scrambled by the bomb, my mind could produce nothing coherent about the anthropology I believed would surely help me to make sense not only of the rituals going on around me but of my own pain.

Months later I reread Rosaldo's essay. I still had not felt the rage that had engulfed him after Michelle's death and that he argues is the irreducible, possibly universal, effect of loss. Another of his ideas impressed me. Rosaldo depicted rituals as busy intersections, places "where a number of distinct social processes intersect." This image aptly captured the matanga where hundreds of people from all parts of Jamal's life, and my own, passed through: the clerk from the Islamic court I had studied, people whose disputes had been data for my earlier research, children from my neighborhood, a British anthropologist who had also married a Swahili man, and Jamal's ex-wife, whom I had never met. The human traffic reminded me of all that Jamal had accomplished and blunted the sense of extreme isolation grief induces. At times, though, I needed protection from the memories brought into the bedroom and from the sheer presence of witnesses to my pain. Even the mildest, most basic request that I greet those gathered around me could feel like an assault. Mary watched out for me, sometimes inventing reasons to clear the room and lock the door, when we needed simple quiet.

Here and there snippets of conversation about the chaos at the site of the Kenya bombing caught my attention. For days after the bombings rescuers continued to search for bodies, and families tried desperately to find loved ones: first at the blast site in Nairobi's city center, then at hospitals, and finally at the city morgue. A neighbor had yet to hear from her daughter who was enrolled in the secretarial college just behind the embassy. I never asked for details about Nairobi. Whenever I consciously thought about the bombings as a double attack, I felt a cold chill.

Fauzia whispered in my ear, "Did you dream about him last night?" "No." "What did you dream about?" A rush of relief, as I answered, "Nothing. I didn't dream at all." I had feared terrible nightmares, exploding bombs jolting me awake. Fauzia reassured me, "Don't worry, you'll dream. You'll see him. You'll dream a beautiful dream." Fauzia was among those friends and relatives who believed that Jamal's spirit—deemed powerful by many—still circulated, just beyond our conscious perception.

Among my visitors was a Swahili woman I did not recognize who stood at the foot of my bed holding her teenage daughter's hand. Through tears, the woman explained that Jamal had been treating her daughter who periodically descended into confusion and terror brought on by evil spirits whose voices her daughter could not silence. "Who will help her now?" asked the distraught mother. "Marehemu's gone; his father's gone. What will we do?" The mother swore that sessions with Jamal who, following his father's teachings, had treated the young woman with herbal remedies and hours of calm talk had kept her daughter out of Port Reitz, a notorious mental hospital in Mombasa.

Jamal's father—whose nickname for the last decades of his long life was Jiddi, meaning "great-grandfather"—had groomed Jamal, his youngest son, to take his place as a Swahili "teacher" (*mwalimu* or *sheikh*), who used spiritual power and practical knowledge to help those experiencing crises. I had watched Jamal counsel clients with great patience and a manner reassuring to those who felt plagued by demons or abandoned by loved ones. Jamal's father, leaning back in his plaited raffia chair, listening to tales of insults and disappointments, would focus his intervention on persuading angry parties to agree that adhering more closely to the values of Islam would bring harmony to their households. He could also be stern, especially when clients disregarded his careful advice. His brand of informal justice, what I called "Swahili ethics" in the book that resulted from this research, espoused principles distilled from the Koran and presented with sensitivity to the local context, including family history.[9] His practice ran parallel to the formal legal processes I was studying in Islamic courts. For Jamal, his father, and other Swahili teachers, the Koran—as God's word—guided and justified their decisions, yet they were always willing to debate interpretations.

When Jiddi was active, clients milled about the family compound waiting their turn to see him. For Jamal, the compound and surrounding neighborhood were a source of strength. He had always lived there, surrounded by a close, extended family and, in recent years, a new generation. The graves of beloved relatives were nearby, not far from the mosques that his family had helped to build and support. Herbs used in various treatments grew alongside paths winding down to the sea. Girls made frequent trips to a plot of fragrant jasmine that they used to make the wedding corsages worn by Swahili women. Jamal had told me that he would never leave permanently; we would have to commute from the United States. In the months before his death, he and Fauzia had many telephone discussions as construction began on a fifth house in the family compound. It was intended as a *waqf* house, a charitable venture undertaken in Jiddi's name. Income from renting out the house would be donated toward the upkeep of a neighborhood mosque. At the time of Jamal's funeral the house foundation had just been laid, and the siblings decided that charity from the finished house would be donated also in Jamal's name.

In the 1990s clients' problems became more intractable, many of them related to the area's economic decline. Tourism had become the primary commercial endeavor, yet it was highly volatile, its success dependent on a healthy global economy and political stability in the region. Both were elusive. Moreover, European developers and organized crime interests skimmed off much of the profits. Tourism brought with it prostitution and drug abuse, which strained relationships in many families. By the late 1990s, problems often stemmed from the frustration of the many young men knocking about Malindi with no income and no job prospects. Jamal tried to figure out how to help young people addicted to "brown sugar" (heroin) and how to keep children in school. The worst effects of the declining global economy were impinging on Malindi and even the compound, and he and others were looking for any means—traditional rituals, Islamic prayer, nongovernmental organizations—to stave off the danger.

On the matanga's third day, a few relatives and friends from far away came to say their good-byes. Everyone reassured me, "God will help you." "Marehemu's in a good place." At some point, Jamal's brothers and sisters gathered at the end of my bed, and the oldest brother conveyed the family's formal offer: "We want to take care of you. In Islam it's our duty to provide for you during your *edda*,[10] to maintain you for the next four months and ten days. Even after that, you can stay for as long as you'd like." Another brother explained, "The Prophet Mohamed always defended widows and orphans. Helping them brings blessing." I told them that, given what had happened, my American family would be distraught until they saw me. After a few protests everyone agreed with my plan to return to the United States in another week or so.

I knew from my research in Islamic courts that a divorcee must observe an edda waiting period, well established in Islamic law, during which she was not permitted to marry. For divorced women, edda lasted three months, shorter than the widow's obligation.[11] Islamic judges offered a simple explanation for edda. During those months of waiting, the widow or divorcee, and those tending to her, will come to know if she is pregnant. If so, then paternity could be assigned without question to the deceased or the ex-husband. Although over the years I had paid my respects to several widows who were observing edda, I had never thought much about what they experienced during the waiting period and the many meanings that edda might hold. If I had, I might have appreciated a comment Fauzia made after the men in the family filed out of the bedroom that morning. With tears in her eyes, she sympathized with me, saying, "You have the hardest burden. We stop mourning today, even though we still feel sad. Only a widow mourns for more than three days. Mourning your husband for four months and ten days is no small thing." If I had thought much about a widow's edda, I would have noted that the simple legal rule of waiting before marrying again was, in fact, an elaborate cultural practice that shaped all aspects of a new widow's life and identity. After the matanga, she becomes the deceased's chief mourner. Soon after this conversation with Fauzia, I began to encounter the many cultural expectations laid onto edda's simple legal prescription and to realize that at the same time that edda guaranteed the support and protection of Jamal's family, it also would require much of me.

Ma Rukia, an elderly neighbor, leaned over me, incanting in her gruff voice how she had "suffered and suffered and suffered" during her edda years earlier. A young widow with few relatives around, no money to hire help, and several children to care for, she had no choice but to leave the house during her edda. But she insisted that her behavior had been above reproach, "I would not speak. Not even in the market. If I wanted one kilo of flour, I pointed like this and put up one finger. If I wanted two kilos, I did like this," she said, thrusting out fingers in a V. "Of course I wore gloves, and socks. No one could see any part of me. And it was so hot."

After Ma Rukia shuffled out, a couple of teens in the bedroom corner laughed with each other as they mimicked her one-finger, two-finger routine. "That's the old days," one said dismissively. But eagerly they listed edda's many obligations on Swahili widows, mostly restrictions, that I would hear about from others: Don't wear makeup or cut your hair or pluck your eyebrows or put on perfume or use scented soap or wear jewelry or fancy clothes—or go out, unless you absolutely have to. All things I could not, at that moment of despair, even imagine wanting to do. "It's hard," said one of the teens. "It will be hard in America," said another, imagining life in the States. "You'll want to go out all the time." It dawned on me that, for the past three days, I had left the bedroom only to use the bathroom nearby.

The image of the widow, secluded in her home, hidden from men's gazes, contrasted sharply with the daily lives of most Swahili women I knew, and yet it reflected a central cultural value: *heshima*, or respectability, so often the justification for keeping unrelated men and women apart. For both genders, behaving with heshima—through obedience to one's parents, speaking in modest tones, showing patience, and, above all, conforming to the norms of sexual propriety demonstrated respect and thereby preserved family and personal honor. The guidelines for behaving with heshima could be specifically articulated—stay away from bars and other places where activity counter to Islamic teachings occurs—but they were also vague, always shifting. As I had learned over the years, in practice, women (especially if younger and unmarried) bore more of the burden of upholding heshima. Potential infractions—talking to boys or roaming into areas where men congregate—could harm family reputation. Yet the myriad connections among extended families living in one or another of the coastal towns meant that Swahili life was characterized by mobility, and seclusion was rarely a practical strategy for preserving heshima. Men and women traveled frequently for weddings (the major social event), funerals, and visiting. Also, women had almost as many reasons as men to leave home each day for school, employment, shopping, and socializing. The mobile Swahili lifestyle posed a constant challenge to heshima that women negotiated by comporting themselves appropriately rather than through seclusion. I knew this well, as I had appropriated certain modest behaviors so that I could conduct my research, which took me into public places such as courts and into conversations with forbidden interlocutors.

The image of the widowed Ma Rukia completely concealed as she shopped in the market was a reminder that wearing a veil can mimic seclusion and thus be a strategy for preserving he-

shima in public. Because so many Western scholars have exot-
icized, misunderstood, or blatantly condemned Islamic veiling,
in my own writing I have argued that veiling has many meanings for Swahili women, and Muslims generally. When I began
my research in the mid-1980s most Swahili women and teens,
when they left the house, wore a long black cloak and attached
veil, called a *buibui*. Some pulled the loose veil across to cover
the face. By the 1990s new styles of veil—see-through cloaks,
head scarves tied under the chin, wrapped headdresses—had
made veiling a fashion statement as well as a continued affirmation of one's respectability and identity as a Muslim. These
new forms rendered the buibui old-fashioned. Also in the 1990s
a small number of women in coastal Kenya began to cover themselves completely. Some did so at the request of husbands or fathers who wanted to emulate the stricter control of gender relations associated with Saudi Arabia and the Gulf States. Some
young women unilaterally adopted more concealing veils, including masks tied over their faces, in order to demonstrate personal piety. Community leaders argued about whether the more
restrictive veiling was appropriate, some insisting that the
Koran did not require a woman to cover her face.

Compared to all other women, the widow in edda faces the
highest standards of sexual propriety. Legally off-limits to men,
she is also the living symbol of the honor of her dead husband.
No wonder Ma Rukia felt that she had to behave with such modesty. For their part most men reacted differently to widows than
to other women. Those few men who chose not to avoid me deliberately averted their eyes in my presence so as not to violate
my widow's seclusion.

Late in the afternoon on the matanga's final day, Fauzia came to
see me. Sitting close, she laid a small wrapped package between
us. "When you leave the house on Saturday, you have to be careful. No one should see you. Because of edda." I opened it partway and saw the familiar black fabric. "It's a buibui?" "Yes, a
nice one. You'll pull it across like this. No one will see anything,"
she assured me. I paused, confusion building, then burst out,
"No, there's no way I'll wear it. I don't want to, I never did be-

fore, I won't now." Looking surprised, Fauzia pleaded, "Please do it for me. Just so people won't say anything." "No, Jamal would never have wanted me to." Fauzia must have seen my tears of frustration and she rose to leave, saying calmly that we would talk later. The buibui remained on the bed.

As I think back our argument puzzles me. Why did I resist so strongly, knowing that how I looked when I first emerged from Jamal's house as his widow would mean a lot to Fauzia? I owed her so much for helping me through the funeral, the matanga, and those first days of my edda, and clearly she would play a crucial role in my recovery and in maintaining my relationship with the family. Even though I have little memory of what I was thinking or feeling at the time, my training as a legal anthropologist tells me that this conflict reflected underlying tensions.

Fauzia wanted to see me leave the family's house looking like a respectable widow. At the moment I appeared publicly as Jamal's widow, with the certainty that others, including men outside the family, would see me, it was critical that I dress appropriately. In contrast to newer fashion, the buibui, when held across the face, covered completely, conveying no hint of the flashiness that a widow was expected to avoid. Wearing the buibui would also display my concern with preserving honor, and indicate my respect for the family and for Jamal. Fauzia would have wanted everyone to witness all those things.

Fauzia may or may not have thought consciously that my wearing a buibui would link me more tightly to the Swahili community in the minds of those who saw me. Because the buibui symbolizes Swahili identity, wearing it would Swahilicize me and, by the same logic, would claim me for the family. My foreign identity, and the brevity and secrecy of our marriage, exacerbated the anxieties widows routinely experience. Widows are always ambivalent figures, their allegiances, especially in relation to the husband's family, always questioned. Part of the family by marriage, and treated as such for the months of edda, eventually the widow, technically, has no legal connection to her husband's relatives. This is especially the case for young widows, who occasion thoughts of remarriage that would further widen the legal rift.[12]

On my part, I know that I wanted to show respect for myself, Jamal, his family, and Swahili Islamic culture. Mary remembers my telling her that covering up completely was not the problem. In fact, I sensed it as a way to protect myself, conceal my pain from public gaze. Why, then, did I reject the buibui?

Maybe I refused because I wanted some control over how I would appear. The complete loss of control I had experienced as both a sudden widow and a victim of traumatic violence led me to grasp, perhaps unreasonably, at regaining power over something. Controlling my attire was a way of managing my shattered self.

Perhaps I refused out of the frustration I felt, because Jamal could no longer help me negotiate requests from his family. Together, we had handled other differences of opinion. His death short-circuited our plans to navigate the complex bargaining over my identity that we would have faced.

I may have refused because it felt a strange irony that, at the moment the community looked on me publicly as Jamal's widow, establishing an identity for me that contrasted with my past persona, I would be indistinguishable from other Swahili widows, not recognized as an individual. The very moment that would highlight my new identity would make me anonymous by clothing me as a traditional Swahili woman, a role I had never played.

Maybe in rejecting the Swahilicizing anonymity of the buibui, I was trying to symbolize the person, the wife, Jamal had chosen. I knew it was important to him that, in marrying me, he had selected someone who behaved with the respectability of a Swahili woman but at the same time differed. My difference— whether it was my American nationality, my Jewish background, or my work as an anthropologist—had to be remembered and marked. Otherwise something important about Jamal would be ignored.

Or more simply, perhaps I refused to wear a buibui because too much had already been asked of me, beginning with the unspoken demand that I continue living, without Jamal. Refusing

Fauzia's sincere request was an act of resisting all that weighed on me much heavier than a veil.

These possible explanations, reached only after years of reflection, may or may not be why I rejected Fauzia's suggestion. A few days later I told her that she had no reason to worry. I would dress modestly; I would cover myself completely. But I would not wear a buibui.

For weeks before the bombings, Jamal and I had been planning all we would need to accomplish before departing for the U.S. After saying good-bye to friends and family in Lamu, arranging for relatives to handle his businesses, and buying the customary parting gifts we would give relatives and friends, Jamal planned our last week in Malindi. The celebratory meals and visits would culminate in a large *dhikri* ceremony held at the family compound on the Thursday prior to our departure. Before leaving for America, Jamal had wanted one last chance to experience the power of dhikri. The word means "to invoke God's name." During a dhikri ceremony, participants gather closely and repeat certain words or phrases, usually "Allah" or another of God's many names. The rhythmic chant, a thumping drum, and deep inhalations between each repetition uttered in a burst of breath can bring those present into hypnotic or ecstatic states. One common dhikri chant, "Allah hai," "God lives," captures the ceremony's intended goal: the quest for direct connection with the Divine.[13] Dhikri, a staple spiritual practice for many Sufis, especially in Africa, offers an intense individual experience; believers focus inwardly, searching for truth and knowledge of Allah. Once Jamal tried to explain what he felt at the height of dhikri: wholeness, peace, connection, uplift. Sensing the inadequacy of his words, he concluded that I would only understand when I felt it myself. Family and friends interpreted our arrangements as evidence of Jamal's eerie premonition of his own, more permanent departure. Mindful of following Jamal's original intentions, the family decided to host a large dhikri to mark the matanga's end on the very night we would have had our send-off to America.

Jamal's family had a reputation for hosting potent dhikri.[14] For me, the highly charged atmosphere had always felt too unpredictable, even a little scary, and I usually stayed on the outskirts of the few dhikri I had attended over the years. The ceremony's intense energy invited spirits from other realms, and, although not a goal of dhikri in its pure sufi sense, some participants invariably spoke and moved as if possessed by spirits. During one dhikri, a young woman, apparently possessed by a spirit, singled me out, calling me "*mzungu*," or "white person," and, in English, demanding money. Her ability to speak English, and her rudeness, stunned me, as she had a friendly demeanor and led a relatively sheltered life. Anthropological interpretations of spirit possession during dhikri depict it as affording participants the chance to negotiate interpersonal and community relations in a public setting, as well as to achieve spiritual goals. But for myself—neither a student of religious ritual nor on a personal quest for the altered state that dhikri promised—I could never seem to "get into it" and always worried that, in the midst of a ceremony, my lack of belief would be exposed.

At first such reservations led me to consider staying in the bedroom rather than crossing the courtyard for the dhikri. I also worried that the sheer volume of the chanting would trigger a panic attack. At Fauzia's urging, I agreed to attend with the proviso that Mary would stick close by, and we would leave if the noise upset me. As the family prepared for the ceremony, the atmosphere changed markedly. The terrible sadness and sameness of the past few days of intense mourning was gently set aside, replaced by a sense of great anticipation. Everyone was looking to the dhikri, searching for something.

Women and teenage girls packed the back bedroom floors; men filled the living room at the front of the house. Once the lights were out, the door between was opened, so that the sound could carry. Saidi, Jamal's niece's husband, led the chant, with a clear voice and steady beat. Unlike some of the others, he could be trusted not to lose his head. Low at first, the chanting grew louder, more breathy, and soon shrieks and the beginnings of testimonials from spirits punctuated the quickening, collective pulse. Eyes closed, I focused on my own breath and low voice. The frenetic noise grew hazy, hard to hear, as I concentrated my energy, something that had been impossible since the bombings. Simply participating, searching for something, I gave myself over to the chant. An enormous rush of bright energy, a wide whoosh of air and light; enlivening, pleasing, empowering sensations. After some time the room and the people became evident to me again, as if I were coming out of anesthesia. Next to me Jamal's sisters were trying to calm a woman who was seemingly possessed; each held an arm until she quieted down. Others around me lurched in the throes of trance. To my utter surprise, I stayed calm throughout the commotion.

When the lights went on, Fauzia knelt in front of me and asked, "Did you *panda*?" which literally means "Did you climb?"—that is, "Were you possessed?" "Maybe. I felt something." She smiled and nodded knowingly. Mary looked at us with dreamy eyes and said, "I don't know, but whatever happened here was very powerful."

After days of submitting my pain to the scrutiny of one person after another, the emotional and physical catharsis of dhikri brought profound relief. Dhikri reverberated with an unstoppable force, pushing back the equally strong force of grief. Dhikri insistently shifted the attention of all of us participating, focusing us away from the worldly realm where Jamal was dead, and we were all bereft, toward a transcendent domain that promised truth, where spirits wrangled with different problems, and where Jamal, we knew, would hold his own. Jamal's sisters professed that his spirit had circulated in the room. Not sure what I thought about that then, I know I took comfort in the possibility that he might have been close to us.

That night I dreamed the beautiful dream Fauzia had promised.

Across the Muslim world those seeking deeper spiritual experience practice versions of dhikri. The incorporation of spirit possession lends a local character to East African dhikri ceremonies. Anthropologists who have studied the spirit possession cults that organize to perform dhikri and other trancing ceremonies have sparked debate over whether, through participating, women and impoverished men gain power denied them at the

mosques controlled by community elites. Others have noted that
the spirits sometimes play out tensions bigger than family or
community struggles: those between Christians and Muslims,
white foreigners and Swahili people, colonizers and colonized.
Dhikri also has its critics. Since its inception and popularization
in early Islam, sufism has garnered skepticism by those who fear
the power of spiritual masters and the inward, almost antisocial
focus of sufi practices. A complex religious and social politics
leads some coastal Muslims to oppose dhikri. Since the end of
the nineteenth century, reformers have tried to rid coastal Islam
of undue influence from surrounding African societies and pre-
Islamic traditions. Their goals are unabashedly to "modernize"
practices viewed as traditional to the point of being backward.
A famous Muslim judge argued for reforms that would avoid
activities undertaken out of the superstition of African ani-
mism.[15] Some reformers, who tend to be from the secularly educated upper classes, seemed most concerned with consolidating
their own power as against that of local leaders, including sufi
practitioners. The long-standing, low-grade struggle between reformers and Swahili people who adhere to local practice has
rarely escalated beyond a strong difference of opinion, although,
arguably, power over mosques and resources has always been
at stake.

In the last decades of the twentieth century, a stronger condemnation of local practices emerged, influenced primarily by
ideology and funding from Saudi Arabia and other international
sources. The new opposition, characterized fairly as fundamentalist, decried the corrupting nature of customs they deemed
"unIslamic," including spirit possession, saint veneration, and
elaborate wedding and funeral rites. The fundamentalists depicted raucous dhikri ceremonies as "innovation," an inappropriate activity in contrast to true Islam, which, in their view,
should consist only of those practices carried out at the time of
the Prophet, preferably by the Prophet and his companions.
Fundamentalist versions of the Prophet's Islam are spare: no
music, visual images, or deviations from adherence to strict interpretations of Islamic law. The arguments made against Swahili practice resembled those mounted by fundamentalists es-

pousing a Wahhabbist version of Islam in many parts of the world; however, their inroads had not penetrated far in coastal Kenya. Many Swahili people, mindful of the coast's distinctive history and convinced of their own piety, refused to view Saudi Arabian Islam as more authentic than their own practices. Yet a small minority willingly embraced new fundamentalist visions. Young men out of work and feeling the discrimination of Kenya's political system turned away from local tradition in an effort to support themselves and as a requirement of connection with purist groups that made attractive promises. With donations to Koranic schools, and with the provision of social services to neglected parts of the community, fundamentalist interests cultivated a few strong allies on the ground. In addition, some young men returning from stints of employment in the Gulf brought back rigid ideas about religion. But any push to radicalize more intensively usually passed quickly with opposition from local leaders, an upturn in the economy, or a crackdown by Kenya's secular central government, which policed any hints of religious extremism.[16]

Throughout my years of living off and on in coastal Kenya, I noticed these intermittent and largely imported fundamentalist voices, but their limited influence in the communities I studied gave me little reason to examine them closely or to fear them. In the years since the bombings, I have wondered whether my inattention to fundamentalist elements missed a critical aspect of local and global politics, a concern explored in a later chapter.

The next morning I heard scurrying outside my room. A niece rushed in, "Are you ready? An important guest is here." Seeing the kindly Islamic judge, called a *kadhi*, moved me to tears. I had spent many months observing cases in his court and talking to him for hours about law, his decisions, marriage, and life. He listened as I blurted out my story of terror and loss and confusion. He comforted me with familiar assurances that the tragedy was part of God's plan and I should just be patient. Anticipating questions that might perplex me, he advised, "Keeping edda is not about what you wear, or whether you stay indoors, but what is in your heart. You've always shown heshima; of course, you will now. Edda has no uniform. Look to your heart." He placed his palm flat on his chest.

The kadhi's faith in my ability to preserve heshima provided enormous support, because it encouraged me to look to my own character and background, as well as to cultural conventions and legal rules, to navigate this emotionally fraught moment. It was crucial that the judge—a representative of the law—endorsed my ability to decide for myself how I would keep edda.

That the kadhi would counsel flexibility and individual responsibility did not surprise me. When I observed cases before his court, he justified hard decisions with Koranic passages as his guide. Yet he remained mindful of the ethical principles that lay behind specific rules: reminding those embroiled in marital conflict that a good marriage requires a tranquil, supportive atmosphere, that abuse is unacceptable and cruelty intolerable, and that fairness in all dealings paramount—the Islamic and Swahili values that outline how people should treat one another, whether they are married, business partners, family members, or friends. His approach placed less emphasis on following specific rules than on acting in good faith.

By embracing an ethical practice alongside of and congruent with legal rules, the kadhi's approach resembled that of Jamal, his father, and others in the community. Individuals were entrusted and empowered to read the Koran, study the Prophet's life, and look into their hearts to find solutions. That multiple traditions and diverse individual experiences could shape belief and action was evidence of a deep sense of tolerance for difference. Watching the kadhi and lay mediators such as Jamal and his father, I gained enormous respect for their ability to interweave law and ethics to confront life's realities and calamities. Jamal defended this approach from detractors. This was his heritage, something that, if lost to an insistence on rigid rules, would erase what he knew to be the backbone of a strong and vibrant community.

Mary returned from the shop where she had gone with one of my nieces to buy an outfit suitable for me to wear in the crucial moment when I would emerge from the house to take the several steps to the van that would ferry twenty of us to the city of Mombasa, the first stage of my journey back to the United States. Watching me closely, she pulled out the long cotton dress and large fringed scarf, both dark blue with tiny flowers. Together they conveyed the required modesty, yet differed from a buibui and other dresses worn by Swahili women. My nieces approved, saying it was a new style from Somalia. More important, Fauzia approved, and when I left Malindi the next day I wore the outfit, which covered me completely.

I arrived in the United States too vulnerable to stay by myself. My brother put my suitcases down in the guestroom of his house, and said, "No one will bother you here. Whenever you need to, just close the door." I remember feeling grateful that he recognized my need to shut out the world, even family. An instinctive reaction to trauma, a blunting of most feelings, had been protecting me. But as this response began to fade—no longer suppressing the force of grief and other powerful emotions—I flinched at every encounter, as if my whole being were a raw wound exposed to harsh wind. Even when I moved back to my old apartment, I established my own version of edda's seclusion. I told a friend that whenever I went out, which was rare, I actually wished I could wear a veil so that no one would recognize me. It was a strange sentiment, because, of course, a veil worn in our small town would have drawn attention to me all the more. My strongest memory of those first weeks back was my desperate desire to control every encounter with others. I craved company and feared being alone but could hardly bear to see my own pain reflected in the eyes of friends, family, colleagues, even strangers, once they learned what had happened.

The forced, ritualized companionship of the matanga in Kenya and the initial days of my return to the U.S. when many friends and family came to pay respects (both resembling the Jewish practice of sitting *shiva*) had provided welcome distraction. But a month or so after the bombing, the really hard work of coming to terms with my loss began. A phalanx of professionals and concerned others explained the clinical terms for my condition: post-traumatic stress syndrome, complicated grief (as if there were a simple variety), identity fragmentation, at risk for depression, and agoraphobia. Their recommended therapies—ranging from grief counseling to sleeping pills to rapid-eye-movement therapy used to treat witnesses to genocide to a support group for young widows—helped me gain some measure of control. I tried everything to combat the pain, even alternated between reciting Islamic prayers and saying Kaddish, the Jewish prayer for the dead. Unable to resume my work, I read advice books about grief and also Swahili poetry. I made phone calls to begin organizing a charity in Jamal's name, to lodge demands for compensation with the U.S. government, and to commiserate long distance with Jamal's family. Late at night I counted worry beads. My simple strategies for getting through each day drew from a variety of traditions, both those that criss-crossed my life and several new ones. I began to believe that the most effective therapy for grief was time, having heard those words so often, and I passed it in any way that sustained my attention and caused no additional pain.

The fragmentation of identity that often follows the death of a spouse was, for me, especially profound. At the time of the bombing I was immersed in a massive personal transition that included the challenge of building a life in two very different places. After the bombing, what was I? A Swahili widow? An American victim of terrorism? The support group I attended for young widows emphasized our status as "young widows" and offered a straightforward way to make sense of our change in identity. Group facilitators, widowed themselves, helped the group to appreciate that it was not possible to return to one's "old self." Emphasizing always that there is no right or wrong way to feel, they gently counseled us to work toward "integrating" the "old self" and the now damaged self into a new life and identity that would embrace both the good and the bad of the past and enable us to move into a positive future.

My memories of the long edda in my house are mercifully vague, each day blending into the next. Often I wondered if recovering from grief and loss might have been easier had I been a strong believer in any one religious tradition. Perhaps deep faith and clear doctrine would have guided me more smoothly through this life crisis. Yet I came to see that embracing a mixture of rituals, traditions, and beliefs ultimately sustained me. Perhaps an eclectic set of therapies reflected my background as an anthropologist who had always sought out and tried to learn from places, people, and experiences different from what I had known. I took comfort that, instead of closing in on myself, finding and protecting putative roots, I continued to reach out, to look across difference for comfort and, eventually, meaning. As the initial grief began to subside, I became focused on the still unanswered questions about the bombings.

CHAPTER TWO
Recognizing New Identities

How sleep these brave
the unredemptive fires absolving them
today three countries inscribe their loss
Is death absolute and is death without memorial and absolute
—Robert Pinsky, from "A Dialogue between Poetry
and Grief on the Anniversary of the Embassy Bombings,
Nairobi and Dar es Salaam, August 7, 1998"

The US appears to be living up to its international image as a lone
ranger, shooting first and asking the world community to condone its
actions, however insupportable in international law and practice. . . .
The sober world must stand up and tell Washington that individual terrorist violence cannot be solved by state terrorist violence for this goes
against all civilised international norms enshrined in the UN Charter,
and other protocols and conventions.
—*The African*, Dar es Salaam, Tanzania, August 24, 1998

LESS THAN TWO WEEKS after the East African embassy bombings,
U.S. Secretary of State Madeleine Albright made brief visits to
Kenya and Tanzania to survey the damage and offer U.S. support in the recovery. A highlight of her trip was the announcement of a $2 million reward for information leading to the ar-
rests and convictions of those responsible for the bombings. At
a press conference in Dar es Salaam, she hung a poster dominated by photos of the Dar and Nairobi bombings. Two declarations emblazoned across the top—"THIS IS NOT POLITICS" and
"THIS IS NOT RELIGION"—were answered below by "THIS IS MUR-
DER." The award announcement boosted the already intensive
criminal investigation led by U.S. FBI agents who had come to
East Africa by the hundreds.[1]

As soon as she disembarked at Nairobi's Jomo Kenyatta International Airport, Secretary Albright was forced to respond to
East Africans' continuing accusations that the United States bore
some responsibility for the tragedy. In a statement made at the
site of the blast, she apologized for the actions of any Americans

who might have caused offense by seeming to impede rescue efforts, as had been alleged. She went on to explain that entrance to the damaged embassy had been forbidden after the bombing out of concern for the compromised structure of the building, the possibility of another attack, and the risk of fuel tanks exploding.[2] Her words satisfied at least one prominent Kenyan pundit who concluded that Secretary Albright "had the decency to admit they got it wrong and to apologize. The Americans are Kenya's friends, so let's give them the benefit of any doubt and assume they were just as confused, shocked and panicky as the rest of us."[3]

In a book about his experiences treating patients in Kenya's largest national hospital on the day of the bombing, Dr. Obwogo Subiri voiced the complaints of insensitivity many Kenyans directed toward the United States. He criticized the U.S. government's offers of financial assistance as woefully insufficient, amounting to "betrayal" of their relationship with the poorer nation. Although at times histrionic, Subiri's charges reflect the pain that can emerge when differences of power and interests divide victims, as illustrated by the following vignette. During her visit to Kenya, Secretary Albright planned a stop at Nairobi's Kenyatta Hospital. Amid the chaos of continuing to treat the injured, intensive effort and expense were required to make the hospital presentable for the dignitary's visit, including extra cleaning, flowers to decorate the rooms, and the purchase of new sheets, which patients usually must provide on their own. Relatives of the sick were sent home, and at least one troublesome patient was heavily sedated so as not to disrupt the visit. Stringent security measures included cordoning off the hospital seven hours before the secretary's scheduled arrival. She and her entourage were four hours late, and, in the meantime, security guards, supervised by U.S. personnel, denied entry to people seeking treatment. Subiri writes: "A woman came in labour but could not be allowed in as the hospital had been sealed off. A makeshift curtain was made around her, and she delivered by the roadside. She named her baby after Madeleine Albright."[4]

In a memoir, written several years later, Secretary Albright recalled the event differently, "I visited a nearby hospital to see

some of the Kenyans who had been hurt. As I went from bed to
bed, I told them how sorry I was. Like other victims of terror,
these were just everyday people who had been going about their
lives, only to find themselves in the wrong place at the wrong
time. Many were heavily bandaged; others had cuts on their
hands and faces."[5] Focused on the human encounter with victims, yet shielded from the preparations required to bring a
powerful official to the powerless, Secretary Albright probably
had no inkling about those suffering outside the hospital or the
woman who gave birth to her namesake. But the secretary knew
well the importance and value of speaking directly to victims
and their families, and expressing, officially, her condolences
and sympathies.

Getting recognition as victims—especially from officials in
power—often becomes a crucial goal for those struggling to
bring coherence to a damaged and wildly fluctuating sense of
self in the wake of a violent attack. Whether or not one's loss
is acknowledged or one's altered self recognized can be key in
surviving a tragedy. From the criticisms East Africans expressed,
and from my own experiences, it was evident that especially important for bombing victims on both continents was gaining recognition for their loss and suffering from the U.S. government,
given its position as both victim and superpower. But exactly
what constitutes recognition for those who have been harmed
varies tremendously. Is it satisfied by pressing the hand of a dignitary? Receiving an official condolence letter? Hearing an apology? Can money or medical treatment be sufficient? Do victims
require press coverage? Information? An explanation? What
about a name on a commemorative plaque? A monument? A
place of honor at a memorial service? Victims might find any or
all these constructive and appropriate recognition at one time or
another, and might also find that each offering fails to fulfill the
deep need to have one's loss and self acknowledged.

After the embassy bombings, financial assistance from official
sources became a critical marker of recognition for both Americans and East Africans. We victims made our needs known and
officials scrambled to apportion limited funds. Perhaps less
overtly contentious than the provision of assistance, recognition

also took the form of rituals that memorialized the tragedy and sought to honor its victims. The provision of government assistance and participation in rituals helped people pull themselves together after the tragic event, yet, as described in this chapter, both also had the sometimes unfortunate effect of defining the relationships of victims to one another in ways that reinscribed hierarchies of class, nationality, and degree of suffering.

For a time my focus on gaining acknowledgment for my loss through requesting and receiving assistance and participating in rituals obscured the crucial role of law in addressing the needs of those harmed by a criminal act. As the investigation proceeded and preparations were made for the prosecution, the legal process came to have an enormous impact on my sense of self in relation to the embassy bombings and my understanding of the crime itself. For these positive benefits, I engaged with the U.S. legal system on its terms, as a "victim." Only later did the consequences of adopting that status emerge.

A month or so after the bombings, Jamal's family asked me whether there was any truth to the rumor that bombing victims in Nairobi were receiving a million shillings each from the U.S. government. The bombings and the bad weather caused by the el Nino effect had hurt the tourism and transport industries they depended on, and, in such tough times, U.S. assistance would help. Even before hearing this rumor, which seemed implausible, I had begun calling offices in the State Department to ask about help for victims. One of the first people I reached brought me up short when I inquired about "compensation." She insisted, "The U.S. government is not going to provide compensation. Compensation connotes responsibility, and *we* are not responsible for the bombings. We can only offer 'assistance.' " Every day for several weeks I faced the demoralizing experience of phoning one government office after another only to receive inadequate or insulting responses. I would call, tell my sad story, and then, once again, be told that perhaps another office could more appropriately handle my requests.

Media reports about the thousands of East African bombing victims in dire need put my own requests, especially monetary ones, in perspective. I knew that, eventually, I would go back to work, support myself, and help my husband's family to the extent that I could. Still, receiving U.S. government assistance was important to me. My persistence in seeking it emerged at least in part from a desire for the government to acknowledge my loss. The tragedy left by the bombings, including unmet needs, constituted my entire world; refusals to recognize that world—including experiences with bureaucrats who made me repeat my story or quibbled with irrelevant details—led to a feeling of emptiness that quickly filled with frustration. After a few weeks the process had worn me down, and I turned for help to an acquaintance who had high-level State Department connections. He said, "Give me some time to think about it. I want to be sure I pull a trigger that will fire." Within a day I received a call from an office where they already knew my story assuring me that assistance would be forthcoming when Congress passed a proposed bill that was expected to include emergency funds for bombing victims (e.g., school fees for dependent children and funeral expenses) and for East African institutions whose ability to provide vital assistance had been compromised by the bombings (e.g., hospitals and security forces). They welcomed me to check back but cautioned that I should not expect too much. The trigger had fired, at least for me.

Months passed before the families of Africans who had died in the bombings received any assistance from the U.S. government.[6] Awards of $5,000, plus a little more for funeral expenses, went to each family who lost a member, including mine. I split ours multiple ways among Jamal's children and siblings. Many East African recipients expressed bitterness at the small size of the awards. Some compared them to the large awards rumored to have been given to those with closer ties to the embassies. In fact, award totals differed depending on whether a deceased individual had been working on a contract basis with the embassy, or was a Foreign Service National (a more permanent position occupied by East Africans and other non-Americans), or an American employee of the U.S. Foreign Service or U.S. military. The latter categories tended to have access to insurance and other standard death benefits that many East Africans lacked.

Just determining who counted as a legitimate victim presented a logistical nightmare, particularly in Nairobi, where the list of East African victims was checked and rechecked for errors in spelling and fraudulent claimants. Cultural misunderstandings complicated the process. For instance, a significant minority of the Kenyan men who had died had left more than one wife and family. After much discussion, State Department officials decided to award funds only to the spouse with whom the deceased had been living at the time of death. Protests erupted immediately. East African men sometimes take a second wife when they move to a job in the city, leaving the first wife in the rural area to raise the eldest children, who as firstborn, are generally considered the more important set of inheritors. Yet, under the State Department plan, second or junior wives would be most likely to benefit. Eventually a decision was made to provide for each spouse. The focus on wives and children as beneficiaries also flew in the face of the cultural practice of many ethnic groups, which award property and death benefits to a man's male relatives, that is, his patrilineal clan. For many years widows across Africa had been struggling against this practice, including in the courts. Embassy officials firmly rejected disbursement to clans but were initially unaware of the intimidation that some widows—depending on ethnic group, religion, and personal relations with the husband's clan—would experience, after receiving a financial award. Stories of tragic retaliation against widows popped up repeatedly in the East African press.

No one took responsibility for conveying the promised education payments to Jamal's children.[7] My frustration at bureaucracy, and at being ignored again, returned and grew. Similar frustration, and, for many, sheer need, led a large number of Kenyans and Americans to join civil lawsuits filed by U.S. attorneys. In addition to blaming the U.S. government for negligence, one suit also charged Osama bin Laden and al Qaeda with causing wrongful death, assault, and battery, and implicated the governments of Sudan and Afghanistan.[8] Becoming a plaintiff initially appealed to me because lone victims commanded so little leverage, but aspects of the lawsuit gave me pause. For one, its logic resembled that of the U.S. government's missile strikes yet offered no more proof, for example, of the Sudanese government's role in the embassy bombings. Although I thought it important to press the U.S. government, especially given controversies over the Accountability Review Board report that had largely absolved U.S. officials from blame, charges of U.S. negligence were more apt with respect to Nairobi than Dar es Salaam. For instance, prior to the bombings Ambassador Prudence Bushnell, the U.S. envoy to Kenya at the time, had written to Secretary of State Albright to express her concern that the embassy in Nairobi was vulnerable to attack. She pointed out that certain security and safety measures mandated by State Department regulations (e.g., reinforced windows) had never been implemented. The embassy in Dar es Salaam, which had been built specially to serve as the Israeli Embassy, was a more secure structure. No one from Tanzania was asked to join the lawsuit, and, knowing that such actions can drag on for decades, I declined to become involved.

In May 1999, the U.S. State Department hosted a "Family Meeting" in Washington, D.C., to address the many issues raised by those affected by the bombings. Victims and their families were brought from all over the country, and from several, possibly related, violent tragedies, including the attack on U.S. Marines in Somalia, to meet representatives from the departments of Justice, State, and Defense, from the Social Security Administration, and from the Internal Revenue Service. Disputes over entitlements expected from these agencies, and the lawsuits filed and threatened against the government, likely motivated those scheduling the meeting. In an individual session with representatives from the Department of Justice's Office for Victims of Crime, I could not decide whether to feel happy or sad when told that they had recently realized both that I was a "special case" and that my case had "fallen through the cracks." I was the only American who had lost a non-American spouse. My spouse was the only Kenyan killed in Tanzania. And as a Fulbright scholar, my connections to the embassy were greater than those of other Americans abroad (e.g., tourists), but I was not a U.S. government employee. Assuring me that my status as an American "victim of crime" was one to which the Justice Department could definitely respond, they eagerly listed what I might expect, including treatment for injuries—physical or mental—suffered in the blast. Then, gingerly, they explained that my newly discovered status as a victim of crime stemmed primarily from my experience of being in the bombing myself, not as a result of Jamal's death. Because Jamal was not American, assisting his relatives (including me) after his death was not part of their purview.

Organizers of the Family Meeting soon found that it was risky to have brought together so many victims. Angry accusations flew, as people stood up one after another to share their stories of insensitive and inept treatment: "You said you would pay this bill, and the hospital keeps sending it to *me*"; "I kept calling and calling. No one would agree to help me"; "They sent his autopsy to me in the mail. Can you imagine how I felt?"; "My kids have nightmares. I have nightmares. I don't know what to do"; "I think maybe I'm depressed." One accusation, directed at high-ranking State Department officials, received applause: "I think you just want to forget about us." Comparing stories swelled the rage that many admitted they had brought to the meeting. I was stunned by their fury. All along I had assumed that victims with government connections would have been well cared for. I first had that impression when attending a memorial service at the National Cathedral in Washington, D.C., two months after the bombings. I noticed that each person who had worked in one of the embassies at the time of the bombings, or who had lost a loved one employed there, had a ribbon pinned to his or her lapel. Those attending had arrived together in vans that delivered them to the doorway, and they had been seated in front of myself and my family, who had come in a taxi. As I watched them file out, headed back to their vans, it occurred to me that, although we were all victims of the same event, a strict rank order divided us. Arrangements had been made for those with embassy connections, their expenses covered; the rest of us were on our own. This realization made me more determined not to be overlooked in the future, and I became increasingly sensitive to markers of my status relative to others. Since then I had assumed that the ribbons worn by some victims at the memorial service were symbols that they had gained recognition. Not only was that a false impression but at the Family Meeting I also learned that their anger differed from mine. Many felt betrayed by the government—their employer—whom they had trusted to protect them and, failing that, to help them recover. Others believed that, having risked all for their country, the service of their loved one should be recognized through any and every means. With no direct connection to the U.S. government, I had never expected much and so did not face the torturous disappointment of those whose convictions and loyalties had been shattered, and their needs unmet.

In the hope of promoting cohesion, perhaps, the meeting had been organized around the metaphor of "family," and materials distributed in the sessions made frequent references to the "Embassy Family" and the "State Department Family." Yet the anger and division typical of real families in desperate circumstances overwhelmed the metaphor's intentions.[9] Comparing our stories both helped and complicated matters for those of us trying to stabilize a sense of self. The meeting displayed the power of our numbers as victims; the horror of the bombings was remarkable because so many of us shared it, and our sense of deserving recognition deepened with this collective evidence. Yet listening to others and acknowledging their losses obscured the recognition we each sought individually. It was hard to face up to one's own relative status as a victim. The presence of victims from other tragedies helped to temper anger and fear of the future. Meeting people who had lost relatives in Oklahoma City put our experiences in perspective. Two, three, or more years out from a violent tragedy, some had found ways of making peace with what had happened and spoke of themselves not as victims but as "survivors."

At a large plenary during the Family Meeting, panelists looked down over more than a hundred audience members and addressed the government's obligation to inform us about the investigation and prosecution. Lucky breaks had jump-started the Nairobi investigation. After being treated for wounds to his face, hands, and back, a young Arab man left behind keys and a bullet in a Nairobi hospital bathroom. Police were tipped off to look for him, and, when questioned, the doctors who had treated him expressed suspicion, having noted at the time that his wounds seemed to have resulted from running away from a bomb.[10] With the assistance of U.S. investigators, Kenyan authorities found the man, Mohamed al-'Owhali, whom they detained along with other suspects. When it was learned that he had connections to others thought to be involved, al-'Owhali became a prime suspect. On August 18 raids on two rooms in Nairobi's Hilltop Hotel turned up more evidence of an active Nairobi terror cell. By the end of August FBI agents had hauled off boxes of evidence, and Kenyan officials brought the hotel manager in for questioning.[11] Within two weeks of the bombings hundreds of pieces of evidence had already been shipped to FBI labs for testing.[12]

Another suspect's route into custody was no less opportune. At the airport in Karachi, Pakistan, on August 7, an immigration officer carefully inspected the Yemeni passport of Abdull Bast Awadah, who had arrived on a flight from Nairobi. Finding that the man's face failed to match his passport picture—an infraction called a "man change"—the officer detained him. Kenyan newspapers reported that the man, who gave his name as Mohammed Sadik Howaida, told Pakistani authorities that he had been involved in planning the embassy bombings and that Osama bin Laden had sponsored them. Further interrogation yielded his real name, Mohamed Saddiq Odeh.[13]

A few months prior to the Family Meeting Jamal's sister, Fauzia, told me what she knew about Odeh, who had married a young woman from Malindi. The gossip mills had established that Odeh, a Palestinian from Jordan, had settled in Kenya several years before the bombings. After marrying and starting a fishing business, he moved to the small village of Witu on Kenya's coast. Fauzia eagerly reconstructed the kinship relations that connected Odeh's Malindi in-laws with one of Jamal's cousins, a young woman I knew well. According to Fauzia, after Odeh's arrest, his in-laws came to their family compound to express condolences and beg forgiveness. They had said, "We had no idea that he was a bad person, that he would do something so terrible. He was very pious, quiet and kind." Fauzia said that she did not know what to believe.

At the Family Meeting the first panelist to speak about the investigation was Louis Freeh, the FBI's head at the time. He announced with pride that, of the twelve individuals already indicted, four were in U.S. custody, and proceedings to extradite several from Europe had been initiated.[14] One of the men indicted was Wadih el Hage, a naturalized American who had been arrested in the United States. Affirming his goal to bring all suspects to New York's Southern District to face trial, he asserted: "Our job is to do justice." Even though, in describing those captured and their current legal statuses, he provided little more detail than the *New York Times* articles I had been following, it was an intense rush for me to be in the presence of the people who had directed the investigation and, more important, who actually knew details about the bombings. For the first time, those who had studied the tragedy, my tragedy, were explaining it. Hopeful that some answers to my "why" questions would finally be forthcoming, I opened my notebook and began to take down specifics. Freeh described the ongoing search for the remaining fugitives, who were probably in Afghanistan. When he looked out at us and said, "This is your case, more than anyone else in the world," I began to question his assertion. All this effort, agents deployed worldwide, and why had none of them ever spoken to me before now? Why had I not been asked if I had seen anything? Could they be doing such a great job, if they had not even interviewed all the eyewitnesses? Was it possible, perhaps, that the Nairobi bombing was garnering all the attention, because Americans had died there, because the U.S. government had lost so many high-level employees, because the casualties were more extensive than in Dar? My victim's sense of entitlement reared up. As Mary Jo White, the U.S. Attorney for New York's Southern District stood before us to say that, for her office, this case was the "highest priority," I began to list questions to ask the panel. White reminded us that her office had previously prosecuted terrorist attacks. By the time the lead prosecutor Patrick Fitzgerald vowed that this would be the "most important case of our lives," I tried to compose myself, writing in my notebook: "Can I get up and ask these questions?"

When the presentations ended, applause was mild, and pointed questions from the audience followed: "Why isn't the American in custody charged with treason?" One woman challenged panelists by saying that if they know that Osama bin Laden is in Afghanistan, then "we should be over there bombing it out of existence, or Iraq, or wherever." As I did not share the view that bombing other countries would be useful, expressions of vengeance brought back the image of me falling through the cracks. Frustration with the questions, and the panel's answers, which repeated platitudes about their commitment and self-congratulations for the progress already made, motivated me to approach the microphone. In a voice that came out less shaky than I had feared, I spoke from the scribbles in my notebook: "I was one of the last people to enter the embassy in Dar es Salaam before the bomb went off, and I was one of the first people to leave. My husband, Abdurahman Mohammed Abdallah, was killed. No one from your office or from the FBI has ever interviewed me about what I saw." There was a collective gasp from other victims. "See," hissed a woman who will never be satisfied that enough had been done to investigate her daughter's murder. I asked whether Nairobi was more of a priority for investigators. The prosecutors clamored to respond after my final question: "If the trial takes place in the U.S., what does it mean for justice for East Africans, like my husband's family?"

Prosecutor Pat Fitzgerald leaned into the mike: "We know about you. You're a college professor in Connecticut. We didn't want to bother you, because we thought you'd be busy." I brushed off his excuse with a frown probably not visible from so far away. Panel members assured me that East Africans would be invited to participate and would get justice along with the rest of us. Catching me on the way back to my seat, a counselor with experience in Oklahoma City asked if I felt angry about the bombing and would I like to talk about it? After falling through the cracks, I had landed right where many expected me to: in the box set aside for allegedly irrational victims assumed to be acting out unresolved anger.

As the session broke up, FBI agents swarmed around me, saying: "Could we talk to you? Won't take long." "We've been wanting to meet you. But we've been investigating in Africa." We ducked into a deserted meeting room. Mike, whom I would come to know well, took off his coat and, turning to hang it, exposed the gun tucked down the back of his pants. I thought, "Who's going to threaten him here?" Then I remembered the fierce anger of disgruntled victims.

Mike introduced Ken Karas, one of the prosecutors, and Abby, another FBI agent. They asked me to describe the day of the bombing. I took my time laying out what had happened. Jamal and I had taken the bus from the university and got off before reaching the embassy. Mike knew the place. "Then we walked along Ali Hassan Mwinyi Drive, beside the embassy fence, and turned in at Laibon Street. We parted at the guard house. Jamal was going to wait for me, to smoke a cigarette. I went inside." They nodded patiently. I continued by describing what happened after the bomb went off, how I ran out a back exit, tried to climb a fence, and then rushed through a gate that miraculously opened onto the street. The agents asked a few questions. Then I asked them something I had wanted to know for a long time: "Where, exactly, was the bomb?" Newspapers had answered this question in different ways. Taking my notebook and pen, Mike drew a diagram of the area around the embassy. I pointed to where Jamal had been standing. Then in shaky handwriting I traced where I had run after leaving the embassy and the paths I took trying desperately to reach Jamal. I drew a bold line to mark where a barbed wire fence had stopped me. Bursting tires, which I and others heard as gunshots, had also forced me back. Even though I had tried going around the embassy another way, I never reached Jamal. I left the scene within a half hour, heading to the hospitals to search for him.

With a sinking heart I realized that, although I saw horrors I wished I could forget, I did not see much of use to the investigation. Mike's and Ken's questions demonstrated that they knew a tremendous amount about the bombings. But they claimed modesty about their understanding of East Africa generally and asked for my help with a problem: "We can't get Muslim people in Kenya to open up to us. We want to talk with more people in the community." I smiled. My book on coastal Kenya had described that reticence as typical of Swahili culture. People are outwardly welcoming, but if those seeking entrée are police or otherwise associated with the government, they will not get very far into Swahili homes, mosques, or social networks. The agents asked whether I had connections with Muslim political leaders, but it turned out that investigators had to avoid the politicians I knew, who were bitterly opposed to the ruling party. Mike said, shaking his head, "We operate in Kenya by permission of the government." "That's part of your problem," I said. "Few people trust them." Then Mike suggested that maybe I could bring a couple of agents to the houses of people I know, introduce them to ordinary people in the community in that way. With visions of protests from parents of young Muslim women, I explained that entering homes for questioning was impossible. But unwilling to depict Swahili culture as inherently conservative, I extolled the moderate qualities of Islamic practice on the Swahili coast, and then talked about how anthropologists, having gained trust in a community, guard against being used as conduits for "outsiders," whose purposes might be viewed as threatening or offensive. As we said good-bye, Abby asked me for pictures of Jamal and his family, saying, "I like to have pictures. It helps remind me of who I'm working for—the victims and their families."

The interview was a turning point for me. Not only was it the first time that anyone official had listened to my story about the bombing, which gave me a satisfying rush of feeling recognized, but I was able, finally, to question people who knew the story behind the bombings. The Family Meeting's emphasis on my entitlement to information as a victim changed how I understood my position. That entitlement, along with my newly found access to those in the know, encouraged me to believe that I might find answers to the questions that haunted me, Fauzia, and others.

During the plenary panel at the Family Meeting, prosecutors explained the indictment issued the previous November, which included more than two hundred criminal counts against twelve suspects.[15] The government's long-standing investigation of Osama bin Laden, described briefly by U.S. Attorney Mary Jo White, had allowed her office to construct a portrait of al Qaeda's complex organization and its history of threatening U.S. interests. The indictment's brief background section asserted that bin Laden, as al Qaeda's leader, or *emir*, along with associates who pledged an oath to the organization, dedicated themselves to opposing non-Islamic governments. The United States was viewed as an enemy because of its infidel status, its support for governments al Qaeda opposed (e.g., Saudi Arabia), and its prosecution of terrorists. This last charge was linked directly to the work of White's office, which had convicted Ramzi Yusuf and Sheikh Omar Abdul Rahman who were serving life sentences for various offenses involving the 1993 World Trade Center bombing and other planned attacks in Manhattan. The indictment's portrait of al Qaeda reflected years of investigation and had motivated a previous indictment naming Osama bin Laden, which had been filed under seal two months before the bombings. Al Qaeda had long been on the Southern District's radar.

Count 1 of the indictment charged the defendants with "conspiracy to kill United States nationals."[16] This section of the U.S. Code was intended to allow for prosecution of terrorist killings abroad, and, in some instances, conviction carried a life sentence.[17] Relying on a conspiracy charge allowed prosecutors to implicate bin Laden and other top al Qaeda officials even though most were nowhere near East Africa at the time of the bombings. Once the al Qaeda organization broadcast its mission to kill Americans through the religious decrees called *fatwas*, many of their actions, even those that initially seemed not terribly serious, such as establishing front companies, providing fake identity and travel documents, and engaging in coded correspondence, became evidence of the conspiracy to murder. The specific overt acts of some defendants began to fill out how the bombings were planned and accomplished. For example, overt acts attributed to Mohamed Sadeek Odeh included his decision to join al Qaeda, his role in establishing a Kenyan base of operations, his presence in Nairobi with other conspirators, and his flight from Kenya the day before the bombing.[18] The indictment focused on those defendants in custody, linking each to al Qaeda, its business or military activities or both, and other overt acts related more directly to the bombings.

Counts 2 and 3 of the initial indictment centered on the bombings. Under the U.S. Code, defendants were charged with "using fire or an explosion" to destroy U.S. property and thereby causing death.[19] Although located within sovereign nations, U.S. embassies, as a matter of international law, are considered U.S. territory, and federal laws apply. These counts therefore focused on the harms to property and the other events (specifically deaths) that resulted from acts directed against that property. Superceding indictments would eventually include additional conspiracy counts: conspiracy to murder, kidnap, and maim at places outside the United States;[20] conspiracy to murder relating to American nationals, military personnel, and diplomats;[21] conspiracy to use weapons of mass destruction against nationals of the United States; conspiracy to destroy buildings and property of the United States; and conspiracy to attack national defense utilities.[22] Some of these charges were later dropped either because of their irrelevance or redundancy.

Immediately after the bombings Tanzanian authorities had arrested more than a dozen people—all foreign nationals, all Muslims.[23] But confusion about what actually occurred in the Dar es Salaam bombing exacerbated the difficulty of determining responsibility. Initial reports claimed that an oil truck, found damaged yards from the building, had delivered the bomb. Once it was sorted out that the truck had carried water, not oil, and was, in fact, the embassy's water truck, suspicions turned to the driver and his assistant; the former had been killed in the blast, and the latter was missing. The investigation honed in on others with access to the truck, including a garage owner and mechanics.[24] Within days, however, the FBI determined that the water truck had not delivered the bomb but rather had been thrown into the air by the blast and hit the side of the embassy.[25] It would be months before authorities confirmed through DNA tests that the driver's assistant had also died at the site. Most of those arrested initially in Dar es Salaam were eventually released, as immigration violations were the most serious charges that could be made against any of them. For instance, a Somali-born Australian working for the UN High Commission for Refugees was unlucky enough to be without his passport and other identification documents when Tanzanian police detained him during a sweep of his hotel. For a time they found unconvincing his insistence that an office in Dar es Salaam was processing his papers.[26] One suspect, Rashid Hemed, was allegedly found with blasting caps in his residence and charged under Tanzanian law with offenses relating to the bombings.[27]

Had the East African governments prosecuted the accused, different legal logics would necessarily have applied. For example, the death of a Kenyan citizen on a bus destroyed by the blast might have been prosecuted as a form of murder, perhaps murder with a weapon of mass destruction, not murder "during the course of an attack on a federal facility." Instead, the crimes charged in the indictment emerged from the intention of those accused to harm Americans and American facilities. This conceptualization of the crime made a clear distinction—legally and thus necessarily—between American loss and other losses. Destructive of considerably more East African than U.S. property, the crime against property was still one that began with the intent to harm U.S. interests. Despite the much higher casualty count for East Africans compared to Americans, it was still the intent to murder the latter that motivated the law's application. The charges further subdivided American victims into military personnel, embassy employees, nationals, and internationally protected persons (i.e., diplomats). My own reaction after reading the indictment was to feel that my interests and experiences, as the widow of an East African, were tacked onto crimes that were more serious because they violated U.S. interests. And yet most important to me was that my husband, an East African, had been killed. It was hard to avoid feeling that the violations against us emanated from acts that were designated criminal by virtue of targeting others.

To counteract the impression that American lives and property figured first and foremost in the U.S. prosecution, Counts 4 through 227 of the initial indictment charged the defendants with the murders of 224 people. Every single person killed in the bombings (with the exception of the suicide bombers) was listed alphabetically, African and American. When I questioned whether American interests were privileged in the handling of the crime, prosecutors referred to these counts, and especially all the names, as evidence that their office was committed to bringing justice to everyone harmed.

Eager to mend fences after the contentious Family Meeting, the State Department invited bombings victims to travel to Kenya, Tanzania, or Washington, D.C., to mark the first anniversary of the bombings in August 1999. When they extended the invitation to me, I viewed it as an opportunity to involve Jamal's family, especially his sons, who had yet to be contacted by anyone from the U.S. government. The State Department arranged for Mary Porter to accompany me to Malindi, where six members of Jamal's family joined us for the trip to Dar es Salaam.

One year after the bombings the U.S. ambassador to Tanzania was political appointee Charles Stith, an ordained minister who had long been active in Democratic politics in the Boston area. He and his wife, a physician, carefully orchestrated three days of commemorative events that melded religion, state, pathos, memorializing, and forward thinking into a healing process. A printed program outlined their intentions: "We meet to remember and honor those who perished, those who were hurt and those who suffered great personal loss. However, while we gather in solemn memory, we want these days also to be a signpost as we move toward our future: A future characterized by a healing spirit and hope out of sorrow."

The first event took place at the temporary embassy where the Dar es Salaam staff had relocated shortly after the bombing. Local religious leaders—two Christians and a Muslim—offered brief remarks to the solemn crowd of employees, victims, and local dignitaries. After some words from the ambassador and a moment of tearful silence at the precise time of the bombings,

Figure 3. Jamal's nephew and sons at the U.S. Embassy in Dar es Salaam, August 1999. Credit: Susan Hirsch

Jamal's youngest son, along with children of other victims, pulled a cord to unveil a plaque with the names of those killed. Jamal's name appeared first; the others following alphabetically. Eventually the plaque, which matched one being unveiled that same day at the State Department in Washington, would stand in the lobby of the new embassy.[28] The ceremony was short and formal, capturing and accentuating our somber mood.

Most of those in attendance that morning were embassy employees. Only a few Americans present at the time of the bombing had stayed on; others had been reassigned during the previous year. Their replacements had not experienced the bombings and thus faced the challenge of empathizing with the colleagues who had. Most Tanzanian staff had continued working for the embassy. Given the high rate of unemployment in Tanzania, one of the world's poorest nations, an embassy job was a precious opportunity, and staff members traumatized by the bombing had little choice but to continue in their positions. Even after moving to the temporary embassy, with heightened security precautions, going to work each day filled many with fear. A month or so after occupying the temporary quarters, frayed nerves snapped during a fluke incident when an embassy security guard, probably overcome by stress, began shooting randomly outside the building.

The past year had been hard on the Tanzanian staff in other ways. Wave after wave of investigators had subjected them to interviews as the investigation proceeded to cast considerable suspicion on local staff. The initial belief that the driver of the truck, considered one of their own, might have been involved in the bombing created an atmosphere of distrust and anguish among embassy employees. Everyone breathed a sigh of relief when investigators determined that another vehicle was involved and the finger of blame once again pointed outward.[29] The Accountability Review Board's finding that security had not been breached through the fault of anyone working at the embassy failed to erase bitter feelings about the breakdown of trust. Some staff—both American and Tanzanian—felt worn down by previous memorial services, which returned them repeatedly to the pain of the original event. Those who wanted to move beyond the bombings came to feel that such events, although well intentioned, pulled them back into the terror and also the debilitating sadness of remembering lost colleagues. Those who suffered from lingering injuries had no reprieve from the effects of the bombings.

The one-year commemoration provided my first opportunity to mark the incident publicly with Tanzanians and the first time for Jamal's family to experience official recognition for their loss. Many of the embassy staff offered their sympathies, though few had met Jamal. We garnered special attention from embassy officials, perhaps because I was the only American victim who had made the trip. When Mary and I realized this, we agreed to avoid attracting more attention than the families of the other victims. Half of those killed had been Tanzanian security guards, employees of a firm under contract to provide the personnel who check IDs, operate the metal detector, and otherwise police access to the embassy.[30] Several of their widows, and other relatives, attended the ceremony, as did the husband of Mtendeje Rajabu, the only woman killed. Many of us had known Mten-

deje by face. Her demeanor was usually sunny as she ushered
visitors into the embassy. But at times she could be all business.
Her husband, looking sad, admitted to me how hard it was to
raise their small children without her and in such tough economic times.

As we left the temporary embassy, Jamal's eldest son asked
whether the actual bombing had taken place nearby. When I told
him that the old embassy was about five minutes away, he and
his brothers insisted on going there. The middle son, nicknamed
Jiddi, said, "We want to see where *marehemu* died. The exact
place." No one was around as we drove in and parked by the
flimsy fence ringing the battered embassy. I pointed to where I
thought Jamal had been standing when the bomb went off. On
that spot, facing the abandoned building with a still gaping hole
blown into its side, the boys were led in a few moments of
prayer by Mohamed Jelani, their older cousin. We all broke
down; I cried at their bravery and my own fear. No one, including me, had thought that they might want to see the embassy.
Earlier I had carefully instructed our driver to take a route that
would avoid passing it, mostly to protect myself. Unbeknownst
to me, the boys had hoped that, in coming to Dar, they would
get the chance to pray for their father, at the very site of his
death. For them, those prayers were the most meaningful ritual
of the trip. When we left, we stopped at the beach; Jamal's youngest son ran with abandon on the sand.

On leaving the hotel the next morning we headed to the National Museum of Tanzania, where Ambassador Stith and Tanzanian dignitaries would launch an art exhibit commemorating
the bombings. In the museum's large courtyard, parts of the exhibit were already visible: car parts and charred bicycles strewn
about randomly resembling the scene just after the bombing. A
sculpture covered with a drop cloth stood tall above a circle of
round flat stones each bearing a plaintive face looking up. Ambassador Stith presided over the unveiling, which revealed an
armless female head and torso. Its creator, Scandinavian sculp-
tor Clara Sornas, called it "Hope Out of Sorrow." A young Tanzanian woman from Bagamoyo, a town just up the coast from

Dar, had been the model for the sculpture, but Sornas insisted that the figure was intentionally anonymous. Someone in the audience questioned her. Why anonymous, when one specific African woman—Mtendeje Rajabu—had died? And why a woman, when mostly men had died? Sornas explained that the statue represented not a woman but Hope. Just behind Hope, Sornas had positioned a large cracked window that had been in the booth where the security guards, including Mtendeje, had been killed. As others debated the meaning of the female figure, I focused on that window, marveling that it had cracked but not broken. It looked just like the visa window that Jamal and I had stood in front of so often while seeking his immigrant visa. To me, the cracked window symbolized the strength of the U.S. barriers that keep people on one side or the other yet cannot prevent their destruction.

My reaction to the window was admittedly idiosyncratic. The experiences that Jamal and I had had seeking his immigrant visa made it meaningful, and objectionable, in a very particular way. No doubt others, including those cut by flying glass from windows shattered by the blast, would react differently to the window. Plaques, sculpture, and other physical memorials are open to multiple interpretations. Their official or intended meanings can be articulated by their creators, but those who view them, whether victims or members of the public, understand the symbols through their own experiences, interests, and perspectives. At the museum, some among the crowd expressed disdain for the exhibit's unkempt appearance, especially the charred car parts. Such struggles implied the impossibility that a material object can contain all the significance of an event like the bombings. The difficulty posed by multiple perspectives, which express the various needs of victims, governments, the public, and the public of the future, pointed to the importance of creating and recognizing multiple memorials. The more material to interpret, the more chance that at least one would resonate. Though I might have created a different sculpture, or altered the wording on a plaque, these objects did me, and other victims, the great service of bearing some of the responsibility for marking and preserving memories of the

Figure 4. Victims and family members gathered for the unveiling of "Hope out of Sorrow" at the National Museum of Tanzania, August 1999. Credit: Mohamed Jelani

bombings. Victims always carry the knowledge that we are the most crucial repositories of such memories. Yet it was a relief to leave behind these material markers, which would carry on the never-ending work of remembering and thereby lighten the burden on ourselves as victims.[31]

At the museum a State Department employee had taken my hand and closed it over a business card, saying, "You remember Mike, from the FBI? He says he met you at the Family Meeting. He's here with Abby, staying out at the Sea Breeze Hotel. They'd like to talk with you while you're here, if you get a chance." Later that day, when we were tired from all the public events, we made our way out to the Sea Breeze. From the lobby phone, I called Mike's number and took some pleasure in surprising him on what had become the FBI's turf. The family sat down at a large table on an open air patio looking out over the water and finally relaxed. Abby and Mike joined us. They were not supposed to be in the country during the anniversary, as a courtesy to those who had felt beleaguered by the agents' endless questions. "But something is up," Mike said with a meaningful look. He and Abby were sure that someone among those involved in the bombing would slip up, possibly one of the young East African suspects. I agreed that it might be hard for them to resist contacting their relatives.

Mike asked me to translate so that he and Abby could tell Jamal's family about their role in the investigation. They explained that they were trying to catch those responsible for the bombings and that they were working on our behalf. At first, the boys looked wary. Mindful of accusations against "Fee Bee," the local name for the FBI, we could all recount stories of bad behavior attributed to American investigators, such as searching domestic spaces reserved for women, or entering mosques with their shoes on and intimidating young Muslim men. Swahili Muslims feared reprisals from their non-Muslim countrymen, and faced the harsh scrutiny of investigation by both Kenyan police, who often abused them, and by Americans, whose power they feared. Backed by some Muslim officials, accusations against investigators were made publicly. In some in-

stances stories of abuse turned out to be exaggerations, designed
to get press attention or galvanize the Muslim community. But
in the months after the bombings, my friends and family had
become frightened and felt at risk that violence would be directed toward them.

Listening to Abby and Mike, two personable individuals who
expressed their earnest commitment to the tasks before them,
the boys softened; their faces betrayed admiration and interest.
For their part, the agents seemed to be watching the boys closely,
especially Ali, the teenager who was having such a hard time
since his father's death. Abby took the two younger boys aside
and pulled out yo-yos. Soon they were happily entranced. At
one end of the table Mary and Mike pushed their chairs back to
talk quietly. Mary explained what we do as anthropologists, that
she and I had each stayed for long periods of time in Kenya and
Tanzania, learned the language, and studied Islam and Swahili
culture. Appreciative of her expertise, Mike asked Mary whether
she would be willing to give a lecture at the FBI's New York
office, admitting, "We're trying to understand. We just don't
know enough. It would help us to hear about Islam and Africa
from someone like you." She told him that she would have to
think about it but that he could contact her once we were all
back in the States.

That night Mary and I talked for a long time. We both felt
Abby and Mike's sincerity in wanting to understand more about
Islam and the East African communities where they operated.
In short, knowing more would enable them to do their jobs more
effectively. But what was our role? I challenged myself aloud,
"Shouldn't I try to do everything possible so that they can catch
the people who killed Jamal? Shouldn't I offer what I know
about Muslim communities in East Africa?" Mary had similar
questions about her own responsibility. And we both knew that
lack of knowledge about the community and its norms was
likely leading to serious misunderstandings. But the initial concern in the eyes of Jamal's sons urged caution. In the days after
the bombings, Kenyan Muslims were warned to reject appeals
to collaborate in the investigation. For instance, a Saudi-based
organization, al Muhajirun, wrote an editorial for a Kenyan

newspaper, which read: "Oh, Moslems, the US government is appealing to you with a two million dollar bribe to spy against your brothers which will lead you to hellfire since spying is forbidden, for Allah says 'do not spy on each other' and 'whoever betrays, deceives or cheats us is not one of us.' "[32] Most Swahili Muslims were unaware of these warnings or ignored them, but many were conscious of their vulnerability and of the lack of protection for those who might cooperate with authorities. Given those circumstances, what kind of information could we provide that would avoid the risk of compromising anyone? Thoughts of collaborating with a U.S. government agency brought up stories of anthropologists accused—some rightly, some wrongly—of, for example, spying on guerilla positions during the Vietnam War. Such accusations turned suspicion onto all researchers, endangering some who had no ties at all to the U.S. government. Moreover, scholars can hardly control how the information we provide is used by an agency or an investigator or how members of a community will ultimately be viewed or treated. But is it arrogant to imagine that we can protect the people we are tied to through research, when bombs have killed some of them, and when they face threats for participating in any investigation? What strategies of ours could protect them? Or ourselves? Mary and I shared our frustration at being in the dark about many issues, not least the troubling reality that some East African men stood accused of participating in the bombings. Mary decided that, if contacted by the FBI, she would decline to lecture on Swahili culture. In her view, the risk of people being harmed by partial knowledge inexpertly applied seemed greater than any help she might offer. In any case, the FBI never contacted her.

On the final day of the commemorative weekend, Ambassador Stith and his wife opened their home for an afternoon reception. The light-hearted tenor of the event contrasted completely with the somber plaque dedication just two days before. No hint of death or fear or funerals. At the reception my stepsons heard for the first time the sweet tinkling of American jazz; we ate petit fours and drank tea from gold-rimmed china cups. The ambassador's wife walked us through an art exhibit hanging in their home. The eleven pieces, all by African American artists, had been selected for their focus on healing, a process the Stiths wanted to encourage while serving in post-bombing Tanzania. Jamal's cousin, Shamsa, stopped in front of a large piece called "Fence with Hands." It was a folding screen made of glass. Pressed between the panes were pairs of ladies' gloves, of various demure colors, some edged with tasteful lace. Shamsa asked Mrs. Stith, "Do American women wear gloves? In Kenya it's only widows and very pious women who wear them when they want to cover up completely." I translated, as the ambassador's wife explained that African American women used to wear gloves to church in order to appear respectable. Shamsa joked about how fashion changes everywhere. We laughed quite a few times that day, without the guilt of grief.

Judging from my own response, the commemorative weekend had achieved the Stiths' sensitive aspirations for us. The events had taken us through a process of solemnly and sadly acknowledging our losses, concretely memorializing the bombing, rebuilding toward the future, and then stepping out and opening our eyes to enjoy life's beauty once again. The experience paralleled the transition from viewing oneself as a victim to embracing the status of "survivor." The weekend played out a time-compressed version of an ideal trajectory of healing after tragedy, one where individuals follow a smooth path from the depths of despair to the dawn of new hope. Anyone who had experienced the bombings, or lost a relative, knew that the path of healing looped back on itself, cut off at dead ends, and forced the victim/survivor to start over, and over again. But somehow the weekend had moved us, had lightened our burdens and made us into survivors, at least momentarily.

Once back in Malindi our own rituals marked Jamal's memory and the anniversary of the bombings. Jamal's sons and I presented a donation to the officers of the Malindi Muslim Orphans Association (MMOA), a local charity Jamal had patronized. Board members shared with us the plans for a new building, and we discussed using funds donated in Jamal's name to include a computer room. As the event broke up one of the officers pulled me aside. Looking embarrassed, he said, "I don't want you to worry, but tomorrow I have to tell the police that you were here and that you gave us money." He explained that, ever since the bombings, American officials had forced the Kenyan police to crack down on all Muslim charities, some of which were believed to have supported violent causes by providing false IDs for personnel and trafficking weapons. After one of the bombing suspects admitted that he had connections to an organization called Help Africa People, FBI agents, along with Kenyan authorities, raided several Muslim charities and shut down five.[33] Closing the charities created a public relations problem as some were actively assisting Somali refugees in Kenya's desperately poor Northeast Province. Through political and religious representatives, the Kenyan Muslim community—which had condemned the embassy bombings—strongly protested the closings, calling them "a continuation of harassment, persecution and intimidation that Muslims in Kenya have been subjected to."[34] A Christian leader complained that "Kenya should not be drawn into the ongoing war between the Western world and perceived Islamic fundamentalism."[35] Charges that the closings violated civil liberties came from prominent Kenyan lawyers.[36] Threats of court cases ended with some charities reopening and the permanent closure of others.

Knowing the reputation of the Kenyan police, I asked the leader of the orphan's charity whether he would have to pay bribes to get the police to leave them alone. He smiled and said, "You know how these things go. But we have a pretty good relationship with the police, and we're getting used to this kind of harassment." The ironies infuriated me. Money collected to ease suffering after the bombing had become suspect because of the investigation.

Two months after the commemorative trip, Mike called to say that he and Abby had just returned from South Africa where they had arrested another suspect. Khalfan Khamis Mohamed, or "K.K." as he came to be known, was accused of participating in the Dar es Salaam bombing, and he was the only Tanzanian in custody thus far. Mike wanted to be sure that I heard about the arrest from him, rather than reading it in the paper. I appreciated being let in on the developments of the investigation. In moments like these I felt a stake in Abby's and Mike's work, which was crucial in helping me to understand what had happened.

The embassy bombings trial would not begin for more than a year after that conversation with Mike. During that period many victims, like me, focused on returning to our careers and continuing the long healing process. Controversies over assistance continued, with no one feeling satisfied. The civil lawsuits moved along slowly. By the time another memorial was dedicated in May 2000—a lone poplar tree planted in Arlington Cemetery next to a simple plaque—the bombings had all but disappeared from public memory.

Being a victim of crime, as defined through the law, meant that I witnessed the growing attention devoted to the bombings case as it moved toward trial. The prosecutors' office in New York sent regular updates about the case to inform victims about, for example, the timetable for the trial, amendments to the indictment, and information about how the prosecutor's office would assist those of us who wanted to attend the trial at the Manhattan court once it began. The frequency of these missives increased as the trial's opening in early 2001 neared, and although they contained no real information about the bombings or what the investigation had found, they enticed me to believe that the trial would be an important event that I would not want to miss. Although the rituals and other memorial events, the assistance provided by the U.S. government, and time itself had put me on the path to becoming a "survivor," the trial would emphasize my status as a victim and, were I to attend, I risked becoming stuck in that identity or re-traumatized. I understood why many victims would choose not to attend (or not be able to). But the trial would direct considerable public attention to the bombings, and, quite simply, I felt I should be present.

CHAPTER THREE
Recounting Chaos

SECURITY WAS TIGHT on the first day of jury selection for the embassy bombings trial. Before passing through the metal detector near the courtroom door, I signed my name in the log book and then, following the lead of those before me, wrote "Victim" in the column under "Purpose." Although I had struggled to assert my agency after the debilitating tragedy, to become a "survivor," I had also learned to adopt the "victim" label strategically, especially when I wanted something, such as access to the trial. On that day, in early January 2001, my preparations to attend court had quite unconsciously resembled what I had done when studying Islamic courts in East Africa. I packed a small bag with the kind of composition book I have always used as a journal and for fieldnotes, a couple of pens, a bottle of water, and something to read during the inevitable periods of waiting that characterized courts everywhere. Just before I entered the courtroom together with several other victims and family members, one of the many federal marshals whose mandate included monitoring security told me to keep my magazine in my bag unless the jury left the room. As federal marshals steered us into the very last rows of the packed courtroom, one young woman complained loudly, "Why are we back here? *We're* the victims." Gesturing at those seated in front of us, she asked, "Why should the press be able to see and not us?" With threatening stares and warnings that the judge was about to enter, the marshals quieted everyone.

Perched high at the front of the court and flanked by flags, the judge's bench was visible, but we could see little else. The largest courtroom in the Manhattan Federal building, the site of previous terror trials, had been specially outfitted for this one. On the left, just behind the rail that separated counsel, defendants, judge, and jury from the rest of us, four large interpreters' booths blocked our view of the defendants and their attorneys.

Judge Leonard Sand entered, and with just a few sentences he explained that jury selection was closed to the public and press, and both were ordered to leave immediately. I had known about these restrictions beforehand, and prosecutors had urged me, and other victims, not to come to court just to be turned away. I had made the trip anyway, sensing the symbolic importance of being present at the very first moments of the trial. As we filed out, several of us tried to catch a glimpse of the defendants. The chance to see them face to face, for the first time, had also motivated my presence.

When jury selection ended a month later, victims, journalists, and the public were welcomed back to the courtroom, which had been rearranged in the interim. The interpretation booths—set behind the last row—no longer blocked our view from the audience. On the left side of the court, the first long row of seats was occupied by the security detail, so that they would be close behind the defendants. The second row was reserved for visiting dignitaries, for example, personnel from the Kenyan and Tanzanian consulates. Victims and witnesses sat in the next few rows followed by associates in the prosecutors' office and the FBI at the back. Across the aisle, journalists filled several rows on some days. But for much of the trial only stalwart representatives of the major outlets turned up.[1] Toward the front, just near the jury box, sketch artists worked quickly to create visuals that ended up on websites and in the newspapers.[2] Members of the public sat at the back or in an overflow room on another floor.

Victims' advocates hired by the Department of Justice provided logistical assistance to victims who attended the trial, such as alerting us about schedule changes and explaining court procedures. A special program paid the costs of transportation and accommodations for some. Victims and family members were invited to gather in the victim/witness lounge each morning and enter court together. One day, early on in the trial, a victims' advocate gave each of us a small lapel pin to be worn whenever we attended court. Bearing the map of Africa, with Kenya and Tanzania highlighted, the pin would alert the federal marshals that its bearer was a victim and should be seated accordingly. Within a week, however, we were told not to wear the pins anymore. Defense attorneys had complained that jurors might see them, figure out that we were bombing victims, and be inappropriately influenced. I followed instructions, hardly giving a thought to leaving the pin at home. For so long after the bombings, gaining my government's recognition as a bombing victim had preoccupied me. But by this point, my place in court was unquestioned, and a physical marker of that recognition no longer seemed necessary.

Among the many reasons I had for attending the trial was my desire to hear the bombings described in public. The agonizing moments of terror and chaos demanded an open hearing, and, by recounting them for all to hear, those testifying would offer the recognition that I sought for myself, Jamal, and other victims. In my view, the trial would not achieve justice unless it provided public recognition for us through telling our story.

Addressing the impaneled jury for the first time, Assistant U.S. Attorney Paul Butler began the prosecution's opening statement right where the story started for most victims: "It's August 7, 1998. It's a Friday, about 10:30 in the morning. It is downtown Nairobi, the capital of Kenya, a country located in eastern Africa. It's business as usual at the American Embassy, which means busy."[3] Speaking calmly, he described bustling activities at the embassy, in the secretarial college next door, and in a nearby office tower. The city intersection came alive with morning traffic, including a bus bringing children to school, and then, "in the blink of an eye, everything changed" (p. 22). A massive blast shattered buildings and left hundreds dead, thousands injured. And, Butler continued soberly, "the horror repeated itself minutes, perhaps even seconds later, in another country in east Africa called Tanzania," where "eleven more innocent people were killed and dozens more were injured" (pp. 23–24).

For scholars in my field, stories are the crucial centerpiece of trials.[4] In many cases, jurors must decide which one is true among two seemingly plausible accounts of "what happened" as put forward by prosecution, on the one hand, and defense, on the other. In their opening and closing statements, and as they question witnesses, talented attorneys are mindful of building and enhancing the "story" they want the jury to remember and embrace. Discrediting the opponent's account is a common parallel pursuit. A trial's opening statement offers the first chance to tell those stories. In his book, *A Theory of the Trial*, Robert Burns makes the point that, while the story told in an opening statement might sound like an objective or "god's-eye view" of the events at issue, it has already been infused with the legal significance that the attorney intends to argue to the jury.[5] Being a good prosecutor Paul Butler, in his opening statement, recounted the bombings as part of a broader story of nefarious deeds attributed to al Qaeda, and from a perspective that had already attached moral significance to those actions. His overarching "theory of the case" shaped how he recounted what happened that day.[6] The delicate challenge, according to Burns, would come as Butler tried to fit the individual stories told by eyewitnesses and others into the larger narrative that would either implicate or exonerate those accused.

Stories told in court differ from those of everyday conversation, and many people find the constraints of testifying difficult to negotiate. A person's ability to testify depends on many factors, including personality, culture, and social position. My research in East Africa showed that when Swahili women went to Islamic court they told long narratives about their marital difficulties in an effort to gain recognition for their suffering and to achieve a remedy.[7] Their stories implicated husbands in desertion, insufficient financial support,[8] and cruel emotional and physical treatment. Their stories were compelling sagas told with all the dramatic features of Swahili storytelling, including sound effects and conversations replayed in the voices of husbands, neighbors, and themselves. Not only did a woman achieve recognition by forcing the judge and observers in court to bear witness to the struggles in her domestic life, but, as I found, women almost always won their cases.[9] Because the stories Swahili women told contrasted so starkly with men's testimony, which tended to offer pronouncements about law and only terse descriptions of married life, I was interested as much in the forms of speech people used in court as in the content of their accounts. The dramatic qualities of women's stories, and their skill as storytellers, contributed to their success. And although they had to overcome shame and shyness, many Swahili women expressed satisfaction that they had found the courage to tell their stories in court. This finding was a cross-cultural affirmation of something scholars had established with respect to witnesses in the United States: getting a public hearing for one's story can be tremendously satisfying, a crucial aspect of achieving justice.[10]

Prosecutors had not asked me to testify in this phase of the trial, and I wondered how the few eyewitnesses selected would approach the daunting task. Their testimony would be guided by Butler and the other prosecutors, who would link individual stories to the government's theory of the case and would help witnesses achieve the twin goals of legal relevance and rhetorical drama. Hearing the accounts of the bombings told in court and observing the collaborative process from which they emerged challenged some of my assumptions about how witnesses tell stories in court while confirming others. The experience of participating in the trial as a victim also compelled me to reevaluate my view of how stories provide the recognition central to justice as I understood it.

Although Paul Butler began by recounting the story of the bombings, another story—one that had to be told, and told well, to gain convictions of all four defendants—described events occurring long before August 7, 1998. As Butler put it, the prosecution's evidence would show that the bombings "were a major strike in an ongoing terrorist plot carried out by a violent worldwide group" (p. 23). Prosecutors would, in fact, devote most days of the long trial to providing evidence of al Qaeda's existence, its conspiratorial operations and its role in many violent acts. Yet the opening statement gave a preview of how the prosecution would return repeatedly to victims' vivid stories of the bombings so as to focus the jury's attention on the concrete horror resulting from an otherwise abstract accusation of conspiracy.

First and foremost on the prosecution's agenda was to prove Count 1 of the indictment, that al Qaeda members conspired to kill Americans. No one knew the importance of proving the con-

spiracy better than Butler, whose career had been shaped by al
Qaeda's machinations. Of the four prosecutors trying the embassy bombings case, Butler was the only one who had been with
the Southern District office during its prosecution of the 1993
World Trade Center bombing, which ended in life sentences for
four defendants.[11] From the investigations surrounding that
trial, Butler and his colleagues became aware of what appeared
to be an international conspiracy against the U.S. government,
and they began a hunt for its leaders, which by the mid-1990s
centered on Osama bin Laden. Even though bin Laden was still
at large when the embassy bombings trial began, proving the
existence of an al Qaeda conspiracy would mean that Butler's
office would finally get to reveal evidence against the man who
had been their target for years.

We watched Paul Butler in profile as he stood at the podium
on the right side of court and spoke directly to the jury. His colleagues—Patrick Fitzgerald, Ken Karas, and Mike Garcia—sat at
the prosecutors' table in front of him; their reactions were rarely
visible as we viewed them mostly from behind. So when Butler
asked, "Why did these bombings happen? Who could be responsible for such horrible acts of violence?" he brought jurors,
victims, and the press to the edges of our seats. We all wanted
to know, and Butler's answers took us to Afghanistan in the late
1970s and then to Sudan and Kenya, tracking bin Laden and his
allegedly expanding organization. While these defendants faced
hundreds of charges, Count 1 was especially important, and Butler carefully laid out the evidence of a conspiracy—numerous
threats made against the United States and Americans, the military training of bin Laden's operatives, the deployment of trainees and trainers to help Somalis oust U.S. troops, and the businesses (some fake) used by the group to fund a worldwide
financial network and to conceal the deadly operations of its
military wing.

Butler confronted the courtroom with a dizzying array of
names unfamiliar at that time: al Qaeda, bin Laden, and Abu
Ubaidah; far-flung places: Kenya, Tanzania, Somalia, and Afghanistan; and esoteric legal concepts: burden of proof, corrobo-
ration, and reasonable doubt. But by the time he warned the jury

that "the story that is about to unfold before you is long, complicated and chilling," he had already presented a simplified version focused on Count 1, the conspiracy (p. 45). And he had fin-
gered each of the four defendants for specific acts: Wadih el
Hage lied to protect people associated with bin Laden; Mohamed Sadeek Odeh trained Somalis who later fought against
U.S. Marines; and Mohamed al-'Owhali and Khalfan Khamis
Mohamed played roles in the actual bombings, which were the
culmination of one goal set by the conspiracy. Sweeping across
years and continents, Butler's broad story was far from complete, and presciently he directed the jury's attention to its gaps,
expressing his confidence in them as jurors and in the clarity of
his case, saying: "Be assured the *important* things you will remember" (p. 46). Butler also mentioned statements given by
three of the defendants, thereby creating an expectation that an
even fuller account of preparations for the bombings would be
forthcoming. The opening statement seemed to promise both the
recognition the victims desired and a detailed explanation of
who was responsible, what they had done, and, possibly, why.

Butler ended by telling the jurors that, if they were patient,
open-minded, and used common sense, they would agree that
the government had proven "that each of these defendants . . .
are guilty beyond a reasonable doubt of entering into an illegal
agreement with Osama bin Laden to kill Americans anywhere
in the world they could be found. They each helped the best
way they could, and in the end 224 men, women, and children
from Kenya, from Tanzania, and from America lost their lives
and Kenya, Tanzania and America would never be the same.
For that this trial seeks justice" (p. 47).[12] Butler deftly directed
attention back to where he had begun: the bombings themselves, the dramatic touchstone of the case. Yet, to convict all
four defendants, his focus had to be the conspiracy. He was both
vague and subtle in his accusations: all four defendants "helped
the best way they could" and—avoiding direct attribution—"in
the end" people "lost their lives." Even Wadih el Hage—whose
connection to the bombings was indirect—could not escape the
impact of their destruction.

The defense teams were quiet and attentive through Butler's opening. Each defendant was represented by several court-appointed attorneys.[13] In their opening statements, which followed Butler's, defense counsel also implored the jurors to strive for justice. But no one who invoked the term during opening statements attempted a definition.

Throughout the trial, breaks were carefully timed so that the defendants would be able to pray at the proper times, which follow the sun's movement, and thus change slightly each day. Moving the defendants in and out of court was a protracted procedure involving multiple federal marshals and correctional guards. Three guards brought in each defendant, who shuffled slowly with feet shackled. Once seated, the men were shackled to the floor and then each held up his handcuffs to be unlocked. All this had to be done before the jury entered, so that they would remain unaware of the extent to which the court deemed the defendants dangerous. A large cloth hanging from the defense tables blocked jurors' view of the restraints. We were told to ignore the usual expectation that "all rise" when the judge entered. Jurors might wonder why the defendants could not or would not stand up. Some old hands around court—especially the marshals—found themselves starting up out of habit and then abruptly sitting down.[14]

Following a brief recess, defense attorney Sam Schmidt rose to say, "I am somewhat humbled to be here as a representative of Wadih el Hage, a forty-year-old nationalized [sic] American citizen, father of seven American children" (p. 49). Schmidt proved to be quite the opposite of humble in his aggressive, sometimes arrogant, defense of el Hage throughout the trial. In his opening statement Schmidt hammered two points: el Hage's good character and the government's lack of evidence for his participation in a violent conspiracy. Narrating el Hage's life story, Schmidt described how his client moved with his parents to Kuwait where he decided, against their wishes, to convert from Christianity to Islam. It was el Hage's commitment to helping fellow Muslims—presented by Schmidt as one of his many positive attributes—that led him to Pakistan to help refugees from the Soviet occupation of Afghanistan. Later el Hage returned to the U.S., took up various jobs, and married an American Muslim named April Brightsky Ray. According to Schmidt, el Hage was hard-working despite a disability, a mediator in the community, honest, and a devoted father. He moved around a lot, traveling several times to Pakistan. Schmidt failed to state plainly how el Hage came to work for Osama bin Laden, living first in Sudan and then Nairobi, Kenya, where he managed bin Laden's commercial interests. In the prosecution's opening statement, Paul Butler had said of el Hage, "On the outside, he was an American businessman in Kenya. On the inside, he was doing secret work on behalf of Osama bin Laden" (p. 31). But Schmidt insisted that el Hage and bin Laden were business associates, not confidants, and he returned again and again to el Hage's positive attributes: he was a relief worker and a devoted family man. Such a man would live "quietly" and "peacefully," and would never have engaged in violence against Americans.

Predicting that the evidence about the bombings themselves was "going to be terrible," Schmidt appealed to jurors "not to let that horror, that destruction, steer you away from your job, your job as the people who stand between each and every American and even non-Americans, and the power, the might of the government when they want to do something" (p. 66). Schmidt had begun his statement by reminding the jurors that el Hage was not charged with the bombings.[15] Yet his concern about their reaction to the graphic evidence of the destruction in Nairobi and Dar reflected the defense counsels' genuine worry that the violent centerpiece of the government's case would overwhelm the jury's ability to appreciate the arguments made in defense of the accused.

Throughout the morning virtually every speaker—including Judge Sand—referred to the eerie, high-pitched whistling from the winter storm worsening outside. Unnerved, many in court glanced at the high ceiling and large windows. Anthony Ricco, defense counsel for Mohamed Odeh, invoked the wind to begin his opening statement, delivered with sermon-quality cadence:

Ricco: I stop and I listen to wind. Hear the whistling? People hear different things, they do things differently. Many of you who have
been in the court never have heard that wind like that. The wind is
here today. Many people say the voices are in the wind, raging in
the wind. There was a lot of suffering in this case, lot of pain in this
case. To avoid it is to avoid the reality that the night follows day.
And to me, you can hear it in the wind today as we start this trial.
It's a reminder. It's a call, a reality check. If you listen, you hear those
voices. People lost, people suffering.

I know, looking in the faces of all of you, that it is going to be
extremely difficult to overcome the reality that so many people died
here, so many young people died here, so many people were injured
here, almost to the point where you would sit back and say, "What
are you talking about? Trial? I'm ready to jump over this bar right
now and end this. Trial for who? For *them*?" (p. 68; emphasis added).

Ricco knew that exposure to victims' suffering might fuel a demand for revenge. But he provided an alternative by reminding
jurors that others who have suffered—"black South Africans,
Native Americans, African Americans . . . Muslims, Hindus, and
Hebrews"—have asked only "that justice be served" (p. 50).

In the day's most theatrical and nuanced opening, Ricco embraced the distasteful task of presenting his client as a committed member of al Qaeda. According to Ricco, Mohamed Odeh
was "a soldier" who later operated a business in Kenya that contributed to al Qaeda causes, which he believed were intended to
better the lives of Muslims. In Ricco's depiction, Odeh, aged
thirty-six, had strong principles; for example, he refused to participate in activities he deemed "Islamically incorrect," such as
suicide or killing innocent people. Thus, Ricco asserted, although Odeh fought for al Qaeda's causes, although he ran an
al Qaeda business, although he stayed in a hotel with the bombers, and although he left Kenya just one day before the August
7 explosion using a fake passport, adherence to his principles
meant that he would never have participated in the bombings.
Ricco took the provocative strategy of warning the jury that they
might not understand this man of principle. And Ricco himself
looked like a man of principle, cutting an impressive figure with

a ramrod-straight back, intense stare, sharp bow tie, and shaved head. He commanded respect, urging jurors to overcome their prejudices and stereotypes, their lack of understanding of cultural and religious differences, and resist taking justice into their own hands. It was a gamble. The jury might admire a principled man, but could they appreciate the principles Odeh stood for?

Keeping track of the main players and arguments was a challenge. The court anticipated the difficulty; Judge Sand's initial instructions granted jurors permission to take notes. Partway through the morning, he reminded prosecutors that they bore responsibility for providing notepads and should be sure that jurors would have them for the next day.

After lunch Jeremy Schneider, Khalfan Khamis Mohamed's counsel at the time, took a very different approach to defending his client, whom he referred to as "K.K." His long opening statement urged jurors to make sure they understood what K.K. was charged with—specific acts associated with the Dar es Salaam bombing—and what, according to Schneider, had no relevance to his case, namely, al Qaeda membership, the conspiracy, and the Nairobi bombing. Admitting K.K.'s role in building the bomb, Schneider portrayed his client with a pile of derisive terms. He was a "gofer," a "nobody," a "fungible worker," and many, many times, a "pawn." Even at the moment of his greatest culpability, others controlled K.K.'s actions: he "is told to rent a little apartment. . . . He obeys. . . . He is given money. . . . Is that the work of someone who is sophisticated . . . or at the very lowest rung of the totem pole or the ladder?" (p. 112). Perhaps because of the humble origins Schneider described, K.K. ended up looking like he could not think for himself. This strategy, too, was a gamble.[16]

Fred Cohn, counsel for the fourth defendant, Mohamed al-'Owhali, surprised the judge with his statement: "I just have to advise the Court that my client has instructed me not to open, and I don't know if I am going to obey that, but I'm putting it on the record that he has made that instruction" (p. 86). It was important to Cohn to make this a matter of record, perhaps thinking of potential accusations about his competence. At the same time, this remark, made out of the jury's hearing, was an early indication of what would soon be evident: Al-'Owhali was difficult and unpredictable. As the twenty-four year old turned around in his chair to look up at the clock, twirling a pen in his mouth, he gave the impression that he seemed out of touch with reality. Cohn waived the opening statement.

Delivered one after another, the opening statements of the defense attorneys were oddly disconnected. The different charges against each defendant made it impossible for their attorneys to offer an alternative, joint defense to counter the prosecution's charge of a broad conspiracy behind the bombings. It might have been a powerful strategy to develop a "theory of the case" that would have refuted the charges against all of them. But, in fact, the interests of some defendants pitted them against others. For example, it was to K.K. Mohamed's advantage that someone like Mohamed Odeh be depicted as a higher-up, as more responsible than a lowly "drone" who merely did the bidding of his superiors. And el Hage would certainly want to distance himself from anyone who had been present at the bombings. The several distinct defense strategies began to emerge over the next three weeks as defense attorneys closely cross-examined government witnesses who gave evidence about the conspiracy. Because of demands at my job, I had to follow those weeks from afar, piecing together the conspiracy case from news accounts and the trial transcript, as described in the next chapter. But even on that first day it was clear that, for many of us, the eyewitness accounts of the bombings would be very significant testimony. That was why each defense team's opening statement included a plea for jurors to hold back from rushing to judgment when they heard the graphic details. In early March the story of the bombings, from the mouths of those who had been there, was what we were all waiting to hear, and—for different reasons—dreading.

Some people are simply gifted storytellers. Ambassador Prudence Bushnell, the first bombing victim to take the stand is one of them. After she described what embassies do, what her embassy did in Nairobi, and who was working there on August 7, Paul Butler invited her to step down from the witness stand and, using a scale model of the Nairobi intersection, to indicate the embassy and two nearby buildings: the seven-story Ufundi House and the much taller Cooperative Bank building. Seated once again, and responding to Butler's calm questions, Bushnell described how, on the morning of August 7, she was attending a meeting at Kenya's Ministry of Commerce on the top floor of the Cooperative Bank building. An initial photo-op produced a cheery picture of Bushnell with the Kenyan finance minister that was shown to her as evidence. Carefully, using a typical legalistic question, Butler asked the ambassador to recall what happened after the meeting began. And she responded with the account we had braced ourselves to hear:

Bushnell: After about 15 or 20 minutes, the minister dismissed the press. Someone came in with some tea. . . . We had only—we were maybe two or three, four minutes into the conversation when we all heard a very loud explosion. I turned to the minister and asked if there was construction going on in the area, because to me it sounded like the kind of explosion you would hear associated with construction. He said no. He got up and walked to the window. Most of the other people in the room went to the window. And it was at that point that an enormous explosion came. I was the last person out of my seat and had just taken a few steps before this huge explosion happened. I was thrown back, and although I didn't think at the time I was unconscious, I must have been because when I brought myself back to reality, I was sitting down with my hands over my head because the ceiling was falling down. I will never for-get the rattling of a teacup, just kept rattling. I thought to myself that the building was going to collapse, that I was going to tumble down all those stories, and that I was going to die, and every cell in my body was just steeled toward waiting for the fall. But it didn't. The teacup stopped rattling and there was quiet, and I looked up and I was alone in the room, which is why I must have lost some consciousness. I was alone in the room. (pp. 1858–59)

Next, an American colleague rushed back into the room, and to-gether they searched the top floor for others before starting down twenty-one flights of dark stairs. With a slight strain in her voice, Bushnell described injured people joining the exodus at every floor, "an eerie silence," a woman's body being passed down over their heads, people praying and singing hymns, and smoke at one point, which convinced her for the second time that she was about to die. She continued, "There was blood everywhere, on the banister, I could feel the person behind me bleeding on my hair and down my back" (pp. 1860–61). And, a moment later, in response to a question about whether she had been injured: "The one that was most apparent to me was that my lip was bleeding profusely. I had a lot of blood on me but I was very unsure as to which was my blood and which was the blood of other people." I winced. Those of us with experience in East Africa knew blood's wretched status as a killer and the palpable anxiety about HIV in any situation when blood can mix, in a car wreck, during a medical procedure, or after a bomb explodes.

Most people who have experienced an overwhelming trauma will remember a tiny detail in vivid relief. For me, it's a man a few yards in front of me, pointing over my head and shouting "Exit! Go that way!" Several of us turned around, saw the door, and escaped the embassy. Such details offer almost irrefutable evidence of the narrator's presence at the scene. After all, who could imagine such a tiny sound as a rattling cup and saucer from morning tea making itself heard after a massive explosion?

When she emerged from the bank building, a colleague who was concerned about the ambassador's security pushed her head down so all she saw at first was broken glass and charred metal. Then, as she narrated, "I looked up and saw burning vehicles. I saw the charred remains of what was once a human being. I saw the back of the [embassy] building completely ripped off, and utter destruction, and I knew that no one was going to take care of me." Bundled into a car, she insisted on being taken to a hotel because she "very much needed to get to work" (p. 1863). By the end of her painful story, told with the emotion of a victim bereft, injured, and scared, she had returned to her role as the official in charge. Resuming her status lent authority to her account.

Pausing so that Bushnell could recover, Butler then prompted her to identify numerous photos that would be introduced into evidence, including shots of the embassy, surrounding build-

Figure 5. The U.S. Embassy in Nairobi, Kenya, after the 1998 bombing. Credit: AP/Wide World Photos

ings, Bushnell herself with bandages and stitches, and finally more photos of the embassy. Small details broke the deadening sameness of the images of destruction. "Is this another photo of the interior of the embassy after the bombing?" Butler asked. "Yes, it is, including somebody's red, white and blue notebook" (p. 1869). Beginning and ending at the embassy, where Americans—her Americans—were attacked, the ambassador's testimony, presented first and in more detail than any account that followed, would stand as an official version of what happened that morning in Nairobi.

Similar to the women who had told compelling stories in Kenyan Islamic courts, Bushnell narrated her experience directly, peppered with details and her own feelings. Prosecutors suspended their usual question-and-answer control, not even stopping her from quoting others and offering her own opinions, both of which usually invite objections. The defense sat quietly during Bushnell's testimony to avoid any appearance of antagonizing her. On cross-examination, defense counsel ignored her chilling narrative. Fred Baugh, an attorney for al-'Owhali, tried repeatedly to question Bushnell about whether she had been aware of threats made against the U.S. Embassy. A previous agreement, unknown to those of us watching, prohibited delving into embassy security or communications capabilities, and the exchange left the impression that something was missing, even though we didn't know why it might be important. Tiring of Baugh's repeated violations, the judge finally ordered all counsel to a closed session to remind them again that the failure of the U.S. government to warn others about threats was neither at issue in the case nor an appropriate defense.

With their "theory of the case" yet to be revealed, it was unclear why al-'Owhali's defense team wanted to establish that Bushnell's embassy had received threats prior to the bombings. Possibly they sought to portray the bombing as a salvo in an ongoing "war" between al Qaeda and the United States, rather than an isolated terrorist act. But it was equally difficult to understand why prosecutors objected to this line of questioning. How could testimony about the existence of a prior threat damage their case? If the threat had come from al Qaeda, it would serve as evidence of the network's conspiracy. Given the lawsuits filed by the bombing victims alleging U.S. negligence, including warnings that had allegedly been ignored, Bushnell's superiors would certainly want this topic off-limits. Remembering the accusations about prior threats made by East Africans after the bombings, and as a victim who also wondered whether the United States had failed to warn us, I resented that this topic would not be broached at the trial.

Impressive as it was, with its calm beginning, frenetic middle, and "back-to-work" resolution, Ambassador Bushnell's narrative risked offering too coherent a story of the explosion's aftermath. Prosecutors turned to other victims to convey the utter chaos. Most of the twelve eyewitnesses who testified that long morning were caught in the embassy when the bomb went off; others were in the Cooperative Bank building, a passing bus, and Ufundi House, the smaller building next door which collapsed completely. The disaster spawned many stories, but almost everyone remembered the same sequence of sounds—

something like gunfire first, then sort of a car backfiring, a massive explosion, and finally dead silence just before the harrowing screams, including their own. A collage of violent images illustrated the moment of impact: being lifted up, thrown down, knocked unconscious, flying; concrete doors blowing out, walls disappearing, and windows shattering. But it is the unforgettable devastation of bodies that grasped victims' memories most insistently. They told about bones sticking out through skin, legs lying on the ground, a man holding his protruding intestines as he ran. Dead and living bodies mingled in the wake of the bombing. Father John Kiongo, who had gone that day with his niece to his brother's office at the embassy, remembered returning to consciousness after the blast and hearing the voices of those who rescued him: "Now it's only after some time then I heard people come, and people yelling, 'This one is not dead, this one is not dead, get this one, and leave those who are dead alone.' So I knew from there my brother must have died, and my niece is dead" (p. 1919).

Some told of almost incomprehensible heroism. Staff Sergeant Daniel Briehl, a marine security guard posted to Nairobi but off-duty on August 7, was waiting outside the embassy for fellow marine Jesse Aliganga, who had gone in to cash a check. Just as Briehl was beginning to get impatient, he heard a terrific explosion. When the debris stopped falling around him, Briehl entered the embassy's front door, which was relatively undamaged. As he climbed over floor-to-ceiling rubble to get farther into the building, he fell through an elevator shaft and landed two stories down. Fearing that the elevator suspended high above him might plummet, he forced his way out the clenched doors and, although injured, began to help others. He ended his testimony by reporting that Sergeant Aliganga's body was found the next day.[17] The marine's story made me think of Jamal waiting for me outside the Dar embassy where I had gone in to cash a check. Like Briehl, did Jamal wonder why I was taking so long? Did he consider going in to find me? I have repeatedly pondered what Jamal might have seen or thought while he was waiting. Did he notice when the truck tried to pull into the embassy gate? Did he watch as the guard checked it for explosives?

Was he curious when there seemed to be a problem? In those hours before I learned he had been killed, I thought he would turn up alive and, for years after, would tell an amazing story about a truck and a problem and a loud noise and on and on to a conclusion very different from the one I had to accept.

Surviving victims—especially those who thought they were going to die that day and yet miraculously lived—radiate a fantastical aura. Their presence in the courtroom is a powerful admonishment to attend to their evidence: although momentarily among the dead, here they are to tell about this terrible crime. An astonishing rescue adds more power to the account being woven, even though it is less relevant in a legal sense than descriptions of damages, injuries, and deaths.

Sammy Nganga had become a hero in Kenya after a two-day ordeal trapped in the wreckage under Ufundi House. When asked by prosecutor Ken Karas to describe his painstaking rescue by an Israeli crew, Nganga said that for many hours he just kept pounding on the walls around him, trying to guide his rescuers as they dug probe holes. After a time he saw their searchlight and then kept talking so they could position themselves directly above him. When they tried to pull him up, he felt tremendous pain. He waited again while they tunneled down to his level and extricated him less roughly. All this time he had been communicating with a woman named Rose who was trapped near him but not visible. As the crew took him out, Sammy promised Rose that they would free her within two hours. It turned out that rescuers could not use the same tunnel to reach Rose. With great sadness Sammy told the court, "She was not saved." Sammy Nganga's rescue was a media event in Kenya, lauded as a success after workers had pulled so many lifeless bodies out of Ufundi House. At the time the Kenyan press focused extensively on the many young women killed in the Secretarial College. With so many deaths to cover, and the embassy as the focus, the testimony by eyewitnesses to the Nairobi blast failed to mention those young women.

In preparing witnesses beforehand, prosecutors first listened to their stories and, after agreeing on the important points to raise and to avoid, routinely urged those testifying just to tell their stories as "naturally" as possible. Prosecutors counted on witnesses to produce elements common to disaster stories, especially some of the dramatic features previously described, and they knew that too much preparation, or telling people exactly what to say, could yield an account that would sound rote and phony. It was a delicate job, but prosecutors Paul Butler and Ken Karas had good instincts. Rarely interrupting a victim's story, they were each steady and genial. Their questions kept the accounts moving in the right direction, although at times against the instincts of witnesses.

George Mimba, a Kenyan working in the Nairobi embassy's commercial office, was a lively witness with a terrible story to tell. He set the scene. It was a morning filled with errands as he prepared to leave for Accra, Ghana, to attend a meeting. He stopped to joke with colleague, Lucy Onono, who teased him about bringing her back a Ghanaian dress as a souvenir. Irrelevant to an account of what the bomb blast caused, the story about Lucy's request was the kind of detour a good storyteller might take to depict the lighthearted atmosphere just before the disaster. Mimba then digressed as he described a phone call from Julian Bartley, the embassy's consul general:

Mimba: The previous night we had stayed with Julian until around
    10:30 at night. He was a good friend of mine. He liked me and he
    used to tell me all about his background, how he was raised up,
    how he admires the way I work hard, and they encouraged me that
    I should keep on working hard, even told me how he was raised
    up, how he went to school. The first day he went to high school, I
    think the [principal] asked him—
Karas: Mr. Mimba, let's move on to— (p. 1902)

Ken Karas stopped Mimba's account just before defense attorney Fred Cohn, who had already stood, had the chance to object to a story with little bearing on the facts of the bombing. Such a digression was not irrelevant to Mimba, nor to others sitting in court, who knew that after a few minutes into the story Julian Bartley—Mimba's friend and boss—would be dead. Several looked annoyed at the interruption. Tributes to those who failed to make it out alive were common in victims' accounts told off the witness stand, including ones written by George Mimba and other colleagues for the two-year anniversary of the bombings. Those accounts included personal reflections, feelings, opinions, conversations, and other features of good storytelling that prosecutors were obliged to limit. Witnesses routinely misunderstand the conventions that limit speech in court and, after testifying, are left feeling that key elements of their story had been left out or cut off.

In setting the scene before the bombing, some victims referred to their own state of mind at the time. Like George Mimba, some described the moment before as carefree, as the absolute opposite of the horror that followed, a normal day gone horribly bad. By contrast, others conveyed a premonition of something sinister looming. Just after Father Kiongo's brother worried aloud about what caused the loud sounds outside the embassy, the priest reacted: "And I sat down, and I held my face like this, and I said a prayer because I knew this was the embassy, it was like the foreign country, and . . . if things go wrong, then we don't know where we are going to end" (p. 1919).

On the morning of August 7 Caroline Ngugi and several other Kenyan colleagues were in their embassy office. Her long account narrated the concern she and a coworker expressed after hearing the first noises: "I stood up from my seat, he stood up and faced the building, and I went and leaned on him like a small baby, I don't know why I did that, and from there I was— I think we were just knocked off. And I was unconscious for quite some time. Then after some time I woke up and I couldn't see" (p. 1954). Like so many others alarmed by the first sound, Caroline and her colleagues rushed to the windows. Inches from the unreinforced glass, they were in the worst possible position when the bomb exploded. As Caroline told the court, everyone else in her office was killed.

The witnesses that morning were each allowed at least a few moments to tell the story from their own perspective. But if that story failed to include enough discussion of the consequences of the bombing, prosecutors ended with pointed questions that got right to the legal heart of the matter. As Ms. Muhoho explained, her bus happened to be sitting in traffic near the embassy when she heard noise like a "thunder storm."

Karas: What happened to you after this thunder storm that you heard?

Muhoho: And after that we was coming, we was running out of the bus, and all of us was fall down. And after that I heard one of the kids crying, "Help me, help me." And the other woman was saying, "Help me." And then I touch my mouth and I found that I don't have no teeth in my mouth. And I asked for help and pray. And one person came and pulled [me] by hand, and then I heard other people crying. And they tried, they pull us to the end of the car.

Karas: And Ms. Muhoho, did you lose your eyesight as a result of the injuries that you suffered in the blast?

Muhoho: In the time they was taking us and another woman to the hospital that I realize I lost even my eyes. (p. 1932)

Untrained and inexperienced, the interpreter translated Ms. Muhoho's Kiswahili into awkward and grammatically incorrect English. But also Muhoho was not reaching the point quickly enough. Taken out of context, Karas's question would have sounded blunt, but with the cushion of the prior narrative, it helped the witness state what was clearly evident to those of us watching in court: the blast blinded Ms. Muhoho.

During his testimony George Mimba also told a story that was missing crucial details. It began just after he had escaped from the embassy and then entered again to help others:

Mimba: . . . another lady called me, "George, George, please help me." I did not want to open my eyes. I did not want to. So I started moving towards—in the direction where the sound had come from. And as I was moving, feeling the bodies, I held to something that made a move and I yelled, I said, "This is the lady who called me." I did not look at what I had held, I just held the object tightly and started pulling the body, heading back to where I had come from. When I came down and people came down to help me, then I realized that the person I had helped was a man. And the lady's voice kept coming back to me.

Karas: Do you know who this person was that you assisted out of the
    building?
Mimba: I don't know. I don't know, sir. It's been haunting me. I really
    wanted to know if he survived. (p. 1908)

In my experience in other courts, attorneys always tried to ensure that witnesses told fully resolved, complete stories. They
feared that a missing detail or an ambiguous outcome would
nag at jurors or confuse them. But an incomplete story has value,
too. Evident in Mimba's uncertainty about who he had helped,
and whether they had survived, was both the terror of the unknown after a disaster and the raw guilt of survivors. His story
illustrated an aftereffect of the blast, one hard to describe in testimony: unanswered questions small and large haunt victims and
shape their memories. His and other incomplete accounts also
hinted that it might not be possible to learn the full story of what
had happened.

Other stories remained partial. We had learned little about
Sergeant Aliganga, who was cashing a check; Lucy Onono, who
wanted an African dress; and Rose trapped in Ufundi House,
waiting to be rescued. Months after, I realized that the prosecutors had intended for witnesses to mention these three but just
briefly; they planned to follow up with fuller stories of their
lives, and their deaths, later in the trial. After the testimony of
the Nairobi victims, the prosecutor read into evidence the name
on each autopsy report. Those two hundred-plus names would
be read aloud again, several times. The twenty-minute recitation
publicly recognized those unable to tell their stories in court.
And it made the legal point that a massive bomb killed hundreds of people.

For several days following the presentation of what came to be
called the "Kenbomb case," the trial focused on the Dar es Salaam bombing. Tanzanian victims and relatives of those killed
had been brought to the U.S. to observe the trial for a week.
Some of us had gone through the bombing together; others were
meeting for the first time. Looking down my row in court and
seeing Nafisa—the only Tanzanian in the visitors' group whom

I had known in Dar—brought back a story I had forgotten. I saw myself being bundled into an ambulance with Nafisa; she was bleeding from cuts on her face. I hadn't yet found Jamal, and I wasn't badly injured, so I banged on the door, demanding to be let out. When guards trying to clear the scene refused to open the door, I pushed it open myself and ran back toward the embassy, frantic. In court my story overwhelmed me, and I repressed this floating fragment by calling up a story from happier times. Nafisa, an employee in the embassy's consular section, had helped Jamal and me to obtain his immigrant visa for travel to the United States. At the beginning of the application process, Nafisa was stern with us, as skeptical as the former Immigration and Naturalization Service demanded. She explained curtly that we had filled out forms incorrectly, that we needed additional documents, that we had to be patient. But when we neared the end of the process, she loosened up and even reassured Jamal as we waited for his final interview with the consular officer several weeks before the bombing. Like many people, she had developed a soft spot for Jamal's genuine charm. Through the visa section's double-paned glass window—it was the side windows that broke on her in the bombing, the visa window held firm— Nafisa mouthed to Jamal the words, "Big smile!" to calm him, to indicate that all would work out. "Big smile!" said with a giant grin became a joke for us for those few weeks before our planned journey to the United States.

Although initially I focused with great anticipation on the testimony of eyewitnesses to the Dar es Salaam bombing, I was struck by the many other stories of the bombing told in and around the courtroom, in the victim-witness lounge, and over tea at the cafeteria. Victims were surrounded by accounts—some unfinished, some they had never heard before, some they had tried to forget. During breaks in the testimony, victims sitting in the audience produced stories for one another, recounting where they were when the bomb went off, what they saw, and, if they had not been present, how they heard about it and what they did when they began to fear for a colleague or friend. Some stories we told by rote—we each had our own—many of us repeating the account verbatim to make the burden of describing the chaos less incapacitating. But others were unstaged accounts that, by intentionally featuring those of us present in court, connected our experiences. Describing how she had helped take a severely injured embassy employee to the hospital later that day, a Tanzanian woman suddenly mentioned that she had seen me there and wondered who I was. Her story made me think that I might have seen her, too, and added a new image to my stories from that chaotic day.

That morning in court I was sitting next to Henry Kessey, a Tanzanian man about my age who introduced himself as an embassy employee. At the next break in testimony, Henry told me his story. When the explosion occurred, he was in an office on the second floor, just down the hall from where I had stood at the cashier's window. The blast knocked him down. He thought he would "just die right there." His colleague, Sam, urged him, "I will support you. I will hold on to you, just try to walk." Unable to see from the blood covering his face, Henry stood, and somehow Sam walked him out the back exit. I interrupted him to confirm that he and I had used the same exit. Once at the hospital, nurses stopped the bleeding from a large cut across his forehead and mopped the blood from his face. But he still had no vision from his right eye. Someone at the hospital suggested, "Maybe there's still blood in the eye." "But up to now," he said, shaking his head and pulling off his glasses to give me a better view, "the sight in that eye has not come back."

These stories expanded my perceptions of the bombings; they resolved some questions and raised others. Stories shared among victims reorganized the horror of that day by exposing previously forgotten facts or uncertainties and by speaking from a future that sharpened hindsight. Some scholars and even therapists make the mistake of treating victims' efforts to tell their stories of suffering as catharsis, a means of purging painful memories.[18] But my experience with storytelling at the embassy bombings trial suggested that victims were interested not in personal unburdening—if only we *could* get rid of these stories that relentlessly dominate our lives—but rather in offering our narratives to one another and to anyone else who might make good use of them. These tellings were as profoundly productive socially as they were personally therapeutic. Sharing our stories forged connections among us as victims of terror, provided company in grief, kept the dead alive in memory, and moved the events of the past into a present that reshaped their meaning. The philosopher Susan Brison has argued that crucial to a victim's recovery and reintegration are people willing to listen with empathy to a victim's story.

Four embassy employees—two Americans and two Tanzanians—testified about the Dar es Salaam blast. Their stories wove around key symbols: "Lizzie," an American woman who was partially buried under the concrete pieces of a wall blasted in by the bomb; sounds resembling gunfire that turned out to be exploding car tires; a ladder that many used to escape over the embassy's back wall; "the gardener," a Tanzanian man who died from terrible burns. Their testimony focused on the small embassy compound and embassy personnel, creating a portrait of a tight community that suffered a horrific assault and then quickly brought the chaos under control.

Similar to the Nairobi testimony, the official story was told first by the American diplomat in charge that day. The Deputy Chief of Mission, at the time acting ambassador, John Lange was meeting with staff in his office when they all heard an explosion, and, "as if in slow motion," he saw large pieces of glass blow over his desk and onto colleagues seated across from him. He got up, made certain that no one was badly hurt (Mylar film covering the windows of the Dar embassy prevented the blinding injuries suffered by Nairobi victims). Then, as Lange said on the witness stand: "I kind of thought to myself, 'I'm in charge here, I better figure out what the hell happened,' pardon my language" (p. 2504). But when he started to leave the room, a colleague warned that the sounds they were hearing could be gunfire. Lange made his way to the second floor where he began to help remove fallen concrete slabs that had trapped Lizzie Slater. Lange interrupted his own story to address Judge Sand:

Lange: —by the way, oh, I forgot something excuse me. I forgot about my phone call.

Karas: You want to tell us about the phone call?

Lange: Yes. What happened was when, after the community liaison of-
     fice when we helped get the rubble away from Lizzy Slater, then,
     and this is something that every State Department foreign service
     officer always has to remember, you have to tell Washington. What
     happened was I went to the phone at [the security desk] and called
     the operations center of the State Department in Washington, which
     goes for 24 hours a day. I remembered the number. The phones kind
     of amazingly were working and I just called the number directly. (p.
     2507)

Lange's lapse and correction made his testimony sound unre-
hearsed, more realistic. Lange next described his exit from the
building and his attempts to evaluate the scene and help others.
Lange confessed that he could do nothing for the man he saw
dying from severe burns, but he was able to assist those escaping
by ladder over the embassy wall. His staff, who were primed to
implement the embassy's emergency plan, helped him establish
his own nearby house as a gathering space and command center.
Here, embassy personnel assessed the damage, treated the injured, and organized call lists to notify victims' families.

Answering prosecutor Ken Karas's questions about damage
to specific areas of the embassy, Lange made legally relevant
points about the bomb's destruction. He also offered more personal reflections: "I've told every Marine I see now the same
story. . . . I still remember the regional security officer coming up
to me on the street to say: 'Sir, the Marines have secured the
building.' And there was something even in this chaos which
was fire engines, smoke [from] earlier explosions, et cetera, with
all that going on, there was something comforting about the idea
that in this chaos we still had been able to secure the building"
(p. 2509). Because the damage in Dar was less extensive than in
Nairobi, survivors were able to begin rescue work immediately.
Lange's emphasis on bringing the disaster under control, although important to him, had less legal relevance than his descriptions of the chaos and destruction. Yet his story, which reflected his need to show that—against the odds—he and his
embassy continued to function, was evidence that a witness's
personality and position shaped the stories told in testimony.

Figure 6. The U.S. Embassy in Dar es Salaam, Tanzania, after the 1998 bombing. Credit: U.S. Government

Stories from the other Dar es Salaam witnesses added different perspectives and ironic twists. Lizzie Slater—only three days on the job as a communications specialist at the embassy—was attending her "Welcome to Dar es Salaam" briefing when the bomb exploded. Like Lange, she described exiting the building to find the gardener just outside. With much of his skin burned off, he lay moaning in the immediate aftermath as other victims stumbled out a nearby exit. Aghast at his agony, Lizzie choked out, "I just wished he'd hurry up and die." At this, the young man sitting in front of me removed his earphones, unable to bear the Kiswahili translation any longer. His shoulders shook as he sobbed in grief for his brother, the gardener. When I looked through the court transcript of Lizzie's testimony, I found no reference to her wish that the gardener would die. The transcribed testimony made no sense, especially a curious line: "He didn't have any—he died." Then I realized that the court reporter, as overwhelmed by Lizzie's story as the rest of us, was unable to take down her words.

As I listened I had vague sensations about a story of my own, one that I can never remember in full. A security guard lay on the pavement, awake and in pain. His lower legs were cut and bloody, a foot might have been missing. All I could think as I stood over him was that he must be very hot lying there. This part of the story always puzzled me. Why would the heat concern me so much? The heat of the sun? Of the pavement? Of nearby cars on fire? Perhaps my fear that the cars would explode led me to urge another security guard to help me move him to the shade? Then the story collapsed, remaining partial. I think that we picked him up. But this may not have happened. I think that, seeing water drip from the water truck parked nearby, I brought him water in my hands and dribbled it on his face. One or two times. I can't remember. In the company of other eyewitnesses in court, I could have tried to reconstruct my story, but I left it, deciding that not knowing would be a continuing reminder of the chaos and of the impossibility of ever telling a complete story of the bombing.

After finishing his testimony, Ambassador Lange joined the audience. As he greeted me warmly, I remembered sitting next to him on a bed in his house, on the day after the bombing, and listening as he told me how sorry they all were about Jamal's death. So empathetic and so able to reach out, he was the definitive diplomat. In court, surrounded by his former staff, he began to tell other stories of the bombing. In these versions he mentioned his encounters with each of us after the blast. His story started, stopped; he told it with uncertainty and pauses, and ceded the floor so we could fill in our parts. Lange must have heard the contrast between the stories that he shared with us and his testimony, which he acknowledged left out many of our experiences. In truth, the stories told by the four eyewitnesses described scenes unfamiliar to me. I had encountered few of the people mentioned in their stories; I had not used the ladder to escape; and I never, I am grateful, saw the gardener. I felt sadness, relief, and a kind of resignation, but with no resentment, to realize that the story of the bombing could be told without me, even though it described the most significant event in my life.

Returning home on the train after court, I wrote about the stories we victims had told one another. These entries contrasted with how I had written about courtroom stories in my work as an anthropologist. In that earlier work I tried to create a thickly described account by filling in as many gaps as possible to construct a coherent picture of "what happened" in a case. But coherence was not the hallmark of our victims' stories. Our stories stopped, leaving a sense of "there's no need to say any more." In writing them down, I, too, avoided resolving gaps and contradictions. I understood in retrospect that establishing the story of what really happened was perhaps what victims (including me) most craved, and most feared, and why my notes and reflections would avoid it. This perspective was a striking contrast to the legal anthropologist's usual project of assembling the pieces of a complex narrative to create an apparently whole picture, not— at least for the professional—a painful void. If all the pieces of the story about the bombings *were* put together, they would depict the loss, the void, the inchoate underlying the experience, a confirmation yet again of absence, of an old self and cherished others. As victims, many of us tended to control tightly when and where this absence confronted us, preferring to acknowledge it only when we felt strong enough.

My defenses against feeling traumatized kicked in when a prosecutor mentioned a videotape filmed in Dar es Salaam. I turned to the young man next to me, one of the victim's advocates, and asked when he thought they would show it. He didn't know. I was apprehensive that the video might contain disturbing images. I whispered again to the victims' advocate that being certain about the video screening was important to me, and he nodded in sympathy. The next day, without warning, the video began. I peeked and turned away, over and over, catching only glimpses of frightful scenes. An ambulance arriving, people climbing a ladder, cars burning. Several close-ups showed the American flag flapping on the embassy roof. With my gaze averted for most of the fifteen minute screening, I saw that Nafisa and Henry and other Tanzanians looked away as well.

Over time, most victims develop strategies to avoid images and experiences that might trigger a trauma reaction. One common trick is to see threatening flashbacks as if they were on a television screen. To make them small, and to wield the power to turn them off. In court I had already faced my nightmare on a video screen, a huge one right in front of me. Then I spotted another option. A smaller, more manageable version played on the laptops used by the defense counsel about fifteen feet away. I started to watch, mercifully unable to make out many details. When he shifted in his seat, blocking my view, I realized that the defendant Mohamed al-'Owhali and I were watching the same small image. Much later I learned that K. K. Mohamed—accused of helping to build the Dar es Salaam bomb—had cried throughout the video.

At the end of the week's testimony in what courtroom insiders called the "Tanbomb case" (in contrast to the "Kenbomb case"), I sat in the victim-witness lounge with Nafisa and her sister and told them a funny story, a rare gesture in this setting. After Jamal's visa had come through, he wanted to thank Nafisa for helping us through the process. He decided that we should bring her a gift, something from his home in Kenya. I said, "No, she could get into trouble." He insisted, "We can just call her outside, tell her we want to meet her briefly after work, and then give her the present." As I related the story, Nafisa frantically waved her hands in protest, "No, no, we cannot accept anything. It would be very bad." We laughed. Just weeks after her return to Dar, Nafisa and her colleagues in the consular office would be processing visas for K. K. Mohamed's family to come to the United States to testify at his trial in an effort to save his life.

Before we left the courthouse that day, members of the investigation and prosecution teams came to the victim-witness lounge to see us. Even with tightly packed schedules, they made a point of meeting each Thursday with the group of East African victims brought that week to observe the trial. They told us that they were hard at work on the case, that they were doing it for us, that they would not stop until they captured and prosecuted all the accused. U.S. Attorney Mary Jo White, looking sharp in a red dress, beamed up at her assistant prosecutors and proclaimed them to be the very best team in the country. Her assistants praised the FBI agents for their tireless work and the paralegals for pulling all-nighters to meet the document requests made by the defense and Judge Sand. They all looked exhilarated, if a little weary. The lead prosecutor Pat Fitzgerald offered us some behind-the-scenes insight into the prosecution's strategy: "Did you see how we kept showing the photos of those guys—Hussein, Fahad, and Ahmad?" He nodded and winked, "*that* will come up later." Having impressed us with their commitment to tell our stories in court, they welcomed us briefly into their inner circle. With all their experience, they must have sensed victims' thirst for two aspects of justice: recognition for our stories and an explanation of what had happened. Before leaving us, they insisted again that the terrible things we had endured motivated them as they worked on our case, that we victims were always in their thoughts.

Prosecutors had faced the burden of advancing stories primarily for the jury's consumption (and for the legal record), while also appeasing a diverse range of victims who sought recognition through those tellings. How prosecutors had managed that also reflected their understanding that, to accomplish legal goals, a story had to be compelling. Although I quibbled with their inclusion of melodramatic references to the gardener, and with the focus on the embassies, U.S. government officials, and patriotic symbols, I was not inclined to criticize the portrayals of the bombings. To the extent that the prosecutors were competent, which by all indications they were, and to the extent that I respected their judgment, which at that point in the trial I did, I accepted the stories told and was grateful to the witnesses who had told them and to the prosecutors who had guided them.

I had come to court to hear the Dar es Salaam bombing recounted and to be sure that Jamal and I gained recognition through the telling. The stories told in court never mentioned us, but, I decided, they more than achieved my goal. At the same time the experience convinced me of two contradictory notions: first, that many other, completely different accounts would also have been equally appropriate and effective, and, second, that no story of the bombings, however encompassing of multiple perspectives, would succeed in representing all that victims found significant in their experiences of the tragedy.

CHAPTER FOUR
Exposing a Conspiracy

To PRESERVE the element of surprise that would make for an effective case, prosecutors had waited until the embassy bombings trial to present their considerable evidence against al Qaeda. Despite some media attention after the embassy bombings and new acts of terror linked to the group (e.g., the bombing of the USS *Cole*), official accounts explaining who constituted al Qaeda and how it operated had not gained public attention.[1] Media commentators' routine conflation of al Qaeda and bin Laden only enhanced the natural skepticism of those, including myself, who found it hardly credible that, from a remote cave in Afghanistan, one man could have accomplished so much destruction. Competing reports that linked al Qaeda to Iran, on the one hand, or to Iraq, on the other, deepened the uncertainty about who comprised the group and what they hoped to accomplish.[2] When Ali Mohamed, among the two dozen indicted co-conspirators, pled guilty to conspiracy and other terrorism-related charges in October 2000, he offered a first-person account of the group's wide-ranging organization and deadly operations. His credibility was undermined, however, by a history of serving both as an informant for the FBI and probably also for the CIA, while at the same time pursuing al Qaeda–related activities. That history included a string of lies told to U.S. authorities.[3] In the first days of the trial it became clear that, through individuals like Ali Mohamed and their own extensive investigations, the Southern District prosecutors's office was well acquainted with al Qaeda's dimensions and delicts, and bent on finally exposing them in court.

After the opening statements, the prosecution devoted the trial's first weeks to proving that the four defendants (along with others) had participated in a conspiracy to kill Americans.[4] As in other cases where conspiracy is a central charge, prosecutors in the embassy bombings case would have to show that each of

the four defendants conspired with others (even those not indicted or not on trial) to commit illegal acts (e.g., killing Americans), that they deliberately joined the conspiracy, and that at
least one among the co-conspirators (not just those on trial) had
engaged in an "overt act" to implement the plans (e.g., surveil-
ling the area around the embassy).[5] Put another way, once prosecutors established the conspiracy's membership and exposed
their illegal plans, they would only need to show that one
among the co-conspirators had committed an act to further the
conspiracy. By foregrounding the charge of criminal conspiracy,
prosecutors took a broad approach to the question of who was
responsible for the bombings, implicating many people beyond
the defendants.

Sometimes called "the prosecutor's darling," because of its
powerful efficiency, and because they routinely include it in any
criminal case involving multiple defendants, criminal conspiracy can, in fact, be difficult to prove. By definition, a conspiracy
is secret, and a successful conspiracy hides evidence of itself. As
we would learn early in the trial, the embassy bombings conspirators communicated in code and operated as isolated cells.
These and other tactics had posed problems for investigators,
but through their witnesses and evidence the prosecution would
show that the conspirators in the embassy bombings case did
not entirely succeed in hiding their deeds.

Sudanese-born Jamal Ahmed al Fadl, the first person to testify,
indeed the government's star witness, had been kept under
wraps before his court appearance, referred to in preliminary
documents only as CS-1 (Confidential Source 1). Through two
days of direct testimony in early February, the public learned
first that al Fadl had been a prominent member of al Qaeda from
its very beginning. As a young man he had answered the worldwide call for Muslim men to help the *mujaheddin* forces drive
the Soviet Union from Afghanistan.[6] He left the United States,
where he had been studying at a mosque, and traveled to Pakistan for military training. After brief combat experience, he
began to work with the victorious mujaheddin, including
Osama bin Laden, who, as the Soviet campaign ended in the

late 1980s, was launching a new organization. The mujaheddin planned to combat Islam's enemies and establish a *khalifate*, a global Muslim government, as had existed after the time of the Prophet Mohamed. Al Fadl was among the first to swear allegiance by taking the oath, called a *bayat* in Arabic, that bound members to al Qaeda, the name chosen for the group after considering "Islamic Army." The reward for this commitment, and for al Fadl's considerable hard work, was a position in the group's inner echelon.

On the witness stand al Fadl explained that, in late 1990, Osama bin Laden, who had assumed leadership of al Qaeda, moved the organization to Sudan, a north African nation positioned closer to the Middle East, the area of interest to bin Laden. Once there, al Fadl took an active role in the group's activities. He found houses for those relocating from Afghanistan, established businesses to provide the financial underpinning for the group's operations, set up "refresh" camps where former fighters could renew their military skills in the Sudanese countryside, and monitored security through, for example, working with Sudanese intelligence officers to evaluate the credentials of prospective members and root out spies. For a time al Fadl's office was in the same building in Sudan's capital, Khartoum, as Osama bin Laden's.

Testifying for the government, al Fadl named names, real names when he knew them, which was generally when he had worked directly with the person. More often he supplied nicknames, known as "Abu names." As he explained, the nicknames given to recruits always began with "Abu" (Arabic for "father of") followed by a name (only sometimes the actual name of the person's son or daughter) and ending with a country, such as Liby for Libya or Lubnani for Lebanon, depending on the person's birthplace. His own nickname was Abu Bakr Sudani, and, like most al Qaeda operatives, he had a few others. Nicknames were among the ruses used by al Qaeda members, who, when traveling, carried fake passports and fraudulent visas and dressed to look more "Western," that is, less obviously religious. As he proffered the names of more al Qaeda members than most observers could manage to take in, al Fadl accomplished the more important task of slotting individuals into the organization's command structure.[7] Al Qaeda's highest-ranking individuals, with whom al Fadl had worked closely, served on al Qaeda's *shura* council, an elite group that deliberated on many aspects of the group's activities. Operating under the shura council, different committees took responsibility for military action, money and business, religious decrees or *fatwas*, and publicity.[8] Indicating who served on each committee, al Fadl recited their names aloud and matched them to photos displayed as evidence.

From his vantage point within al Qaeda, al Fadl pulled back a curtain to expose not only its multiple operations and underlying missions but how al Qaeda's conspiratorial world had been transformed from the initial years of the group's development after 1989 until his own departure in 1994. Critical to that transformation were the fatwas issued by the group's scholars. These articulated and justified the group's overarching goal, which was phrased as *jihad*.[9] Abu Hajer, the top-ranking official depicted by al Fadl as Osama bin Laden's "best friend," announced one especially notable fatwa, which declared that killing civilians in battle was not a sin in Islam but rather a regrettable outcome of armed struggle. He justified this conclusion—controversial within al Qaeda and among Islamic scholars generally—with his own interpretation of scholarly and religious sources, including the Koran.

With proving Count One of the indictment—the conspiracy to kill Americans—at the forefront of his agenda, prosecutor Pat Fitzgerald asked al Fadl several times about any fatwas that advocated violence against Americans or the United States. According to al Fadl, in its initial years al Qaeda had had little interest in America. Moreover, al Fadl contended that al Qaeda was not overwhelmingly opposed to U.S. involvement in the Gulf War of the early 1990s. Some members supported the attempt to quash Sadaam Hussein's advances on neighboring Muslim countries, given his questionable religious credentials and the predatory intentions of his Baathist party. However, when the deployment of U.S. troops in Saudi Arabia extended long after the end of the Gulf War, al Qaeda opposition to

America increased, and Abu Hajer announced a new fatwa opposing the U.S. presence on the Arabian Peninsula. Over the next few years the commitment to fight against American influence in Muslim regions gained strength, to the point where bin Laden declared that America was a snake that had advanced too far into the Horn of Africa. As al Fadl recounted, bin Laden called for al Qaeda members to "cut the head of the snake." That menacing remark resonated as evidence central to Fitzgerald's task of proving al Qaeda's intention to harm Americans.

Al Fadl's own career in al Qaeda played like a thriller. After the group's move to Sudan, he worked with al Qaeda companies in Khartoum and the countryside, where the organization had business interests in construction, currency exchange, leather tanning, and agriculture, among others.[10] As the commercial enterprises flourished in the heady days of the early 1990s, al Fadl traveled extensively, mostly to keep an eye on business but sometimes for so-called jihad assignments, when the group's focus turned more concertedly toward military activities. Al Qaeda officials did not always fully explain these errands to him and may, at times, have used him callously.[11] Although some duties may have remained murky to al Fadl, by his own admission he was a conscious, informed, and active participant in any al Qaeda endeavors, including the recruitment of members, the development of security measures to protect bin Laden and the group's activities, and the traffic in arms.

For quite awhile al Qaeda leaders failed to realize that al Fadl was double-crossing them. Taking advantage of his position, al Fadl had been demanding kickbacks from clients seeking business with al Qaeda companies. His was a brand of petty corruption common in that part of Africa and many other places in the world, but—once they found out for sure—his superiors were furious. Al Fadl had managed to swindle more than a hundred thousand dollars, which was enough to purchase land for family members. As his testimony described, when first confronted, he denied any wrongdoing. Later, realizing that al Qaeda leaders had proof, he begged forgiveness. Everyone insisted, with bin Laden as the final arbiter, that he could only redeem himself by returning the money. Describing bin Laden's reaction, al Fadl said that the emir had seemed deeply puzzled and hurt that someone involved with the group from the beginning would undermine it by stealing. Unable to repay the money, al Fadl fled Sudan and, by traveling frequently, managed to evade the group's wrath. Knowing that two members had been executed for betraying group confidences, al Fadl must have been terrified. By June 1996 he was desperate enough to walk into an American embassy—its location was intentionally withheld in court—and tell the clerk behind the visa counter that he had information about a group planning attacks against the United States.[12] For the next thirty days American officials—diplomats, FBI agents, and prosecutors—interrogated al Fadl. Realizing his value, they brought him to the United States and took the highly unusual step of assigning FBI agents to protect him twenty-four hours a day for two years. At some point after the 1998 embassy bombings, when it became clear that alleged al Qaeda members would face prosecution and al Fadl could testify against them, he entered a witness protection program and was reunited with his wife and children brought from Sudan. By the time he testified in February 2001, the U.S. government had spent hundreds of thousands of dollars to support al Fadl. For his part, al Fadl pled guilty to charges of transporting weapons for the purpose of harming Americans.[13] While not exactly quid pro quo, by testifying al Fadl hoped to receive a much lighter sentence than the fifteen years he potentially faced.[14]

It was in those first weeks of the case, as prosecutors focused on exposing the conspiracy, that I most regretted the rules against televising federal trials. Watching the testimony would have enormously improved my ability to follow the trial and to feel involved. Demands at my job precluded my attendance most days during the trial's first month. I kept up as best I could by following media accounts, which not surprisingly highlighted dramatic moments in court, such as al Fadl's identification of defendant Wadih el Hage. As al Fadl explained, he knew el Hage quite well. After el Hage arrived in Sudan, al Fadl trained him to take over some business responsibilities. As a naturalized

American, el Hage was a special asset for al Qaeda ventures requiring international travel.

I suspected that the press accounts, necessarily concise, offered only a glimpse into the world of al Qaeda conspirators being described in al Fadl's testimony. Craving more elaboration of al Qaeda's means, motives, and deadly ends, more information as to how its members operated as an international network, and more evidence of a direct connection between the world of al Fadl's description where leaders launched grand conspiracies and the four defendants in court, I turned to the trial transcript, which was posted nightly on a website sponsored by a group devoted to exposing U.S. government secrecy.[15] As soon as I began reading al Fadl's transcribed testimony, I wanted to pull my hair out in frustration. Although an Arabic-language interpreter stood at the ready, al Fadl insisted on testifying in English. But as the transcript showed, he had trouble understanding questions and repeatedly produced inaudible and incoherent answers.[16] Admonishments to slow down and to speak up peppered the transcript and made reading it more difficult.[17] Typos, missing words, and misheard utterances compounded the difficulty of figuring out what al Fadl and his questioners had said. Some of these mistakes, which are common and understandable in a trial where witnesses speak multiple languages and refer frequently to foreign names and places, were merely annoyances. For example, "Coast Province" in Kenya, an area frequented by some al Qaeda operatives mentioned by al Fadl, appeared as "Khost Province," a mix-up with the city in Afghanistan already mentioned several times in the trial and probably keyed into the transcription machine. But other mistakes were more consequential, such as long, convoluted renderings of the al Qaeda definition of "jihad."

Given my previous research, the opacity of courtroom language was no new discovery. My frustration over the impediment it posed to evaluating the prosecution's evidence stemmed partly from the fact that al Fadl's testimony touched on such crucial issues. Not least, it implicated al Qaeda in multiple illegal activities. According to al Fadl, the group had cultivated relationships of mutual support with many other organizations that, at one time or another, had advocated violence, such as Hezbollah, the Algerian and Philippine resistance movements, Egyptian Islamic Jihad, and the Sudanese National Islamic Front. They had tried to buy uranium to make an atomic weapon (al Fadl did the groundwork for this transaction but was uncertain about whether it had been completed); they might have been making chemical weapons (al Fadl could not confirm this); and they had moved weapons from one place to another by boat, plane, and camel. A plan to blow up the U.S. Embassy in Saudi Arabia was rejected by some Saudis in the group who were concerned that civilians in their country would be killed. (The group lost members over this issue.) If the group members had conspired to commit even a fraction of the acts described by al Fadl, and if members held the beliefs about the United States that he insisted they did, then this was a very dangerous conspiracy. For that reason I craved the clearest possible, least disputable, demonstration that these and other assertions by al Fadl were more than idle chatter among a radical group that, because of a short history of perceived affronts and betrayals, had obviously come to hate the U. S. government.

Defense counsel had had some difficulty preparing for al Fadl's testimony. The defense attorneys had been informed of his identity just four days before his scheduled testimony, and a Protective Order forbade them to share this information with their clients until the day before al Fadl appeared in court. Throughout the trial considerable discovery material was labeled "particularly sensitive" and thus subject to the restrictions of the Protective Order. This meant that the material was provided only to those pre-cleared by the government (e.g., the defense teams) and had to be kept confidential, including from the defendants themselves.[18] Further, defense attorneys complained to Judge Sand about the Classified Information Procedures Act (CIPA). Much of the material prosecutors had used to prepare the case was deemed to have national security implications and was classified according to the categories—unclassified, secret, and so on—used by government agencies such as the CIA and FBI. Only those individuals who had been cleared by government security procedures could examine classified documents, and such material could not be made public. Accordingly, some documents were entered into evidence with portions blacked out, and areas of inquiry touching on national security concerns had to be avoided during testimony. A few topics, whenever mentioned in open court, led immediately to sealed discussions, such as al Qaeda's activities training fighters in Somalia.[19] Many conferences and hearings were held in the judge's chambers, and those transcripts were never made available. For any observer trying to sort out who was who in a complex conspiracy and to determine the relative guilt of all those mentioned, there always seemed to be more to the story and yet little chance that everything would be revealed. Knowing that the story was incomplete tempted me at times to turn away from the seemingly impossible task of figuring out how it all added up. I hoped the jurors would resist that temptation.

In cross-examining al Fadl, Mohamed Sadeeq Odeh's attorneys returned several times to a question that had begun to concern me: given that al Qaeda was organized hierarchically and was generally secretive, to what extent did information—about plans, goals, strategies, and so forth—pass down the ranks? Under cross-examination by attorney Carl Herman, al Fadl described al Qaeda's structure as a "pyramid," but he was reluctant to agree with the statement that "not everybody in the organization always knew everything that the organization was doing" (p. 443). Even when confronted with examples of times when superiors had kept *him* in the dark, he insisted that members talked among themselves about group activities. Herman, who was seeking support for the position that his client Odeh had never been told about the Nairobi bombing, was frustrated by al Fadl's refusal to affirm this point. After trying several times, he finally ended by saying: "But as far as the organization was concerned, for security purposes some activities that al Qaeda engaged in were not told to everybody on the pyramid." Despite his difficulties with English, al Fadl showed his savvy when he answered: "You're right, that's correct, but sometimes they talk" (p. 448).

Although defense attorney Sam Schmidt, representing Wadih el Hage, pursued many topics with al Fadl, he often returned to questions which would build his argument that the U.S. government had influenced the witness in his testimony, especially his incriminating evidence against el Hage. For instance, Schmidt was able to get al Fadl to admit that he had not even mentioned el Hage until well into his interviews with U.S. officials and even then he might have confused el Hage with another person named Wadih (p. 960). For his part, al Fadl kept insisting that he had trained el Hage and thus knew him well. As prosecutor Pat Fitzgerald tried to protect al Fadl, his own tough demeanor, and a bit of a temper, became more evident. Attacks on al Fadl's credibility occupied most of the cross-examination, but such attacks had begun during his direct testimony through defense objections repeatedly demanding that Fitzgerald establish the foundation for al Fadl's knowledge of particular events.[20] In his responses, al Fadl confirmed that he had learned much of what he testified to by being privy to conversations among al Qaeda's elite and by reading documents produced by the group's upper echelon. These vantage points authorized his knowledge, but at the same time his high rank made him culpable. By sitting in when destructive plans were hatched, he could hardly flee from his own role as co-conspirator. The defense attorneys did not encourage respect for al Fadl. Fred Baugh asked him perfunctorily: "Would you prefer to consider yourself an informant, a snitch, a turncoat, what?" (p. 489). An objection sustained by Judge Sand protected al Fadl from the unsavory choices.

Prosecutors had already helped the defense in their strategy of questioning al Fadl's character by intentionally revealing several aspects of his checkered past that they believed would come out anyway. He had been jailed a couple of times, stolen, lied to many people, and withheld information, including from his U.S. interrogators. Yet, curiously, a prior delict unconnected to terrorism or to al Qaeda operations grabbed the attention of defense attorneys and the media: al Fadl was a bigamist. He married a Sudanese woman in 1986. Not long after that, he entered the United States to study and promptly married again. On cross-examination, the defense hammered him with questions about

Figure 7. Courtroom sketch of Judge Sand, Patrick Fitzgerald (standing), Mohamed al-'Owhali, and Mohamed Odeh (*first row*), and K. K. Mohamed, David Ruhnke, Wadih el Hage, and Tony Ricco (*second row*). Credit: Christine Cornell

this, insisting that, although polygamy was legal under Islam, he should have told his first wife about the second marriage at the time. They went back and forth about the practice of "informing," which, as al Fadl pointed out, depends on national legal statutes rather than on some generic version of "Islamic law" which seemed to have shaped the defense counsel's view. In many contexts where Muslim family law applies, informing one's wife about a subsequent marriage is a matter of courtesy rather than of law. But these legal technicalities were of little interest to the defense counsel who knew that the simple fact that al Fadl had multiple wives would shock most Americans, jurors among them. While I have always condemned gender inequality in any society, I have been especially sensitive to how often inaccurate stereotypes of women's negative treatment under Islam are used to deflect attention from other issues and, simply, to make Islam and Muslims look bad. In this instance, why not impeach al Fadl's character by bringing out his willingness to consider poisoning the former prime minister of Sudan or his failure to challenge colleagues who advocated deploying chemical weapons against southern Sudanese Christians? On al Fadl's twisted resumé, that he was a bigamist hardly stood out.

The defense counsel's cross-examination made clear that the government was relying on someone with a terrible reputation. Al Fadl had left the conspiracy not out of any awakening to the immorality of the group's planned violence but to save his own skin. In testifying, he was still trying to protect himself. Aggressive cross-examination emphasized that al Fadl had much to gain by telling a story useful to the government's case. Defense counsel also alluded to the tainting effects of four years of opportunity for debriefing by FBI agents and questioning by prosecutors.[21] Even knowing that the best witness to a conspiracy is an insider to its secret activities, I found it hard to trust al Fadl. I complained to friends about my reluctance to believe him. One questioned my skepticism, asking, "Do you really think the prosecutors would put on a witness they had trained to lie?" I did not have enough experience with these individuals to judge their morals or ethics, but railroaded witnesses and faked evidence were not uncommon in other prosecutions. More practically, I could argue it either way. On the one hand, such manipulation would be risky in a high-profile case. On the other hand, an attack on U.S. government interests was at the center of this trial, and the prosecutors were under pressure to bring in a conviction. I wanted to trust them to uphold their office, but I could not let go of the skepticism I would bring to any legal proceeding, especially one where secrecy had been a tactic pursued by so many involved.

That said, al Fadl's testimony was so filled with jaw-dropping details about al Qaeda's elaborate operations that I felt compelled to believe his story or at least parts of it, however wrenching it was to depend on someone with his checkered history and questionable motivations. Al Fadl's depiction of the world of al Qaeda was crucial to the case, and this depiction stood relatively unchallenged, despite virulent defense attacks on his character and credibility. When subsequent witnesses corroborated al Fadl's account about forming the initial group, training in Afghanistan, and then working for bin Laden interests in Africa, the details they offered fit neatly into a familiar narrative. The alleged conspiracy, linked to al Qaeda, was becoming a reality of specific people, places, plans, and actions.

By mid-February 2001 the focus of testimony was shifting from the organization's broad history to the specific events in the years preceding the bombings and to East Africa. Evidence from this time and place was needed to connect the al Qaeda leadership with the men on trial. A witness named Essam al Ridi, who represented himself as a former pilot for bin Laden's business interests, confirmed much that we had already heard about al Qaeda's activities in Sudan.[22] In interviews with FBI agents shortly after the embassy bombings, and in his testimony, el Ridi provided damning evidence against defendant el Hage, whom he said had inquired about buying Stinger missiles for al Qaeda. Defense counsel took the thunder out of this point by insisting that the prosecution agree to a stipulation confirming that the U.S. government had provided Stingers to the mujaheddin fighting against the Soviets in Afghanistan. El Hage watched impassively as the case against him mounted. He looked thin and pale, his face framed by long hair flowing over his shoulders. Mostly he sat motionless and rarely talked to his attorneys.

The story that Ashif Mohamed Juma, a young Tanzanian, had come to tell was not immediately apparent. But things got interesting when he readily identified Government Exhibit 103 as a photo of Adel Habib, his brother-in-law, who had married his sister in 1993. Through previous testimony, we knew that Exhibit 103 depicted Abu Ubaidah al Banshiri, bin Laden's military expert, second in command of al Qaeda, but Juma did not know his true identity. In 1996 Adel Habib helped Juma with a family errand by traveling with him to Bukoba, Tanzania, a town on the far side of Lake Victoria. The next day they began the return trip from Bukoba to Mwanza on the other side of the lake by boarding a ferry even more massively overcrowded than the one they had ridden the day before. They took the top bunks of a small first-class cabin shared with seven other men. Juma woke up in the night when he felt the huge ferry list steeply. Habib tried to calm his fears by reminding him that all was in God's hands. Then, suddenly, the craft turned on its side; Juma looked through the door, which was now above their cabin. He wriggled up and out. Standing in the corridor, he reached back through the doorway to help Habib, who was clinging to the door itself. It might have been the others in the cabin, pulling on Habib's clothes, or Habib's own weight—he was a big man— that pulled the door from its hinges and sent him crashing onto those beneath him. Looking up he urged Juma to save himself. As Juma felt the ferry start to turn upside-down and saw water rushing in from all directions, he frantically climbed out a window and eventually mounted the hull, the only part of the vessel above water. A bungled rescue effort sank the ferry, along with some victims still alive in an air pocket. That made Juma, who was pulled from the water hours later, one of only 114 survivors of the 1,200 that packed a ferry designed to hold 480.

Juma broke down while describing his escape from the sinking ferry. After he recovered, he explained that, of course, his family had been distraught, especially because they were unable to locate Habib's body, which was among hundreds still missing. Then, as Juma continued, his brother Sikander, who lived in Nairobi, brought one of Habib's business associates to Mwanza to help with the search. The man's name was Haroun, a figure familiar to us from previous testimony, which mentioned him as a member of an al Qaeda cell based in Nairobi. After two weeks of searching daily for Habib's body, Haroun was joined by Wadih el Hage, who was introduced as another of Habib's associates. The family had not been previously acquainted with the two men, who stayed in the area for a month. He recounted conversations with Wadih, whom he identified in court.

I was fascinated by Juma's testimony, mostly because an apparently humble young man's observations further established the links between Wadih el Hage, Haroun, and someone as high ranking as Abu Ubaidah. Whether the connection between these three constituted a criminal conspiracy was still unclear, but their close involvement was becoming indisputable.

On the day after Juma's testimony, prosecutors turned to the reading of a transcript from 1997 when Wadih el Hage had been brought before a New York grand jury for questioning about his possible connection to al Qaeda in Nairobi and Sudan. His testimony to the grand jury directly contradicted what we had heard from Juma. After telling the grand jury that he was involved in al Qaeda business ventures but had never sworn allegiance, el Hage described his relationship with Abu Ubaidah as "casual." And he asserted that, as far as he knew, Abu Ubaidah was still living in Sudan or maybe Afghanistan. He denied knowing that Abu Ubaidah had drowned on the ferry and maintained that he had gone to the accident site to investigate the death of a man named Adel Habib, whom he portrayed as a colleague in the relief agency he ran, a person altogether different from Abu Ubaidah.

El Hage's denials to the 1997 grand jury would seem even more bizarre later that week, when we heard testimony from L'Houssaine Kherchtou, another government witness with long-time involvement in al Qaeda. After swearing an oath to al Qaeda in Afghanistan in the early 1990s, Kherchtou worked with bin Laden supporters in Sudan and Kenya, including the defendants Odeh and el Hage. Asked about el Hage's reaction to the news that Abu Ubaidah had died on the ferry, Kherchtou said, betraying some emotion himself, "Abu Ubaidah al Banshiri was loved by everybody. He was a very good person, and everybody was upset. Wadih, I saw him cry." Questions remained about why Haroun and el Hage had gone to investigate the ferry accident. Had they intended to recover and bury Abu Ubaidah's body? Or to recover and protect the briefcase Juma said was always at his side? Or were they, as prosecutors asserted, trying to make sure no one discovered that bin Laden's military commander was operating in East Africa? It was surreal to contemplate al Qaeda members frantically searching for their drowned comrade and helping his widow and family. I had trouble admitting that they were vulnerable to disaster and capable of grief, like the rest of us. Yet, if the prosecutors were right, they recovered from their grief in time to plot the events that would plunge others into mourning.

L'Houssaine Kherchtou was the last of several former al Qaeda members to testify for the government. By advancing the narrative up to the moment of the bombings, his testimony was extremely important. He told us about his activities in 1996, when, under pressure from the United States, the Sudanese government asked al Qaeda to leave the country and Kherchtou disobeyed bin Laden's orders to move to Afghanistan. He was concerned about educating his children in such a remote area, and perhaps still angry over an incident when group leaders had refused him financial assistance for a family emergency. As he confirmed on direct testimony, staying in Sudan violated his al Qaeda oath, and he no longer considered himself part of the group. Despite this break, he had intermittent contact with former al Qaeda colleagues and, for a time, continued to conceal what he knew about their activities while trying to develop his own business ventures in Khartoum.

In June 1998 Kherchtou was contacted about a job possibility and traveled to Nairobi to meet with an executive from a tourism company with interests in Sudan. By chance, he said, he ran into Haroun and Ahmed, another al Qaeda colleague, in downtown Nairobi and then met up with them later at Mercy International Relief Agency (MIRA). One of them dropped him at the airport for his flight back to Sudan. After completing some research on Sudanese tourism, he contacted the businessman who set the date for a second meeting: August 6, 1998. Kherchtou returned to Nairobi for the meeting and, after it ended, tried to locate Haroun. When he reached Haroun's wife by phone, she said they were about to leave on a trip. He left his hotel address at the MIRA offices. As he prepared for Friday prayers the following day, he noticed that traffic into the city was backed up. At the mosque a Kenyan man told him that the U.S. Embassy had been bombed. When he ran into Ahmed later that day, the young man insisted that he knew nothing about the bombings but, in Kherchtou's opinion, behaved suspiciously.

Kherchtou's testimony cast suspicion on Haroun and Ahmed, indicted co-conspirators, yet it also begged some serious questions about his own role. How was it possible that Kherchtou had been present in Nairobi in early August 1998, had met with his former co-conspirators, had visited offices linked to al Qaeda, and yet had known nothing about the planned bombing? Was it a coincidence, a setup, or rotten luck that his behavior so resembled that of other conspirators? His nefarious past led authorities at Nairobi's airport to detain him when he tried to leave for Sudan four days after the bombing. Testimony offered a sketchy story of how he had worked as an informer for at least two other governments (not identified in court) before he eventually agreed to cooperate with U.S. officials in 2000.[23] If Kherchtou had not cooperated, perhaps his actions on August 7 would have led to conspiracy charges.[24]

From his experience defending Mohammad Salameh, accused of conspiracy and other crimes related to the 1993 bombing of the World Trade Center, attorney Robert Precht expressed concern that "even minor players in a terrorism plot can easily find themselves charged in a conspiracy indictment and facing death."[25] The risk of assuming guilt by association is a strong tendency in the prosecution of conspiracy cases.[26] The examples before the court in the embassy bombings trial highlighted the difficulty of determining when a person was a full-fledged conspirator (probably Haroun), a business associate (such as el Ridi), a former conspirator turned associate (Kherchtou's representation of his role) or an innocent in-law (presumably Ashif Juma). The secretive nature of conspiracies compounds the problem of establishing whether any individual is "in" or "out." The secrecy surrounding the information released in court also made it more difficult to know with certainty what roles individuals such as Kherchtou, Ali Mohamed, or al Fadl had played before or after their involvement in the conspiracy. For example, connections they may have had with foreign governments were well protected by the procedures for concealing sensitive materials.[27] Having to rely on former members of the conspiracy with murky connections themselves to illegal activities, as well as overlapping tales of deception and secrecy, was fraught with dismay for those of us who craved an untainted explanation.

While negotiating a legal point concerning Kherchtou's testimony, Judge Sand mentioned the name Haroun, and prosecutor Pat Fitzgerald interjected, "the principle organizer of the bombing." Although Haroun's name had come up several times in relation to activities among al Qaeda associates in Nairobi, the evidence had yet to establish the role he had played. Fitzgerald's remark revealed how prosecutors viewed the Nairobi group. This offhand reference to Haroun's central role, made outside the jury's presence, was for me an important shortcut to understanding how the pieces of the prosecution case would ultimately come together, including how some of the defendants would be positioned with respect to Haroun.[28] At the same time this reference heightened my interest in learning more about Haroun in particular. The conspiracy charge set up a curious situation. Haroun, still at large, had been indicted but was not on trial. Even so, because of his role in the conspiracy, and his connection to the defendants, he would be mentioned many times in the coming weeks. Similarly prosecutors offered some limited evidence of the roles played by some of the two dozen other indicted co-conspirators. Bin Laden's ideology came through clearly in a lengthy CNN interview from 1997 that was played in court. His anger at U.S. policy and his intent to attack Americans, especially those in Saudi Arabia, was unquestionable, as were his efforts to place responsibility for any future harm to Americans on the U.S. government.[29] A fatwa issued in February 1998 clarified his plans: "The ruling to kill the Americans and their allies—civilians and military—is an individual duty for every Muslim who can do it." His ideology was becoming crystal clear; we might have wanted to know more, however, about the actual role he played in planning attacks. Yet the prosecution's job in establishing the conspiracy was to focus primarily on the participation of the four defendants. To do so, they might avoid overemphasizing the role of those in charge in order to be sure that the jury would not excuse those in the lower ranks. Robert Precht argues that conspiracy law can treat defendants unfairly for the following reason, among others: Because it only takes the overt act of one co-conspirator to prove a conspiracy (if the other elements have also been proved), "the level of the defendant's actual participation is immaterial."[30] Judging from my own experience, this bedrock of conspiracy law contrasts with how a lay observer in court might evaluate an individual conspirator's actions. Learning who had performed which specific actions was important to me, out of a belief that the behavior of some individuals (namely, organizers such as bin Laden, Abu Ubaidah, or Haroun) would make them more responsible than others. Using the wide net of conspiracy to pull everyone in risked blurring the differences between them and diminishing the culpability of some.

While we had learned a considerable amount about al Qaeda in the course of the embassy bombings trial, the puzzle built through the evidence would eventually foreground the four defendants' participation and leave behind the other co-conspirators. This emphasis was both unavoidable and entirely appropriate, given the nature of trials, and yet made it more difficult for anyone trying to apportion responsibility for the bombings among the whole range of actors and to answer the question of why the group conspired to carry them out.

A few weeks later I was in court when two clerks again read grand jury testimony into the record. Gerard Francisco played the prosecutor, and Abigail Seda was Wadih el Hage. It was el Hage's second appearance before a New York grand jury, this time in 1998, a month after the embassy bombings. Many of the same questions he had been asked in 1997 were posed to him again, and, by reading both transcripts into the record, prosecutors meant to show that some of el Hage's answers had changed and others had been contradicted by the testimony of prosecution witnesses we had heard from between the two readings. Either case would make him guilty of the perjury counts charged in the indictment.

What had seemed in 1997 a juvenile ploy by el Hage to create confusion by insisting to the grand jury that business associate "Adel Habib" had drowned in the ferry accident sounded malevolent after the 1998 bombings. The clerk read Pat Fitzgerald's question, "Do you recall telling the last grand jury that you appeared in front of [in 1997] that you went to Lake Victoria to see about someone who died in that ferry accident?" "Right." El Hage next confirmed that he had gone to Tanzania to meet Haroun so they could search together for their colleague from the relief agency. When prompted, el Hage could not recall the colleague's name. Fitzgerald must have been annoyed when he asked el Hage, "So you flew to the scene of a ferry that sank. You spent two or three days looking for someone and then you returned to Nairobi." "Right." "And you can't remember to tell the grand jury the name of the person you were looking for?" Although the clerk played him deadpan, I imagined Fitzgerald's voice dripping with sarcasm, his face scornful, as he disparaged el Hage's faulty memory. Was el Hage baiting him or trying to be helpful, when he replied, "I told you the name last time in front of the other grand jury. If you tell me now, I would remember it." Next el Hage was asked whether he had reported back to anyone, including Osama bin Laden, after returning from his trip. El Hage's negative response led Fitzgerald to press him: "As you sit here before this grand jury, you don't recall who sent you to the scene of the ferry incident, you don't recall reporting to anyone, and you don't recall the name of the person you were looking for; is that correct?" "Right now, I don't." I wished someone had made a videotape of Fitzgerald asking the next question, "How many ferry sinkings have you gone to, to investigate, in your entire life?" "Just one" was the answer. On being shown Abu Ubaidah's picture, el Hage remembered the name right away: "Adel Habib." When asked, in a few different ways, if Adel was also known as Abu Ubaidah, each time he replied, "Not that I know of."

Given his responses, it seemed a good bet that el Hage had perjured himself. Yet, for several reasons, this part of the case failed to hold my attention. Perjury charges based on multiple appearances at hearings or grand juries are a routine, relatively simple means of convicting someone of a lesser crime, especially when proof of a more serious offense might be lacking. Other aspects of el Hage's role in the conspiracy and in the activities in Nairobi seemed more important. For instance, I was eager to know whether he had been an authority figure in the Nairobi group. I must admit that simple impatience also circumscribed my interest in the perjury case. The hours spent reading the grand jury testimony into the record prolonged the trial for seemingly little gain, as proving el Hage's perjury was, in my view, less relevant than proving his role in more serious offenses. El Hage's counsel, prone to repeated interruptions and objections, wore my patience even thinner.

I came to realize that it was precisely el Hage's evasive and dissembling manner in grand jury testimony that motivated the prosecutors to work as hard as they could to convict him not only of perjury, which would not be difficult, but also of conspiracy. After the embassies were attacked they must have looked back many times at the 1997 grand jury testimony to search for clues that el Hage had known about the bombings and had concealed that knowledge. Perhaps they wondered whether, in their questioning of el Hage, they might have found a way to get him to reveal what he knew. Could they have turned him? Could they have exposed the plot and prevented the bombings? By September 1998, just back from viewing the horrific destruction at the bomb site, listening to a similar performance by el Hage at the grand jury must have infuriated Pat Fitzgerald and the other prosecutors, and fueled their resolve to bring him to justice.

Only partway through the prosecution case, I had already begun to ignore some lines of inquiry and wish that other issues were getting more attention. In short, it was impossible to follow every issue, or even every defendant. Something so simple as the demeanor of a particular attorney made it too burdensome to pay close attention to his client's defense. Likewise, too much concealed information made it difficult to follow certain issues, such as the role al Qaeda may have played in the attack on U.S. troops in Somalia. I was especially concerned that I had to drop my interest in some of the co-conspirators, such as Haroun, as the trial's narrative moved past their roles and prosecutors worked their way down the conspiratorial network to those operating in the cells active at each bombing's ground zero.

CHAPTER FIVE
Proving a "Jihad Job"

FBI SPECIAL AGENT Leo West took the stand to describe the Dar es Salaam bomb scene from the perspective of a forensics expert. A veteran of many bomb investigations, including the 1993 World Trade Center bombing and the bombing of TWA Flight 800, West had traveled to Dar es Salaam just two days after the embassy bombings to spearhead evidence collection. On the afternoon of his arrival, he and his team established a perimeter around the embassy blast site, checked the area visually, and began swabbing for residue that would eventually reveal the bomb's components. The blast had thrown pieces of evidence more than six hundred yards from its epicenter near the embassy's north corner. On questioning from prosecutor Ken Karas, West identified evidence collected at the site, including parts of a Nissan Atlas truck and pieces of metal cylinders, which appeared to be components of the bomb situated on the truck's twisted rear axle. With help from engineers at the Nissan corporation, FBI forensic analysts eventually created a "skeletal structure" of the truck. As we viewed the photo of the truck's fragmentary remains, West confirmed that the blast from the bomb would have obliterated anyone sitting inside.

West's calm description of the force of the blast—a detonation that sheared and pitted the truck's metal—took the wind out of me as I struggled to imagine what Jamal might have felt so close to the truck at that horrific instant. During Jamal's matanga, Mary Porter told me something she had learned from her father. He said that during World War II it became clear that troops were being killed by the blast of a bomb itself, that is, by the force of the torrential energy unleashed rather than by wounds from flying shrapnel. Knowing that such force could itself cause instantaneous death provided me some comfort as it pushed aside more agonizing thoughts about the possible suffering Jamal or other victims experienced. Having seen the mangled truck parts displayed before the jury, I better understood what a bomb's energy could accomplish.

I had high hopes that evidence in the Tanbomb phase of the case would be as detailed and sophisticated as what we had heard in previous weeks when prosecutors presented witnesses who linked two of the defendants to the Kenya bombing. Over several weeks in early March they had offered a staggering amount of physical evidence, which included explosives residue found on the bag their defendant Odeh had carried out of Kenya, bullets left in the hospital where al-'Owhali had been treated after the blast, records of phone calls from cell members to numbers in Afghanistan, Yemen, and London, and material from hotel rooms where conspirators had stayed just prior to the bombing. Before the prosecution rested its case, a phalanx of technical experts would testify, patiently explaining, for example, the technology used to analyze DNA, fingerprints, fibers, and chemicals. Computer-generated displays on the courtroom's video screens were impressive and effective means of organizing hundreds of phone records, the transcripts of conversations collected through wiretaps, and the many documents both seized and prepared specially for the trial. The level of technology used in court lent the presentations a scientific efficiency that encouraged an unconscious assumption of their reliability.

As a highlight of the Kenbomb case, prosecutors revealed statements made by the defendants Mohammad al-'Owhali and Mohamed Sadeek Odeh under interrogation by FBI agents and other officials after their capture, in which they admitted to activities on behalf of the organization and long involvement with its members. From Odeh's account, as presented through the FBI agent who had interrogated him, we came to understand the operation of the intelligence and planning cells that established al Qaeda in East Africa and accomplished the groundwork for mounting an attack.[1] From al-'Owhali's questioner, we learned about the execution cell assigned to enter Kenya at the last minute to perform the actual crime. Even as I experienced a growing certainty that prosecutors were amassing incontrovertible proof of who had carried out the Nairobi bombing, the evidence raised some questions. Physical evidence never "speaks for itself" but rather must be introduced through testimony, which, like other forms of speech, always occasions multiple interpretations. Moreover, the defendants' statements, also linguistic in nature, led me to questions about truth, interpretation, and power which I had been trained to ask of all language produced in court. From the evidence previously presented, we knew that some al Qaeda writings and speech were deliberate manipulations, like the silly code used in a letter warning one al Qaeda member not to trust another because he was working for the "Food and Beverage Institute." Laughter broke out in court as people noticed the crude reference to the FBI. Many key pieces of evidence were linguistic, including transcribed phone calls, letters, conversations between conspirators, phone records, and the defendants' statements themselves. Previous testimony led me to conclude that Mohamed Odeh's guilt turned on conversations. His negative answer to one question seemed crucial: Had he ever discussed plans for the bombings with his cell members?

The testimony of al Fadl and Kherchtou had primed us to remember that the word of some people was less than trustworthy and that the conditions under which a statement was made might skew the story told. Such issues have always intrigued me in my research, as guilt or innocence can turn on the subtleties of language. At the embassy bombings trial I found myself listening closely to evaluate the stories being told about the defendants. As much as I needed to learn what they had done, I wanted to be certain that I could believe the stories, that they had not been coerced or fabricated. Only then would I feel that the trial might bring justice.

The day after Leo West's testimony about the Dar es Salaam bombing, witnesses who had been brought from East Africa began the legally crucial task of connecting the physical evidence from the bomb site and other places around Tanzania to the accused, namely, K. K. Mohamed and co-conspirators not present in court. Dar es Salaam resident Mohamed Zaidi described the sale of his Nissan Atlas truck to two men, one tall and one short. He knew the latter as Ahmed, whom we in court

could identify from previous evidence as the man who had purchased the truck used in the Nairobi bombing. Zaidi's plans to
start a fishing business had fallen through, and, in July of 1998,
he was forced to sell his refrigerator truck only a month after
he had bought it. In describing the sale, Zaidi emphasized the
suspicious behavior of Ahmed and his tall companion. First,
even though they had agreed on a time to meet, he had to track
them down to complete the sale, finally ending up in the tall
one's room at the al Noor Hotel in Dar es Salaam. Then, just as
he was about to sign the papers, Zaidi discovered that the two
had not given him enough cash. He threatened to leave. The tall
man reassured him that he would get his money and then answered an almost immediate knock at the door. Reaching out
without looking, he took a bag from whoever stood there and
handed it to Zaidi to complete the sale.

The short one and the tall one—named Ahmed and Sheikh—
figured in the testimony of several other witnesses. Each mention occasioned the display of their photos. As witnesses recounted, the two were seen around town together and with
other alleged cell members, including Fahad and Hussein, who
traveled frequently in a white Suzuki Samarai. Witnesses linked
each of these individuals to K. K. Mohamed. One witness said
that K.K. had translated for Hussein, who spoke only Arabic.
Demonstrating an association between K.K. and those who had
purchased the truck cemented an important element of the case
against the defendant.

As Paul Butler's opening statement promised, K.K. had performed tasks related to the bombing. For instance, he had been
responsible for paying rent money to the landlord of a house at
22 Kidagalo Street, in which K.K. had lived along with Hussein
and his family. While living there, the tenants had constructed
high walls around the front. When K.K. was told that the house
on Kidagalo Street was no longer suitable for the group's purposes, he had to find another house. A real estate broker reported K.K.'s request that the new house needed to be surrounded by high walls. This was the house at 213 Ilala, where,
as subsequent witnesses would claim, cell members built the
bomb and loaded it into the Nissan Atlas truck. Another wit-

ness, attesting to K.K.'s property management duties in the group, mentioned that, when K.K. asked him to take charge of finding new tenants for 213 Ilala in July 1998, he insisted it should only be rented to "people with light skin like us." That remark, although unconnected to issues in the case, was likely elicited by Karas to paint K.K. as a racist.

At times, interpreters failed to recognize the need to translate across cultural as well as linguistic divides. For example, one witness's response to a question about his occupation was rendered: "I sell juice with bites." "With snacks" would have been a better translation for the American audience. Those of us who spoke Kiswahili, including about a dozen observers brought from the embassy in Dar es Salaam to observe the trial for a week, grimaced, giggled, and shook our heads violently when the interpreter summarized one witness's long mumbled answer as, "He says, 'yes.' " In other instances, his word-for-word translations produced awkward English sentences from people who were articulate in Kiswahili. By contrast, another set of interpreters hired by the court to translate from English into Arabic and Kiswahili for the defendants and, at times, the audience, were very skilled.[2] Other misunderstandings were less the fault of interpreters than the inevitable misspeech of nervous witnesses unfamiliar with the court or with English. In response to a question about how he received rent from K.K., Mr. Said replied in English, "He paid me cash." "Do you know where that money came from?" "He took from his pocket" (pp. 2660–61). Further probing established that K.K.'s superiors had given him the cash.

Julius Kisingo, a welder working in Dar es Salaam, took the stand to describe how he had outfitted the Nissan Atlas truck. He had no trouble remembering that job because, in his seven years of welding, it was the only time he had ever worked on a refrigerator truck, although the cooling unit had been removed. Frustrated in his attempts to explain how he had connected long steel bars into partitions and then fixed them into the truck bed, the welder cast his eyes about for something to indicate length and grabbed the paper tape coming from the court reporter's machine. Pulling it up and holding it against the witness stand, he showed how he had positioned the fittings. Glancing up to see the court reporter's shocked expression, the lead prosecutor quickly ripped two pages from a yellow legal pad and rushed them into the hands of Mr. Kisingo, who dropped the tape and stabbed a Bic pen through the pages to connect them. A craftsman, for whom words were more difficult than fashioning with his own hands, he held up his creation. Ahmed, the truck's owner, had told him that the welded bars would be used to brace containers of fish. Instead, they would hold crates of TNT and other bomb components.

The next witness, soft-spoken Amina Rashid, had worked as a housegirl (the East African term for domestic worker) in a Dar es Salaam home where Ahmed had lived. She identified his frequent visitors, including Fahad and Hussein. When asked if she would be able to recognize another of the visitors, K.K. Mohamed, she said, through the interpreter, "If he didn't change, I will be able to recognize that person, to know that person. But if he change, I will not be able to do that" (pp. 2634–35). When asked to point him out, Amina looked around the room and then focused on K.K. for what seemed like a full minute before saying that she did not see him. Surprised, observers gasped and laughed at the same time. Even K.K. shook his head and smiled slightly. Another witness who had known K.K. well also failed to point him out. Did K.K.'s new glasses and dapper clothes throw them off? Even so, two witnesses managed to identify him.

On cross-examination, K.K.'s attorney, David Ruhnke, avoided antagonizing the witnesses but rather drew on their knowledge to fill out details of the culture and history of coastal Tanzania. Through the witnesses he educated jurors about the significant role played by Arabs on the coast of both Kenya and Tanzania. Ruhnke was using the anthropological tactic of making a remote and foreign place into a familiar scenario. Establishing in jurors' minds a strong, positive identification with East Africa and the lifestyle of people in K.K.'s community would be useful when it came time to present mitigating evidence about the difficulties in K.K.'s life. I had been wondering what images jurors would fix on as representative of East Africa. During his cross-examination of the FBI agent who had searched Odeh's home in a place called Witu, defense attorney Carl Herman had tried to depict the house as a "hut" in a village "back into the interior of Kenya." The agent carefully corrected this impression, saying that the home and other buildings had "stucco wall construction" and that Witu was a "fair-sized village." Herman's desire to create the impression that Odeh lived in a poor and isolated village would serve his client's contention that the distance between his home in Witu and the cities where the other cell members lived made contact between them difficult.

As witness after witness implicated K.K. in activities leading up to the bombing, I stared at him. Once our eyes met, as he looked over at the lineup of victims. I registered no expression; neither did he. In truth, I felt nothing at that time. Although young, K.K., with his neat haircut and trendy, black-rimmed glasses, looked like a defense team associate. His passport photo, an evidence exhibit projected on the wide screen, was not particularly flattering. It had appeared on his application for a second passport, which bore the name of a family friend about K.K.'s age who worked at the Zanzibar Registry office. Zahran Nassor Maulid testified that he knew K.K. as an old school and soccer buddy and had been persuaded, by K.K., to help him obtain the false document.

As the Tanbomb case proceeded, prosecutors were calm and solicitous, never visibly ruffled by the complications of translation and misunderstanding. They had moved so swiftly through the case that Judge Sand canceled court for the next day. The jurors looked pleased. During the break, attorneys would negotiate stipulations that could, in the end, save even more time. One stipulation had already established that K.K. was the buyer in the purchase of the white Suzuki Samarai we had heard mentioned several times. The actions admitted to in the many stipulations already agreed upon seemed to confirm the culpability of a defendant even as it showed his willingness to facilitate the fact-finding aspect of the trial process. The basic outline was becoming clear: K.K. was on the scene in Dar es Salaam prior to the bombing and had associated with others who were actively planning it.

The Al Nur Motel rang a bell for me. Jamal and I had walked in that area and knew people who lived nearby. Watching the trial, I found myself making strange "small world" connections to K.K.'s activities before the bombing. He had mailed a package—a farewell missive from the driver of the truck bearing the bomb to the driver's Egyptian family—at the DHL Express office where I was a regular. That we had traveled the same paths made K.K. seem increasingly like a typical Dar es Salaam resident going about his errands on familiar streets, and this image made it harder for me to understand how he could have participated in the bombing. As I heard these faraway places being mentioned, all so familiar to me, I also gave myself credit for "knowing" Dar es Salaam in the way that anthropologists want to know a place better than its inhabitants might. Yet I had lived right there and had no idea what someone like K.K. was doing.

In my notebook I identified the gaps in the story emerging from the witnesses' evidence, and questions I sought to answer: What role had K.K. played in the bombing? Was he a full-fledged member of an al Qaeda cell? When did he learn that the embassy was the target? Where was he for a year after the bombing, before he was captured in South Africa? What caused this young Swahili man to become involved in al Qaeda?

At the end of a short break in the afternoon, Steve from the FBI leaned up to the back of my seat to pass me a message: "Abby wants you to know that she'd be very glad if you were in court when she testifies next week." Abby was the FBI investigator who had often said that thinking about the victims motivated her when working on the case. I wondered if seeing me in the audience during her testimony might bolster her sense of purpose. I also knew that the government positions victims prominently in court during such testimony so that jurors will notice them. In any case, I looked forward to Abby's testimony about the first FBI interrogation of K.K., which I believed would connect the still disjointed evidence from witnesses such as the welder and the landlord into a more coherent account of what K.K. had done. With all that the witnesses had said about K.K., what would he have to say for himself when Abby and Mike asked him about the bombing?

I was present when Abby took the stand. After establishing the basic facts of Abby's service at the FBI, and her involvement in the Dar es Salaam investigation, prosecutor Ken Karas asked, "And did there come a time when you were in Cape Town, South Africa, that you met Khalfan Khamis Mohamed?" (p. 2795). Abby said that she and her colleague, Mike, had met K.K. in a holding cell at the airport in Cape Town. Before relating what K.K. had told them, her answers addressed the concerns about suspects' statements that had come up in previous testimony by FBI agents who had described their interrogations of Odeh and al-'Owhali. For example, FBI Special Agent Steven Gaudin testified about Mohamed al-'Owhali's statement, given under questioning by American and Kenyan officials after he was picked up in Nairobi. Al-'Owhali's account of his experience with al Qaeda was a sick but fascinating tale in which he admitted coming to Kenya in August 1998 as part of the "execution" cell that would detonate the bomb that others had constructed. Someone named Saleh showed him around Nairobi and explained the logistics, and al-'Owhali confirmed that Saleh was a lead planner of both the Nairobi and Dar es Salaam bombings. He also confirmed Haroun's central role. But before Agent Gaudin could testify about the substance of al-'Owhali's statement, the defense counsel led him through a long voir dire to establish the authenticity of a document that the defendant had signed prior to answering any questions. The scrutiny directed toward the document, which was the version of Miranda rights used to advise suspects of their rights when outside the United States, drew attention to the conditions under which al-'Owhali had given his statement. Those conditions were already the subject of a defense motion that would ultimately alter how such speech was treated under the law. At this point it raised questions about how the power dynamics between interrogators and suspects influence speech, and, in my view, those questions intersected with the concerns about truth and interpretation that testimony routinely occasions.

With these previously aired issues no doubt in mind, Abby described how they had first determined that K.K. could understand English. Then they advised him of his rights and watched as he signed a form indicating his comprehension. He had also confirmed his understanding that he would receive no benefit by speaking with them. Abby continued, "At that point he asked us, 'Does this mean I'm going to see America?' " They told him that there was a "good chance" that he would (p. 2800). K.K.'s compliance led to an interview lasting from one o'clock in the afternoon until after ten that first night. Following a shorter interview the next day, K.K. agreed to accompany the agents to the United States. The questioning continued on the flight but, as Abby carefully noted, only after K.K. had signed yet another sheet advising him of his rights, which had changed now that he was in U.S. custody rather than South African.

After these preliminaries, Karas questioned Abby about substantive issues. In 1994 K.K.'s friend, Fahad, whom he had met at a mosque in Dar es Salaam, raised the possibility that they could both go to Afghanistan for military training. As Abby recounted, K.K.'s activities at a remote training camp resembled those of al-'Owhali, Odeh, and thousands of other young Muslim men who went through basic and advanced military instruction. When departing Afghanistan to return to Tanzania, K.K. left his contact number hoping that those who had trained him would call him up for future assignments. At this point in Abby's testimony, the extent of K.K.'s connection to the conspiracy was still unclear. He appeared strangely detached and ill-informed in comparison with more central players, such as Odeh, who had admitted to being a military man serving bin Laden. For instance, after K.K. returned to Dar, he waited for the call but for years heard nothing from his former trainers. Key concepts—like *bayat* (an oath of allegiance)—were unfamiliar to him. He had not heard of "al Qaeda" as the name of a group. When asked about bin Laden, K.K. told Abby and Mike that he respected bin Laden as a *sheik* (a learned elder) but had never met him. Abby later recounted that K.K. eventually said that he had assumed a link between the group he had worked with in Dar es Salaam and bin Laden's organization.

As Abby recounted, K.K. acknowledged that his training, and his subsequent activities, constituted "jihad," the purpose of which was to help his Muslim "brothers." After meeting up with Fahad in Mombasa, long after his return from Afghanistan, K.K. traveled by boat to Somalia for jihad with his brothers there. K.K. would have said the word "brothers" in English during his interrogation, but what Swahili meaning motivated this use? The Swahili term *ndugu*, a plausible translation, is notoriously polysemic. Most often it means "sibling"—plural and singular—regardless of gender. But *ndugu*'s reference expands to mean cousin and even anyone of the same generation, and can also have the political connotation of "comrade." Just considering what K.K. might have meant by saying brothers, let alone his understanding of jihad, a much more complex notion that Abby's testimony never broached directly, made me more aware that we were learning K.K.'s multicultural and multilingual story through a reconstruction controlled entirely by Abby and the prosecutor. So when Abby stated, "He said that he was involved with a group of what he called brothers, and that they were involved in a jihad against America, including the bombing of the American Embassy in Dar es Salaam" (p. 2813), I felt at once confirmation that K.K. was involved directly in the violent conspiracy, and yet I questioned whether I fully grasped what K.K. believed he had signed on to. Some slippage in meaning seemed inevitable as K.K.'s story emerged through Abby's testimony. But her account of his words was all we had to go on.

During the interrogation K.K. had identified many brothers through photos. On the back of each he wrote the name of the person depicted—Hussein, Fahad, Sulieman, Sheikh, Ahmed Khalfan—and then signed his own name to confirm he had known them as brothers in the cell that had arranged the Dar bombing. As Abby recounted, it was Hussein who approached K.K. in March 1998 to ask "if he would assist with a jihad job" (p. 2816). Hussein had been quick to add that if K.K. had no interest he would still need to keep secret that Hussein had asked him. Threat seemed to hang behind Hussein's request, but K.K. agreed to take the jihad job, even though he knew no details. Even after living and working with the cell members and

participating in the construction of the bomb, he remained unaware of the target until five days before the planned detonation.
But, as Abby carefully pointed out, K.K. had insisted that neither
he nor anyone else involved had been duped into participating.
Everyone played his part; everyone was willing; everyone knew
that this jihad job would be violent.

With each response, Abby was snapping together pieces of the
puzzle depicting K.K.'s role. Some pieces confirmed evidence
we had already heard from previous witnesses. For example,
K.K. had purchased the Suzuki Samarai that was used in the
planning stage and had also rented houses for cell members; he
paid for both with money from Hussein. It seemed plausible that
he had indeed done those things, because we had heard them
multiple times. As the story came together, my scholarly training led me to focus on what made Abby such an effective witness. For one, she listened carefully to each question and then
answered slowly, briefly, and to the point. To my ears, the calm
clarity of her measured responses imbued her testimony with
sincerity. Jurors would be hard-pressed to envision her as the
kind of cowboy agent who might coerce a suspect or cover up
a mistake. It helped that Abby, with short blond hair and a trim
figure, was attractive in a fresh-faced way, although the drawing
posted the next day on CNN's website made her look sallow
and grim. Almost every one of Abby's answers indicated that
she was merely reporting what K.K. had said during the interrogation. Her responses began with "he said" to indicate that she
was not describing what K.K. had done but only what he told
his interrogators. This repetitive linguistic feature oddly increased her credibility (at least to me), because it drew attention
to her precision as a witness. In contrast to other witnesses,
Abby refrained from impersonating K.K.; she stuck to indirect
reports, not direct quotes. Scholars of linguistics argue that direct quotes are generally more credible than indirect ones; however, it would have been unacceptable to those listening in court
had an FBI agent mimicked a defendant. Although an appropriate compromise, indirect quotes distanced those of us observing from the defendant's admissions; we had the vague feeling

that we could hear his words but, because we heard them through a filter, we may have only gotten their gist.

Abby continued in her calm, matter-of-fact tone even as she described how K.K. and the other cell members had built the bomb. As Abby explained, K.K. worked with another Ahmed, this one sometimes referred to as "Ahmed the driver" or "Ahmed the German," and also with Abdu Rahman, the bomb engineer who had come to Dar to assemble the device, as he had done in Nairobi. K.K. had helped prepare the TNT. With more than four hundred pieces of explosive, each the size of a soda can, grinding the TNT and sealing the powder into special wooden crates, which were then nailed shut, were formidable tasks, although ones that puzzled experts, who claimed afterward that the TNT would have exploded just as effectively had it been left whole. According to Abby, K.K. knew little about how the other parts of the bomb worked—for instance, the cylinders and the fertilizer—but he had watched as the engineer connected the wires of more than a hundred detonators without consulting any instructions. In describing this hive of demented activity, which Paul Butler's opening statement had called a "bomb factory," Abby merely reported K.K.'s words without saying, for example, "yeah, it really made me angry, or sick, to hear this." Her testimony offered no evidence that she was incensed, or horrified, which I imagined she was. On the witness stand, any reaction she might display had no legal relevance and could have been seen as prejudicial. Controlled emotions were also required of us listeners; I felt I had to stifle any overt reaction to the revolting image of cell members hard at work constructing the deadly device.

In K.K.'s account, as the day of the bombing neared, cell members began to leave Dar es Salaam one by one, some taking family members and all bound for Mombasa. I remembered that Jamal had planned to leave by bus for Mombasa that Thursday, the day before the bombing. He liked to be in Malindi for Friday prayers and lunch with his brothers and sisters. But when he had tried to buy a ticket for the bus he normally took—a comfortable minibus that made the grueling eight hour trip more bearable than crowded, slower buses—he was told that it had been chartered by a large family traveling to Mombasa for a wedding. Chagrined that he had become so accustomed to comfort, Jamal decided to wait until Saturday for the next minibus. Had he left sooner, he might have ended up next to one of the fleeing bombers instead of blown up by their handiwork.

As the others departed, Hussein asked K.K. to stay behind to help Ahmed the German, who would drive the suicide bomb truck. Unable to speak Swahili, Ahmed, an Egyptian, might run into trouble. In those last days, K.K. helped Ahmed by mailing a DHL package to his family in Egypt.[3] But a couple of days before the bombing the two faced a crisis. Laden with cylinders, bags of fertilizer, crates of TNT, and two big batteries, the truck's wheels had sunk, and became stuck, in the sandy driveway. K.K. and the driver dug frantically to free the vehicle but, as a result, became concerned that the same predicament might arise on the day of the bombing. A telephone consultation between higher-ups and Ahmed yielded the instruction that K.K. arrange for a tow truck to stand by on Friday morning, just in case.

On Friday, August 7, 1998, K.K. rode down the street in the truck and then hopped out, leaving the suicide driver to make his way to the embassy several miles away. Ken Karas asked Abby what K.K. did next. She replied, "He said that he went back to the Ilala house and prayed for a very long time for Ahmed the driver, and he waited to hear the sound of the explosion" (p. 2841). No one saw him do this; only his words through Abby attested that prayer for the driver and for a successful outcome were his concerns. By his account, he never heard the bomb go off. Was K.K. so deep in prayer, shock, or denial that he failed to hear what startled everyone across the city? Colleagues at the University of Dar es Salaam—miles from downtown, further from the embassy than the Ilala house—panicked when they heard the blast. Eventually emerging from his reverie, K.K. became anxious that the plot may have failed. First, he turned on the radio and, hearing nothing unusual, the TV, which had begun to report on the explosion. Only then did he learn that the U.S. Embassy in Nairobi had also been bombed.

K.K. cleaned up the house, throwing waste into a garbage pit out back that was later excavated by the FBI. He contacted his

Figure 8. Courtroom sketch of Ken Karas displaying evidence, including the food grinder, with Judge Sand and defendants K. K. Mohamed and Mohamed al-'Owhali looking on. Credit: Christine Cornell

nephew, Sleyyum, and told him to come by to pick up some household items, including the grinder used to prepare the TNT, and take them to K.K.'s sister. Sleyyum was instructed to tell his aunt to be sure to clean the grinder well, because it had been used for "unclean" purposes. Abby then recounted K.K.'s circuitous trip to South Africa, traveling by fake passport and fraudulent visa. Once there, he was on his own, save for several phone numbers he had been given to call in an emergency. Investigators found the numbers written backward—al Qaeda code—in papers seized in K.K.'s Cape Town bedroom, where he had lived for almost a year with the family that employed him at their Burger World franchise. When shown this evidence, K.K. confirmed that he had once called one of the numbers—just to see if it worked—but it cut off right after the other party answered. A twenty-rand phone card paid for only a short call to Yemen.

The flow of K.K.'s story ended there. The last part of Abby's direct testimony reported many observations that directly addressed the charges against K.K.: "He said that based on his study of Islam, he felt it was his obligation and duty to kill Americans." He also said that the bombing "sent a message to America that bombings were the only way that America would listen and that it also kept the Americans busy investigating" (p. 2841). He said that "Allah would take care of the [Tanzanians killed in the bombings]." Strung together outside a narrative structure, these points fell short of illuminating his purposes. The effect for me was that, although Abby's testimony explained a lot about K.K.'s concrete actions, it left questions about what he thought he was up to. I became further confused when Karas asked Abby, "Did Khalfan Khamis Mohamed tell you why it was important for Americans to understand his motivation behind these attacks?" And she replied, "He said he wanted America to understand that these Muslims weren't crazy, gun-wielding Muslims but they were in fact working for a purpose" (p. 2862). He wanted us to understand his purpose, but what was its substance? What did he think this action would achieve? I, for one, was still inclined to view him as crazy, not someone with rational plans. Abby's mandate was to tell a story that fit the prosecution's theory of the case and that complied with the legal rules governing evidence. It was becoming clear to me that what I wanted to know, including about K.K., went well beyond that story. I was already moving past the issue of what he had done and on to the question of why he had done it. My inability to learn the answers to critical questions from the testimony led to dissatisfaction with experiencing the trial passively, primarily in my role as a victim. As my questions about K.K. and other aspects of the case became clearer and more urgent, I acknowledged that I needed to use my anthropological skills to ferret out information and analyze it. Only then could I satisfy myself that I was getting answers to questions that mattered at least partly because they involved people like K.K. who had grown up in communities I thought I knew well.

A stiffer, more reserved Abby resumed the witness stand after the break. I felt confident that her legal training would help her weather the tough cross-examination she was likely to face from David Stern, one of K.K.'s attorneys. But Stern's cross began inauspiciously, when he asked, "The bombing in Dar es Salaam happened October 7, 1998; is that right?" and Abby corrected him, "August 7." Abby's fine instincts emerged early when Stern posed a seemingly benign question about navigating Dar es Salaam's roads:

Stern: About how long do you think it would take to go from Uhuru Road up to Oyster Bay where the U.S. Embassy was?

Abby: That would be hard to predict. It is kind of like talking about driving in New York City, getting from one point to another. Depending on traffic, it could be anything.

Stern: Why don't you give me a minimum and a maximum?

Abby: I wouldn't be able to guess that. (pp. 2865–66)

Abby's firm resistance to several more attempts forced Stern to drop this issue, even as some of us familiar with Dar es Salaam were mouthing answers to what seemed a simple question. Technically Abby was correct: the amount of time it takes to drive anywhere on the sometimes jammed Dar streets can vary considerably. But why would Abby be so uncooperative? Her clarity and lack of reticence on direct examination did not prepare us for her demeanor on cross, when, representing the government's side, she stonewalled on point after point.

In an odd way, Abby's reluctance to answer Stern's questions contrasted with K.K.'s alleged openness during his interrogation in South Africa. Stern drew Abby's attention to K.K.'s cooperation, his lack of resistance, his ready admission to involvement in the bombing. As Abby confirmed, K.K. agreed that he had bought the Suzuki Samarai, had rented the two houses where cell members lived and where the bomb was built, had ground the TNT, had cleaned up the house once the suicide bomber set out on his mission, and had also engaged in a few other activities that painted him more sympathetically, such as working in his brother's grocery store. Stern used Abby to depict K.K. in as positive a light as possible, leaving the implication that, despite his criminal behavior, at least K.K. had told agents the truth. But Abby dug in her heels when Stern tried to draw any conclusion that minimized K.K.'s culpability:

Stern: He was the guy who had up to that point done fairly menial jobs
   in preparing this thing, wasn't he?

Abby: I don't know if I would describe them as menial.

Stern: Well, would you describe cleaning up the house as menial? I
   don't mean it's menial if you clean your house. I mean in this—

Abby: I clean [my] own house.

Stern: I clean my house, too, but I mean in this context considering
   there is like technicians and people buying you know TNT and this
   and that, cleaning up the house would you consider that one of the
   lesser jobs? Maybe menial is a poor word.

Abby: A lesser job than one of the others.

Stern: He'd done lesser jobs than one of the others, right?

Abby: Necessary jobs I would say.

Stern: But you would say lesser?

Abby: For all of them or for that job? Cleaning up or getting the
   Suzuki, getting the house? Are you just talking about the cleaning
   up?

Stern: All of them.

Abby: All of them I wouldn't describe them as menial, no. (pp. 2894–
   95)

Stern then tried to cast doubt on Abby's claim that K.K. had said
that "he would have done it again, that he'd kill Americans, that
he helped with bombing Americans, that if released he would
kill them again" (p. 2987). Creating a moment of high drama,
Stern charged that this critical statement was nowhere to be
found in Abby's notes taken during the interrogation. When
Abby insisted that she could find it, Stern thrust out the thick
sheaf of notes and said, "Here you go." We waited as she flipped
through pages, continuing to answer Stern's questions on other
matters. After several minutes, she paused and then read out the
disputed remark: "Okay. Page 77. Is that? My handwriting is—
it says here: 'KK stated if released from custody or if never
caught would do it again, would kill Americans and do bomb' "
(p. 2899).

   This strange fragment offered an answer to Stern's challenge
but, given the issue's gravity, left me unsatisfied. Stern followed

up by asking Abby to describe what question led to K.K.'s response, but he did little with her answer that the agents had simply asked him what he would do if he had never been caught or were released. I wanted to ask a different question that would have taken us far beyond Abby's testimony: What did K.K. believe now? Away from the world of jihad, and brothers with a purpose, and Dar es Salaam, would he still "do it again"? The answers to these questions, had it been possible to pose them, would have touched on the important legal issue of whether K.K. posed a future danger.

Earlier Stern had asked Abby to describe the interview process. She explained that she and her partner, Mike, had taken notes by hand, and then, after the interview, one of them wrote up a report condensing their questions and K.K.'s answers into a shorter, summarized version, called a 302 in FBI parlance. As Stern pointed out, the organization of Abby's 302 reflected neither the flow of the interrogation nor even the chronology of K.K.'s actions but rather the categories, such as logistics and motive, that had legal relevance for the prosecution's case. Having laid this groundwork of skepticism about the record left after the interrogation, Stern turned to a more direct attack. His aggressive demand for reasons why the agents had failed to tape record or videotape K.K.'s confession yielded the simple answer that FBI policy requires that all interviews be recorded by hand. After establishing, rather facetiously, that the FBI did, in fact, possess tape recorders, video cameras, and even stenographers suitable for recording an interview, the defense attorney astutely analyzed the policy's limitations, noting that it shielded important information from jurors, namely, the suspect's tone of voice and demeanor. Stern's strategy interjected the notion that the jurors, and everyone in court, should wonder whether we had missed something important because no audio or visual record of the interview existed. Given the high-level technology in use around us and the sophisticated forensic tools that had been crucial to the success of the investigation, it was not hard for Stern to depict the FBI's policy as antiquated and to imply nefarious motives and consequences.

Anthropologists interested in language have a pithy saying that sums up my concerns about Abby's rendition of K.K.'s statement: form is substance. While the substance of K.K.'s answers was certainly important, and I was grateful to hear it, meaning would also have been conveyed through the structure of his grammar, the sound of his voice, and the context in which his words were spoken. This latter observation raised bothersome questions: What had K.K. been asked? In what tone? What words were offered to him, as a speaker unfamiliar with the language? As I realized how much of K.K.'s meaning had been lost—first when no recording was made and then when the conversation was reordered as the 302 was typed—I began to resent the FBI's interrogation practices, which others have noted pose barriers to justice for a defendant.[4] As court ended that day, I remarked to a victim seated nearby that it would have been interesting to hear a tape recording and judge for ourselves what K.K. meant. "It makes you wonder," I went on, "about how language can get twisted and distorted in testimony. And how things can be left out." From her disapproving expression I realized that my American interlocutor was not wondering about these issues and was adamantly uninterested in hearing more from K.K. For her, and for some other victims, a critical analysis of the trial process was in itself insensitive. But, in my view, justice required not only that victims learn a plausible story of what happened and who did it but that the process through which this story emerged be fair to all involved.

I learned much later that the defense attorneys, having pored over Abby's notes numerous times in preparation for cross-examining her, were convinced that the notes did not include the statement about K.K.'s continued violent intentions. They simply had tremendous difficulty deciphering her handwriting, which was, by everyone's accounts, atrocious. There was also another reason why Stern zeroed in on that remark: K.K. had told his lawyers repeatedly that Abby had not understood what he had meant when he said it.

At the time I didn't question why it seemed so important to me to learn as much as I could about K.K. Mohamed and why he had become involved in the bombing. Most likely it was my long-term research and personal connections to the East African Swahili Muslim community—of which K.K. and his family are members—that made me especially interested to learn more about his motives. Given my knowledge of the area, I wondered how K.K. could have developed such extreme views. Who else around him in coastal Tanzania expressed or encouraged such views? The defense account that might answer some of my questions was months away. Using my composition book, I listed the people who could enlighten me further regarding K.K.'s background and motives. A diligent anthropologist would seek out the defense counsel, the social worker who had interviewed K.K.'s family in Tanzania, prison guards, and certainly the defendant himself. I wanted to be that anthropologist. But, as a victim, I was physically and ethically separated from those most likely to have such information. And were I to ask others to whom I had access—the FBI agents who had interrogated him or the prosecutors—I would come under suspicion as expressing interest in subjects unsuitable for a victim. Anthropologists often face difficulties gaining access to information; sometimes our interlocutors refuse to talk to us or barriers of language, gender, religion, and hierarchy of various sorts preclude or circumscribe open exchange. At the embassy bombings trial my role as a victim stood in the way more directly. Prosecutors and other victims expected that I conform to the unspoken rule to avoid contact with the defense. I complied, even as I watched the defense attorneys intently, sometimes trying to read their lips, or their minds. For some victims, the defense attorneys were devils incarnate. Several who acknowledged that they were "only doing their job" went on to ask angrily why the attorneys would put a hand on a client's shoulder or laugh with him. Of course, good defense attorneys try to enhance the humanity of clients through their solicitous treatment of them in front of a jury. Yet, I, too, became annoyed when one of the young defense assistants sat with her back to the audience and played solitaire on the laptop at the counsels' table. Next to her, Mohamed al-'Owhali leaned over slightly so that he could watch the game's progress.

The day after Abby testified, she and Mike asked to speak
with me during lunch. They were trying to fill in the background
of each victim and had questions about Jamal's family. I said I
wanted them to know how important it was for me to be in court
and to hear about their investigation. I also took the opportunity
to tell them about my research on courts. I explained that, since
my undergraduate days, I had been studying how people use
language in court, especially when telling their stories. I told
Abby that I found her to be a model witness, especially in her
responses on cross-examination. Then, I described the problem
with K.K.'s story as she had told it: an obvious piece was missing. Her story failed to include a description of how K.K. Mohamed had come into U.S. custody or even into South African
custody. Immediately Abby interrupted me to say, in her most
legalistic voice, "We are not under any obligation to account for
how suspects come into custody." I acknowledged that I understood this as a legal matter and tried again to convey what it
means in a linguistic and cognitive sense to leave out part of a
story. People are made curious when parts seem to be missing.
Listeners experience doubt; they feel a little nag about whether
everything in the story is true or whether more has been left out,
including details that might put the whole story in a different
light or require an alternative interpretation. Thinking about it
afterward, a juror might wonder, "K.K. got all the way to South
Africa, and then what happened?" Looking at Mike across the
table, Abby repeated firmly that the government was under no
legal obligation to account for how someone had come into FBI
custody. Abby had missed my point, or was evading it, and I
was not going to learn how they had gotten hold of K.K.

During the interrogations that produced the defendants' statements, each was asked why he was willing to admit involvement in an al Qaeda cell or in the bombings. Their answers reflected differences in the roles they had played and in their
personalities. K.K. Mohamed said that, since the investigators
already seemed to know what had happened, he might as well
tell them everything.[5] Odeh admitted that he decided to talk to
the investigators because his cell members "were pushing him

and pushing him and pushing him and they're all gone and he's left . . . facing big problems" (p. 1692). At first al-'Owhali refused to tell the investigators anything. Then, when he realized how much they already knew, he agreed to talk but made it clear that he would only tell part of the story. In the end, he gave an account packed with details. Outside court, one FBI agent described al-'Owhali as so full of himself that he couldn't resist bragging about his role. Stories motivated by delusions of grandeur must have been hard for al-'Owhali's interrogators to witness, although suspects routinely tell elaborate tales, especially when they've had to be very secretive about their criminal activities.[6] The fight was still in al-'Owhali when he insisted on being taken to America for trial.[7] He claimed that Kenyans were not his enemies (he had spent only a week in the country); America was his enemy, and he wanted to face his enemy.

The embassy bombings investigation would have been much more difficult had FBI agents not obtained statements from three suspects, and the trial would have been different altogether had prosecutors not been able to introduce these statements into evidence. In a motion to suppress the statements, attorneys for al-'Owhali and K.K. Mohamed argued that the suspects had not been properly informed of their rights before being questioned in Kenya and South Africa. Judge Sand began his lengthy and controversial ruling by reviewing the interview process, noting first that both foreign and U.S. law enforcement officers had been present during questioning. Citing the famous *Miranda* case that guards against self-incrimination by insisting that suspects be warned of their rights (including to counsel) and then offered an opportunity to waive them, Sand ruled that American investigators rightly attempted to offer each suspect an explanation of his rights, and to admit that they could not provide an attorney at that time under the aegis of the U.S. government. However, according to Sand, the explanation the investigators provided was "an entirely faulty one." The American officials should have informed the suspects that local laws might entitle them to an attorney, which was the case in South Africa and to a lesser degree in Kenya. As a result of Sand's determination that the intent of *Miranda* applied even in foreign interrogations, he suppressed the statements made by al-'Owhali on five of the days he was interviewed. The ruling dismissed the U.S. government's contention that foreign suspects[8] have no Fifth Amendment rights during questioning by U.S. agents abroad.[9] Moreover, Sand's decision rendered "baseless the Government's claims that a warning/waiver requirement will impose intolerable costs to both international investigatory cooperation and America's own ability to deter transnational crime," a view he called "apocalyptic" (p. 55).[10] Judge Sand's opinion probably had little effect on the outcome of the trial. Al-'Owhali had talked so much on the other days he was questioned that those interrogations alone provided enough to incriminate him. At the same time Sand held that K.K. Mohamed had effectively waived his right to an attorney and thus his statement was admissible. However, the ruling charted new legal territory with respect to the conduct of U.S. law enforcement abroad.[11] As Sand wrote bluntly, "To the maximum extent reasonably possible, efforts must be made to replicate what rights would be present if the interrogation were being conducted in America" (pp. 52–53).

Proving that the bombing of the embassies was a "jihad job" required an international effort. As such, it momentarily trained a spotlight on issues of concern when U.S. law enforcement operates abroad and in collaboration with local authorities. In his ruling Judge Sand noted that, in such situations, determining appropriate roles and practices was not easy. Nor could American investigators acting abroad always guarantee the rights of the accused, even though Sand believed they should try. He worried about the great "threats of compulsion" suspects faced in some foreign contexts, including incommunicado detention, substandard conditions, and aggressive practices (whether legal or illegal), noting that "by the time U.S. agents are finally on hand to ask questions of their own, strong countervailing forces will already have run head first into the free will of the accused" (p. 47). During his interrogation by Pakistani authorities, defendant Odeh had experiences that were "unspeakable," as one attorney claimed. Judge Sand noted generally that some suspects may be "unduly predisposed to talking to U.S. agents in the hope that doing so provides a means of relocation to the United

States, where criminal defendants enjoy greater protection from governmental overreaching" (p. 47). The bombing suspects held in Nairobi may well have thought that American custody would offer them the protection they were unlikely to get through the Kenyan authorities, if only because local experience of the Nairobi bombing was still so raw. By that logic, the suspects may have agreed more readily—and against their own interests—to speak with the American officials.

Defense counsel tried several times to depict the Kenyan police as unscrupulous and capable of brutality. During L'Houssaine Kherchtou's testimony, Odeh's lawyers brought out that cell members routinely bribed the Kenyan police, including once when they sought the release of three al Qaeda "brothers" (pp. 1476–80). Questions arose about whether search warrants had been legally obtained before Kenyan police entered the premises of suspects, including at the request of the FBI, and concerns were expressed about the treatment of evidence. An objection cut off defense attorney Ed Wilford's attempt to get a witness to agree that "the Kenyan police enjoy a well-deserved reputation as brutal thugs." Amnesty International and other rights groups had long documented abuses by Kenyan police and prison officials, including many forms of torture inflicted on suspects and detainees. Kenyan scholars and activists had spoken out against such tactics, which were routinely used to intimidate the many political prisoners detained without trial during the years that President Daniel arap Moi ran Kenya as a one-party state.[12]

By the late 1990s the Kenyan police had already begun to reform, having realized that a more democratic Kenya lay in their future, but leftists and radical Muslims remained targets of state aggression. That said, the example of the embassy bombings interrogations warns against drawing too sharp a dichotomy between the Kenyan police (or other foreign authorities) and U.S. investigators, if the intent is to depict the former as brutal thugs and the latter as champions of democracy and due process. Any claim that U.S. officials would never rely on the physical coercion of a suspect or, more pointedly, the threat of such coercion, was belied by the clear presence of that threat in their dealings with Kenyan, Pakistani, and other foreign law enforcement. In

recognizing the inextricable connection between U.S. and foreign tactics of custody and interrogation, Judge Sand opened the
door for the conclusion that in such situations no party can keep
their hands clean. Sand valiantly insisted that U.S. law enforcement should hold to its principles of preserving suspects' rights
as much as possible. And yet Sand's opinion nodded to a loop-
hole that investigators could exploit by reminding everyone that
investigations can proceed according to any rules, or none at all,
because the Miranda warning/waiver becomes relevant only
when prosecutors seek to bring defendants' statements into a
legal proceeding. If the intent is to gather information to be used
for purposes other than a trial, then all bets are off.

The confessions and their presentation in court were crucial elements in proving the defendants' participation in a jihad job.
The government's proof, however, rested on much more. In the
last days of the prosecution's case we heard testimony from
many witnesses who further established the presence of the defendants in East Africa and their connections to al Qaeda leaders. Phone records indicating calls from the defendants to prin-
cipal parties to the conspiracy were especially revealing.[13] Paralegals read from transcripts of phone calls intercepted through
wiretaps. Wadih el Hage's Nairobi phone had been tapped by
Kenyan police since at least 1996.[14] As testimony about the
phone calls continued to the end of the prosecution's case, one
day in early April something clicked in my mind. I felt my
breathing quicken, and at the first break I rushed out of the
courtroom, looking for any FBI agent I could find. I buttonholed
Mike in the hallway and asked, with some impatience, "How
can you have had all those calls and no one knew that the bombings were about to happen? How could you not have known?"
Mike's quick response, "I wasn't involved then," was not an excuse; he was just being clear about his own knowledge before
he speculated, "Well (pause) they knew something was going to
happen," and looking straight at me, said, "but they didn't
know what, or when."

CHAPTER SIX
A Victim's Burden

JUST AFTER THE TRIAL began I was surprised by a conference call from the prosecutors' office. Mike from the FBI asked: "If the defendants are found guilty, would you be willing to testify in the trial's penalty phase?" At once uneasy, I answered with a question: "But doesn't that mean I'd be supporting the death penalty for these defendants?" "Not necessarily," said a prosecutor who was also on the line. "You can hold whatever belief you want and still testify." My continued hesitation led Mike to a second strategy: "Here's another idea. Would any of Jamal's relatives be willing to come to the U.S. to testify?" Other than my brief reports to my husband's family about the trial's progress, no one had involved them in the case. The chance to represent the family at the trial might appeal to them, but I felt compelled to raise again the contentious issue, saying, "I don't know, maybe they don't agree with the death penalty." "Maybe they do," Mike countered. He went on, "We found Muslims who are willing to have these guys put to death by the U.S. government." We talked more about whether Jamal's family might agree and who might be available for the trip. As the conversation wound down, I agreed to call Jamal's relatives and report back. Then I chided them, "So now you guys don't want *me*, because I'm opposed to the death penalty." The prosecutor paused before pushing on, "Oh, not necessarily. We can get you up there and ask you about the impact of your husband's death without ever touching the issue of the death penalty or your beliefs about it." Chilled by that scenario, I had the unwelcome sensation that I was being recruited for a task not in my control, and not to my liking.

As far back as I can remember, I have always believed it wrong for governments to execute criminals, no matter how terrible their crimes. My views were formed as a young teen, when—I vaguely remember—I followed the national debate over Supreme Court decisions on capital punishment.[1] In 1972 *Furman v. Georgia* resulted in a ten-year respite from executions and, at the same time, hardened pro- and anti-death penalty positions. My earliest perspective was less a moral stance than a strategy of self-protection. I believed that, as a citizen, I would bear responsibility for an execution carried out by my government, and I was simply unwilling to have any part in the killing of another human being. At the time, my perspective on killing through war was similar, forged out of my growing awareness of the destructive conflict in Southeast Asia. That a tiny bit of responsibility for killing by the government would fall on me, an individual citizen, was too much to bear.

As I faced the prosecution's request, I was aware that, over time, my opposition to the death penalty had embraced more sophisticated arguments encountered in my studies. However, other than adolescent pronouncements and random attendance at a few candlelight vigils, this conviction had never led me to work actively against the death penalty in my professional or personal life. As the trial began, I told a friend that my opposition to the death penalty was so strong that it would likely stand in the way of my testifying in the penalty phase. He said, "Well, that's really it, isn't it? People always say, 'If it were *your* family member, you would feel differently. You would want to see them put to death.' And you don't feel that." It was true. With no desire for violent vengeance, I worried that killing the defendants—with all the fanfare of a national execution—would only make me more distraught.

In the trial's two penalty phases, victims of the embassy bombings would inform the jury about the impact of the crime on their lives so as to influence whether that impact, along with other factors, such as the gravity of the crime and the future dangerousness of the defendant, was sufficient to warrant the death penalty. The prosecution's account of the bombings in the guilt phase had been satisfying. But I wondered how I would feel if the trial ended without Jamal ever having been mentioned. Participating in the penalty phase would provide recognition for Jamal, our stories, and the grief his family and I felt. Although routinely depicted as an opportunity for just such recognition, and also for victims and their family members to experience therapeutic catharsis, victim impact testimony, from a legal perspective, would be presented primarily to convince the jury that the crime was so heinous that it demanded their vote for death. Given that purpose, I had to ask myself: Was achieving recognition by testifying in the penalty phase worth enhancing the possibility of a death sentence? During the next weeks my confusion over this question generated other hard questions: How solid was my opposition to the death penalty? Was there any merit to the prosecution's view that I could oppose the death penalty and yet still testify? Was it appropriate for me to refuse to participate, if it would mean that my story and Jamal's would not be told at the trial? Which was the greater burden: telling our stories in the penalty phase or not telling them?

Long before the embassy bombings trial began, Attorney General Janet Reno had approved the prosecution's request that two of the embassy bombings suspects face the death penalty for their crimes. Her decision not only raised the stakes for Mohamed al-'Owhali and Khalfan Khamis Mohamed, whose direct involvement in making and deploying the bombs was alleged, but also shaped the whole trial for all four defendants, from beginning to end.[2] Reno's decision also stalled the extradiction of several others being held in nations that oppose execution.

As a federal death penalty prosecution, the embassy bombings case differed from other trials. First, the two defendants who faced the federal death penalty were each provided an attorney experienced in death penalty defense, specifically David Ruhnke and Fred Baugh. Second, that the other two defendants were being tried within the framework of a capital case raised serious concerns for their ability to receive a fair trial. Because Mohamed Sadeek Odeh and Wadih el Hage were charged in the conspiracy (with the implication that they had played roles in planning to harm Americans), and yet because the death penalty was requested only for those at the conspiracy's lowest levels, the two higher-ups might be subjected to harsher scrutiny by the jury. Motions to sever the cases of the two non-capital defendants had been rejected, and the trial went forward in the unusual circumstance of a mixture of capital and non-capital prosecutions.[3]

Having the death penalty at stake had already altered the trial process. From the beginning, attorneys for K.K. and al-'Owhali had had to spend considerable time preparing for the possibility of a penalty phase when they would have to persuade jurors to reject a death sentence. As these experienced death penalty attorneys also knew, almost every move made by defense, prosecution, and judge in a capital case is calibrated with the appeals process in mind. Capital convictions and death sentences are followed routinely by a lengthy two-pronged appeals process during which most aspects of the trial are reviewed.

The jurors selected for the embassy bombings case had to be "death qualified," a strange and haunting phrase that indicates their stated ability to impose the death penalty if, in their estimation, the legal requirements have been met. Potential jurors who had contended that they could never, under any circumstances, impose the death penalty had been eliminated from the jury pool of thirteen hundred. "Death-qualified" jurors tend to share other characteristics, such as relatively conservative attitudes toward law and order, more trust in the police and other government officials, and heightened interest in convicting defendants and imposing harsh punishments. These characteristics of the jury must have concerned the two defendants who did not face capital charges and, if tried separately, might have had their cases heard by more lenient jurors. Choosing the jury pitted the interests of some defendants against others. After the voir dire, during which jurors were questioned by all parties, each defense team made a list of its preferences for particular jurors. Defense attorney David Ruhnke's list included three jurors whom all the other attorneys had placed toward the bottom of their lists. One of these jurors had expressed a belief in reincarnation, which several defense attorneys thought might make him less reticent to impose a death sentence. Ruhnke insisted that this juror, and the two others, could be critical assets in a penalty phase. Ruhnke's experience persuaded the other defense attorneys, against their intuitions, to leave these three on.[4]

Defense attorneys for K.K. and al-'Owhali were also mindful that, if their clients were found guilty, the trial would include two penalty phases, the most distinctive, and controversial, feature of federal capital cases. Until the last decade Supreme Court decisions had expressed ambivalence about many aspects of the penalty phase. During this part of the trial, jurors weigh the impact of the crime as expressed by victims—emotional damage, financial losses, and so on—against mitigating factors introduced by the defendant—for example, abusive childhood experiences, lack of education, indoctrination, and so forth. Part of the justification for impact testimony is that each victim's "uniqueness as an individual human being" should have as much place in the penalty phase as the defendant's unique qualities.[5]

The opportunity for victims to represent themselves and their loved ones at the penalty phase was a hard-won achievement of the American victims' rights movement, which sought representation for those who had suffered as a result of murder. Some embassy bombings victims hoped to get the chance to speak at the penalty phase. By contrast, the request that I do so plunged me into a crisis. Because my opposition to the death penalty had been merely a theoretical stance, untested prior to this intimidating challenge, I felt obliged to make sure that my position would serve me as I sought justice. After all, most Americans can rattle off an opinion about the death penalty, but few face the prospect or obligation of acting on that view. My struggle to decide whether representing myself and my husband through testifying outweighed my determination to remain staunchly opposed to the death penalty forced me to examine my beliefs about capital punishment, the trial process, and justice. To develop a defensible position, I engaged in extended conversations about the death penalty and turned to writings that expressed a range of religious, ethical, practical, and political positions. My views of the death penalty were greatly influenced by my experience attending the trial, which daily confronted me not only with weighing the prosecution's evidence against the defendants but also with assessing the trial's fairness given the government's enormous power and the horror of the crime.

When prosecutors rested their case after presenting extensive evidence against all four defendants with few objections from defense attorneys, I became curious about how the defendants' seemingly indisputable guilt could be challenged with any credibility. I was concerned that the prosecutors' power not overwhelm the defense. It was not that I wanted the defendants to mount evidence so compelling that they would be found innocent—unless, of course, they truly were. Verdicts of "not guilty" would make death sentences impossible, but wishing for that outcome solely to appease my concerns about the punishment would have trampled on my other aspirations for justice. The lack of fairness that characterizes many criminal trials underpins an important argument against the U.S. death penalty. Coerced confessions, incompetent counsel, and other chilling abuses have often led to the wrongful conviction of defendants and eventually to unjustly imposed death sentences. Unfairness that begins as error—faulty witness identification or mishandled evidence—can become an abuse when a prosecution too caught up in the zeal to convict and execute fails to investigate or admit mistakes.[6] As officers of the court, backed by the power of the state, prosecutors' decisions to ignore abuses and errors not only entail serious consequences for defendants but constitute clear miscarriages of justice. To satisfy my own quest for justice, I needed to believe that the prosecutors were above such behavior.

From my perspective, a vigorous defense would be one measure of a trial's fairness, an indication that those accused had counsel willing to advocate for them. Yet my interest in hearing how the defendants might contest the evidence against them had no support in law. In a criminal trial the prosecution always bears the burden of proving a defendant's guilt, and defendants are not obligated to offer evidence in their own defense. Remaining quiet is often a defense counsel's best tactic, especially when the state's proof is weak. Given the mountain of evidence against their clients (including the statements made by the defendants themselves), the attorneys had to make tough decisions about what to say, especially on behalf of those facing the death penalty.

K. K. Mohamed's attorneys had decided on their strategy well before the trial began, after efforts failed to suppress K.K.'s interrogation. They knew from experience that challenging K.K.'s statements to the FBI would destroy their credibility and make them ineffective at the penalty phase. Moreover, after the prosecution's case, any defense—for example, countering specifics of the interrogation or recalling to the stand a witness as unflappable as FBI agent Abby Perkins—might have been interpreted as wasting everyone's time, including the jurors, who would hold the client's life in their hands. Consequently no witness appeared on K.K.'s behalf; no alibi was offered.

Wadih el Hage's counsel took an altogether different approach. For months el Hage's attorneys had been trying to get certain charges against their client dismissed. When prosecutors rested their case, they again requested dismissal of the conspiracy counts, arguing that the government had presented only circumstantial evidence against their client. Their request caught Judge Sand at an opportune moment. Outside the jury's presence, he said, "I was driving last weekend and I was behind a car that had a bumper sticker on it which had a quote from Thoreau on it—will someone explain to the defendants who Thoreau is—and it said 'Simplify.' And as I read the indictment, and as I read the Court's proposed charge, I really wonder whether this is not the time for the government to simplify the burden on the jury by abandoning some of these counts" (p. 3932).[7] Some counts deemed redundant were removed, but Sand refused to support el Hage's attorneys' request to dismiss the conspiracy charges, noting that the nature of a conspiracy usually ensures that circumstantial evidence is the only kind available.

El Hage's counsel put on the most extensive defense, offering a half-dozen witnesses and considerable evidence. They focused on proving the claims they had advanced in the opening statement: el Hage's dealings with bin Laden, although ranging over several continents and many years, all contributed to building bin Laden's businesses and managing charities. To counter the government's contention that el Hage's offices and telephones were used not only for business but also to plan acts that furthered the criminal conspiracy, his counsel introduced into evidence documents and other communications relating solely to business and personal concerns.

One witness spent considerable time attesting to el Hage's pursuit of a business trading in gemstones. During testimony about deals with miners, trips to view gems, and phone calls between buyers and sellers, we learned that Judge Sand considered himself an amateur gemologist. Testimony hinted at the seamy side of the African gem business: those involved found it hard to trust new people; they relied on corruptible police to help them out of jams; and they sometimes got stuck with bad deals. For me, this testimony confirmed that el Hage and the witness participated in yet another murky, semi-illegal network, which did little to boost either of their reputations. If the prosecution's rationale held sway, jurors would view the telephone calls and other evidence as merely irrelevant to the conspiracy charge against el Hage. Even Judge Sand cautioned that demonstrating that most of el Hage's phone calls dealt with legitimate business would leave untouched the accusation that all the rest furthered the criminal conspiracy.

The strategy taken by el Hage's counsel—contesting many minor points made by government witnesses—was designed to overwhelm jurors with a barrage of small doubts so they would conclude that the whole story lacked credibility. Yet defense attorney Sam Schmidt's refusal to cut short his march through the evidence revealed this strategy's downside. Everyone became annoyed—at the time he was taking, at his halting language, at long passages read into the record. But by never letting a point go uncontested, theirs appeared to be a vigorous defense, even though they had difficulty refuting the evidence of conspiracy that had emerged in the testimony of al Fadl and Kherchtou, the al Qaeda insiders who had allegedly seen el Hage in action.

Judge Sand could barely hide his concern as the month of April ticked away. On his mind was the trial's overall length and concluding it before losing another juror to illness or stress. Two had already been dismissed, and he routinely urged those left to "Stay healthy!" Prosecutor Pat Fitzgerald was especially exercised that el Hage's defense team was taking so much time to prove points that the government had already conceded. He was also quick to protest questionable defense strategies. For example, he objected to several attempts to depict el Hage sympathetically through photos. Sand agreed and, expressing concern about "[turning] this into a circus," disallowed such photos, including one of a little girl standing beside a dog, which he acknowledged was "cute."

Prosecutors complained that el Hage's defense had not complied with discovery requests, which obliged them to turn over materials to the prosecution for review prior to offering them into evidence. Defense counsel had made the same accusation against the government. Fitzgerald addressed this issue during the first day of el Hage's defense case:

Fitzgerald: Before Mr. Schmidt puts on exhibits, I think there are some pictures . . . of ostriches, perhaps children riding ostriches. So if we can have a brief moment to confer before the exhibits go to the jury when we get to the stage today when he offers transcripts and exhibits—we were served with three feet of paper late last night. I just wanted to make sure we don't object to what goes in.

Court: People riding ostriches? I recall there has been some ostrich testimony in the case.

Schmidt: There are going to be lots of ostriches. (p. 4380)

Schmidt quickly corrected himself, "Not lots." Judge Sand was remembering the mention made by the witness Kherchtou that el Hage had once talked about a business venture involving ostriches. After two more days of testimony in el Hage's defense, prosecutor Fitzgerald sounded stressed as he complained again that the defense had failed to provide documents in a timely manner: "Notwithstanding this, we haven't objected to most of it. I realized at one o'clock in the morning yesterday ostrich photographs were in evidence yesterday when those piles [of unreviewed documents] went in." Did Fitzgerald sit straight up in bed remembering the ostrich photos? More likely, he was still at his courthouse office where he and his team kept long hours reviewing defense submissions. With many photos already ruled inadmissible, el Hage's team asked for special consideration of just one more. Without seeing the photo, Judge Sand asked why they sought its inclusion. Dratel said, "To corroborate and amplify the conversation about ostriches." To which Sand replied, "This is on the theory, having been deprived of the opportunity to introduce a picture of a dog, you would be entitled to introduce a picture of an ostrich?" His remark drew laughter from spectators exhausted by the trial's gravity. But el Hage's team was serious, so Sand inquired further:

Court: What does this picture purport to show?
Dratel: This is Mr. El Hage and an ostrich, date stamped July 13, 1997.
Court: [Looking to Pat Fitzgerald] Government object?
Fitzgerald: I can't see Mr. El Hage. I can see the ostrich.
Court: [Squinting at the photo] Is Mr. El Hage *on*the ostrich?
Dratel: Yes, he is. Your Honor, he's astride the ostrich.
Fitzgerald: Is this the last exhibit you'll be offering respecting an ostrich?
Dratel: Yes.
Fitzgerald: No objection. (p. 5005)

Judge Sand complimented Fitzgerald's generosity and remarked that he himself would refrain from lodging an objection. Perhaps he anticipated the press coverage that the ostrich received, which briefly turned the trial into the circus he had been guarding against.[8]

As I contemplated the request to testify in the penalty phase, several friends posed the same wise question: "Why don't you consider what Jamal would do?" This strategy was familiar to me (and to others I knew who had lost a spouse). Since Jamal's death, whenever I faced a difficult problem, I would speculate on how he might have tackled it. Would Jamal have wanted me to testify? Were the situations reversed, would he do so himself? Pondering the question "What would Jamal do?" made me think of fundamentalist Christian students across the U.S. who, when contemplating ethical dilemmas, such as whether they would lie to protect a friend, asked one another: "WWJD? What Would Jesus Do?" Jamal would have been the first to note that his life had not been exemplary and would never have pretended to have the wisdom of a prophet. Yet looking to him for guidance made sense, as he had always relished the challenge of responding to a hard problem with a reasoned opinion.

Although I do not recall that we had ever discussed the death penalty, Jamal would certainly have begun any consideration of the issue by referring to the law of talion—that is, "an eye for an eye"—and would probably have quoted the Koranic verse: "O ye who believe! The law of equality is prescribed to you in cases of murder: The free for the free, the slave for the slave, the woman for the woman" (II:178).[9] He would have reminded me that this law first appeared in the Torah. But he would also have noted that the harsh punishments meted out by the community of believers merely foreshadow the suffering that an offender should expect in the afterlife. Jamal was never one to stop at abstract principles; he would have immediately considered the mechanisms whereby a community would arrive at a judgment and, if necessary, implement a penalty.

Searching for the perspective Jamal might have taken, I began reading deeper into the various Islamic approaches to punishment. I immediately encountered the problem that always emerged when I sought a definitive account of an area of Islamic law. Which schools of law? Which commentators? Under what kind of legal and political system? Across Islamic societies and eras jurists and commentators disagreed over and debated many aspects of Islamic law, which makes it difficult to establish either a universally accepted set of legal principles or a means of applying them to suit all contexts. The differences in opinion—not unlike those in other religious or secular legal traditions—required reading a variety of sources, distilling a general set of guidelines, and then qualifying those by considering specific, contextualized examples. The Muslim legal scholar Khaled Abou al Fadl justifies this approach by arguing that even when Muslim jurists routinely affirmed a general principle they "went on to riddle the field with qualifications, exceptions, and provisos, so as to render the general principles quite complicated, and to elicit the classic legal response to many legal issues—'It depends.'"[10] By contrast, fundamentalist adherents (e.g., Wahhabbists), including some al Qaeda members, might insist that certain of their leaders could articulate a true and unambiguous Islamic law of punishment.

With the idea "it depends" in mind, I explored Islamic penalties for homicide. By prescribing equality in punishment—a life for a life, and no more than that—the Koran set limits on the destructive cycles of retaliatory violence that had pervaded pre-Islamic Arab tribal societies. The idealized principles drawn from the Koran, the Prophet Mohamed's example, and a range of early legal scholars do not treat homicide among crimes against society, which include a disparate set of offenses (e.g., adultery, theft, and defamation) that threaten the public order. By contrast, homicide, in its various degrees reflecting levels of intention—murder, voluntary killing, involuntary killing—is an infraction of private law, that is, a wrong of one individual against another. Similar to physical assault, homicide can be punished either by retaliation (*quesas*) or by compensation (*diyya*) to the victim's family.[11] The equality principle governs retaliation, and it can be carried out only if requested by male relatives of the victim. Context determines the implementations of these general approaches. For example, an authority connected to a state or a community can act on a victim's behalf by prosecuting the offense and carrying out the punishment.[12] Rather than exacting retribution, the victim's relatives can elect to pardon the offender and accept compensation, also known as "blood money." The rationale is that, although blood money can never appease the loss of a person, it can help a family recover the material contributions lost through the death.[13] Despite intricate discussions of penalties and how to carry them out, Koranic passages implore victims' family members to show mercy, an act said to be rewarded in the hereafter.[14]

The emphasis on mercy and restraint in scholarly discussions of homicide contrasted sharply with the images of Islamic punishment circulating in the Western media where examples included the stoning to death of adulterers in Nigeria and amputations facing recidivist thieves in Saudi Arabia. Human rights groups had long protested the application of Islamic punishment to non-Muslims. Opposition had also been directed both at the forms of punishment, often depicted as cruel and unusual, and also at the offenses punished, especially when they included moral infractions (e.g., adultery, blasphemy, and apostasy) rarely prosecuted in other legal systems.[15] It bears remembering that the most extreme examples apply only to a tiny minority of Muslim populations and that Muslims have been among those protesting their application. Moreover, lost in the media frenzy to condemn "sharia" punishments is an analysis of the political context in which such punishments are instituted.[16] Oppressive and exploitative applications of Islamic law are usually rooted more in politics than in abstract legal principles or religious piety.

Some Muslims explicitly reject those nations that apply Islamic punishments inappropriately, that is, without proper authority or for political purposes. Others note that the legal systems purporting to be Islamic are actually a mixture of various historical legacies—Islamic (including multiple legal schools), colonial (British, French, Dutch, etc.), and customary (based on precolonial or preIslamic practices). Governments that have instituted religious law in the late twentieth century handle the punishment of homicide in different ways that mix Koranic interpretations with existing statutes. Still others propose modifications to create fairer systems (particularly with respect to due process), which may or may not include the death penalty. The questions of legitimacy raised by these ad hoc amalgams lead some Muslim scholars and activists to argue that the death penalty should never be imposed.

Human rights claims against the death penalty, including the American death penalty, routinely raise important questions: When is it justifiable to violate one set of principles (e.g., religious tenets or cultural relativism or state sovereignty) to preserve another (e.g., a commitment to human rights)? The issues at stake have challenged anthropologists and legal scholars. Even harder questions also come to mind: Should adherents of one legal (or religious) system accept the rationale or practice of another? Should they be compelled to do so? Answering such questions in the abstract is deeply unsatisfying in part because the context in which such decisions are taken so shapes the range of legal possibilities, the mechanisms of implementation, and the legitimacy of the whole process.

Muslims in Jamal's coastal Kenyan community have faced such questions since colonial times, if not before, as populations mixed in the towns along the coast and leaders of different faiths and sects vied for authority. Searching for guidance in resolving disputes, many have looked to Islamic law. However, the Kenyan secular legal system recognizes Islamic law only for family matters. Replacing Kenyan secular criminal law with Islamic law has rarely been a topic of discussion among Muslims, and their status as a minority community makes this improbable. Given their suspicion of the Kenyan state, Kenyan Muslims tend to avoid secular courts, but as citizens they accept the state's authority over many legal matters. In offering an opinion about the death penalty, it is unlikely that Jamal would have invoked Kenyan criminal law.[17] He might have turned to Islamic principles to defend execution as an appropriate punishment for some crimes under certain circumstances. The crimes of the embassy bombing defendants would likely have qualified. Yet I imagine that Jamal would have raised questions about the mechanisms for implementing those principles. He would have asked about the legitimacy of leaders who would carry out harsh penalties. I would never know what he thought of the situation at hand, whether he would have agreed that the U.S. government should be entrusted to punish his killers with death. He may have urged caution. In many interpretations of Islamic legal precepts, any killing—even one by a judicial authority—must be treated as suspect until a determination is made that it satisfied appropriate regulations; that is, any killing must be done correctly and fairly. The trump card in the debate would be the considerable reward for showing mercy.

Presented on two days in late April, Mohamed Sadeek Odeh's defense hinged on the notion that any act of killing could be viewed as either "Islamically correct" or "Islamically incorrect." Although religious teachings can justify the former, as in self-defense, criminal penalty, or justifiable war, good Muslims should never engage in incorrect killing. This idea emerged in the opening statement when defense attorney Tony Ricco said that Odeh had joined al Qaeda, "and he agreed to follow bin Laden, but only to the extent that bin Laden would engage in acts that were Islamically correct" (p. 72).[18]

Prosecutors had presented considerable evidence linking Odeh to the business of killing. Much of it came from the defendant's statement to FBI agent John Anticev, who had questioned Odeh for the better part of ten days after his capture in 1998. Anticev had begun his testimony by describing Odeh's personal history. He was a Palestinian born in Saudi Arabia and raised in Jordan. He did well in school and went for further studies in the Philippines, where he became involved in an Islamic center sponsored by the Kuwaiti government. Exposure to radical versions of Islam fostered Odeh's interest in being part of an international effort to promote Islam. By 1990 Odeh had decided to join other Muslims in the Afghan conflict, where he worked as a medic and was wounded.[19] Former fighters reorganized after the war effort, and Odeh was among those who swore bayat to al Qaeda in 1992. His career as an al Qaeda recruit resembled that of others who, after training, had been sent on jobs in Somalia and Sudan. Eventually assigned to the group that undertook logistical operations in Kenya, he started a fishing business on the coast and, at least initially, worked closely with other cell members in the country. They set up businesses and charities, facilitated the transit in and out of Kenya of people associated with al Qaeda, and also, apparently, planned violent attacks. From Anticev's testimony it was clear that Odeh was trained to kill; he believed in killing to further al Qaeda causes; he trained others to kill (e.g., clans fighting in southern Somalia); some of his best friends were killers (e.g., Abu Hafs); and he frequented places where killing had occurred, including Somalia and Nairobi. Although Odeh told agent Anticev that he felt "morally responsible" for the bombings, he insisted that he had known nothing about them.

Odeh's account was not without its ambiguities. The events just prior to August 7, 1998, confused the issue of whether Odeh should be held responsible for the bombings. Odeh had told Anticev about a conversation in which he had disagreed with his fellow cell members over whether it was appropriate to mount an al Qaeda attack in Kenya. He had become fond of the country and agreed with another cell member that they should avoid harming Kenyans (p. 1670). Anticev described how cell members prepared in haste to leave Kenya in early August 1998 and related Odeh's own reluctance to leave even when badgered by the others. To dispute the prosecution's claim that Odeh had provided technical advice to the cell members who had planned the Nairobi bombing, Odeh's defense team held that their client would never have involved himself in such an attack. Odeh would have realized that a bomb detonated in Nairobi's city center would necessarily kill innocent people, an Islamically incorrect act, by his estimation. Ricco's team had built an image of Odeh as his own man, someone unwilling to "follow blindly like a cat," as he had told FBI agent Anticev. Higher education and travel experience made Odeh valuable to al Qaeda; however, these factors, along with his intensive study of Islam, also fostered the independent thinking that might have led him to break with the organization. When Ricco cross-examined agent John Anticev during the prosecution's case, he emphasized that once Odeh had married a Kenyan woman and established a home in coastal Kenya, he had become more identified with the local population and thereby less valuable to al Qaeda. Ricco also drew attention to a point made by Robert Miranda, an FBI agent who had interrogated Wadih el Hage. When shown a photo of Odeh, el Hage "smirked." In cross-examining Miranda, Ricco tried to tease out the meaning behind the smirk, finally getting Miranda to admit that, in his estimation, el Hage thought Odeh was a "fool" (p. 5734). Odeh's counsel wanted the jurors to wonder: If his al Qaeda cell members had held Odeh in low esteem, would they have entrusted him with the tactical plan for the bombing, as the prosecution alleged? Even so, physical evidence—a notebook and drawings—found at Odeh's house on the coast were hard to explain away. Prosecutors argued that a drawing in one of the notebooks was a map of the U.S. Embassy in Nairobi, including a "blast cone" indicating a detonated bomb. Odeh's defense team faced a hard task. Jurors would have to believe that cell members had visited Odeh at his house and left behind precious belongings, while through it all Odeh remained oblivious to the task they were engaged in. Furthermore, could he have been oblivious a few months later when he stayed with the bombers in a Nairobi hotel room before they whisked him out of the country?

On April 25, defense attorney Tony Ricco called Imam Sirhaj Wahhaj to the witness stand. Imam Wahhaj was an American-born convert to Islam, known and respected for his long leadership of a Brooklyn mosque.[20] His credentials included serving as an expert witness in the very same New York courthouse at a previous trial of accused Muslim extremists. Prompted by Ricco's questions, Imam Wahhaj first explained the meaning of the term "Islam" and the central features of the faith, including its authoritative texts—the Koran, Torah, and Gospel—and its adherents' obligations such as belief in Allah, obedience to the prophet Mohamed's teachings, prayer, fasting, and pilgrimage. Touching on legal aspects, he indicated that, in Islam, some acts are *halal*, or approved, and others are *haram*, or forbidden. Asked about *bayat*, the imam's definition located its origins at Islam's birth, when devotees pledged allegiance to the Prophet Mohamed and, after his death, and in a different way, to the succession of heads of the Muslim community called *khalifa*. After defining *fatwa*, another concept central to the case, as "a legal opinion among the scholars about a difficult issue" (p. 4625), the imam honed in on a central theme of Odeh's defense:

Ricco: When a Muslim seeks a fatwa, is that Muslim obligated to question his leader or must that Muslim follow the leader in blind faith?
Imam: It is absolutely against the religion of the Islam to follow anyone blindly. . . . when our religious leaders or anyone, even our parents give us, you know, a verdict, that verdict must be substantiated by the words of Allah, by the words of God as they appear in the Koran, and the words of his messenger Mohammed as they appear in the [stories about the Prophet's life]. So, you know, blind following goes against Islam. (pp. 4625–26)

As Ricco ventured further into highly disputed and frequently misunderstood concepts, the explanations grew longer. Admitting the difficulty of translating *jihad*, the imam started with its simplest definition: "jihad only means to struggle" (p. 4631). Then a full panoply of interpretations emerged as he translated phrases from Arabic texts and told vivid, illustrative stories. Jihad is a struggle within oneself to be a good Muslim, to pray regularly and to fast, even when these obligations prove inconvenient or difficult. Jihad is also a struggle with others, especially against oppressors, and it can sometimes require force. The imam described his own mosque's jihad to drive drug dealers from their Brooklyn neighborhood. Then Ricco asked, "Now, if a Muslim gives bayat, does the Muslim have the right to question the order or direction of the person to whom he is giving bayat?" The imam's pointed answer articulated the core of Odeh's defense: "No, he doesn't have the right. He has the *duty*" (p. 4633). Human fallibility (to which even leaders succumb) together with Islam's stricture against blind obedience require Muslims to question authorities and their decisions. According to his lawyers, this was Odeh's behavior precisely.

Ricco had encountered little interruption from other counsel until he said: "Imam, I just have a few more questions, and I want to ask you whether or not there is any Islamic authority that endorses the killing of individuals like, for example, Americans, anywhere they can be found?" The imam's answer, "Absolutely incorrect," came out too quickly for defense attorney Fred Baugh's objection to stop it (p. 4634). In order to further his own client's contention that some causes are worth defending, even by killing, Baugh needed to discredit the imam's answer. Centering his challenge on the imam's claim to authority, he argued that this leader was offering merely one interpretation of matters highly disputed by Muslims. Questioning stopped while Judge Sand addressed Baugh's objection. Counseling the jurors to treat the imam's words as an interpretation, one that other scholars might contest, Sand mentioned aloud that the imam was vigorously shaking his head in protest. The imam did not wait for Sand to finish to insist that Islam's rejection of killing "is not a matter of opinion" (p. 4634). By talking out of turn, the imam generated more confusion and additional objections, leading Baugh and Sand to tussle over his status as a religious authority. Ricco jumped on the chance to draw a lesson, saying, "Imam, we have to wait. It's okay. Now, very interesting dynamic. Isn't what's going on here supposed to happen in Islam? In other words, a person says 'this is Islamically correct' and an individual like Mr. Baugh has a right in Islam to say, 'I challenge that'?" "Absolutely," replied the imam (p. 4636).

Several times Imam Wahhaj insisted that, to be successful, an individual's challenge to a leader's decision or viewpoint must be supported by authoritative evidence. For the imam, any individual Muslim should study the Koran, the Prophet Mohammed's teachings, and the decisions of legal scholars to determine, for example, if a leader's fatwa includes forbidden acts that should be rejected. The imam's image of an Islam where believers debate interpretations furthered Odeh's defense that his religiously informed understandings of killing led him to oppose al Qaeda plans and also presented the court with a flexible depiction of Islam. At the same time the imam's emphasis on individual empowerment and responsibility to interpret missed a crucial aspect of Islamic practice: each individual exists as part of one or more communities.[21] An individual Muslim's location within a community of believers could have bearing on interpretative practice and the ultimate conclusions drawn. By ignoring the communal aspect of interpretation, the testimony left the odd juxtaposition of Odeh interpreting in isolation and bin Laden decreeing for a secret, conspiratorial community, with nothing in between as a more appropriate approach. These may have been the options at the time, but the imam missed an opportunity to emphasize the value of communal decision making in Islam.

Al-'Owhali's attorney, Fred Baugh, was concerned that Imam Wahhaj's testimony threatened to undercut his own client's defense, which contended that an individual, who was following a leader's orders, could engage in killing that would be deemed Islamically correct. The imam conceded that calls for jihad by legitimate leaders might have to be obeyed. Somehow Baugh got him to admit that Sadaam Hussein, president of Iraq at the time, had to be viewed as a legitimate leader for these purposes.

Baugh next sought the imam's agreement that, in situations such as self-defense, a good Muslim would elect to kill innocents and, because the killing was Islamically correct, he or she would remain a good Muslim. Baugh asked the imam, "For example, if there is an airplane, hypothetically, coming at the City of New York, and on that airplane is a nuclear device, 2 terrorists and 250 innocent children. It is going to crash in New York and kill every child in the New York school system. Shooting that plane down will kill those 250 innocents. I know it's a hard question. I struggle with it. It gets closer and closer. I decide that it is a decision I must make. Have I violated the faith in killing those 250 innocents?" Smiling slightly, the imam ventured, "That's like a movie I saw a couple years ago. Really, *Armageddon* or something like that" (p. 4656). Five months later, as they watched airplanes smash into tall New York buildings just a few blocks from the courthouse, some trial participants would remember the release of laughter occasioned by the imam's flip reference to what seemed at the time a hokey Hollywood scenario.

Baugh made good use of the mention of Sadaam Hussein by prodding the imam to provide details about the suffering of Muslims in Iraq as a result of U.S. sanctions and bombings. The testimony took an odd turn when the imam mentioned that he acted on his own disapproval of U.S. policy toward Iraq by sending medicine and food. Baugh jumped to accuse him of violating U.S. sanctions. Ricco had a hard time protecting his witness, and it seemed for a moment that the imam's admission would tarnish his credibility. Baugh then made the point that good people might violate the law in order to help other Muslims. But, quick on his feet, the imam refused to have his actions, and those of many other U.S. citizens, compared to those of the defendants, saying, "I can say this to you, Sir, you take great men like Martin Luther King Jr. who fought against unjust laws and did it in a just kind of way. So you take a man like Martin Luther King, so if you want to say he broke the law and he was put in jail, I guess you can say that. But I think people would agree that that kind of nonviolent struggle against unjust laws,

I think you would call him a hero" (p. 4663). The two men glared at each other. Many in court realized that one African American had just played the race card on another and won the hand.

Prosecutor Pat Fitzgerald began his cross-examination of Imam Wahhaj with a crass question: "What is your understanding [of] what the prophet Mohamed would say about whether it is proper to drive a truck into a building and blow up everyone inside?" In response to Baugh's predictable objection, Judge Sand ordered Fitzgerald to ask a different question. Muslims routinely ask themselves a version of the WWJD question: What Would Mohammed Do? Depending on who is asking and answering, the Prophet's life can yield many options. Fitzgerald might have been hitting hard because the prosecution case against Odeh was somewhat shaky. The sketch found in Odeh's home that allegedly depicted the Nairobi embassy—something a technical adviser might possess—was incorrectly drawn. Explosives were found on Odeh's shirt but only after it had been mysteriously separated from his other clothing, none of which had tested positive.

In the event that jurors remained unconvinced of Odeh's participation, Fitzgerald used the imam to build a secondary argument. He asked about a time when the imam had dealt with a fellow community leader who had expressed an interest in robbing banks:

Fitzgerald: You obviously confronted him and challenged him and said "that's wrong."
Imam: Yes.
Fitzgerald: Would it also be your duty if there were people going out to rob a bank, to stop those persons and say don't carry out that act?
Imam: I must do that. If I don't do that, I am derelict in my responsibility. I have to do it. I have to stop them. (pp. 4688–89)

This was exactly where Fitzgerald wanted to end the imam's testimony—with the assertion that when the defendant Odeh realized that those around him were involved in a criminal act, he was obliged to stop them, a duty he had shirked.

Several days after the imam's testimony, during a discussion of the laws that would be explained to the jurors before their deliberations, Fitzgerald asked Judge Sand to consider mentioning "conscious avoidance" with respect to Odeh. He wanted the jurors to understand the law that makes it wrong for a person to consciously avoid figuring out when suspicious activity swarming all around him is, in fact, criminal behavior that should be exposed to the proper authorities:

Fitzgerald: I could easily foresee the way the summations might play out that there may be an argument by the government that [Odeh] can't be in the middle of things and, pardon the expression, "stick his head in the sand."

Court: Like an ostrich. I was thinking about all our ostrich discussions, that we'll not be able to get through closing statements without somebody making the analogy to ostriches.

Fitzgerald: I jumped the gun, I guess. (p. 5195)

Ostriches would come up a few more times before the trial's end. Even the jurors were asked not to be ostriches, when Fred Baugh implored them to look at the evidence, not avoid it. Although seemingly appropriate, the ostrich analogy was also vague. Did refusing to be an ostrich imply that one had to seek the truth, rather than hide from it? Did it also imply that if truth seeking revealed something illegal or objectionable, one must act? I wondered if Odeh had struggled with either of these questions. Judge Sand denied the request that conscious avoidance be explained to the jury, citing the nature of the cell structure, which discouraged members (e.g., Odeh) from inquiring into the activities of others.

In an effort to demonstrate that their client had been unaware of the bombings, and had separated physically and ideologically from his al Qaeda cell members, Odeh's defense counsel recalled to the stand FBI agent John Anticev. Ultimately the agent's testimony left the important question still unanswered: When cell members rushed Odeh to Nairobi, when he stayed at the hotel with the man who had trained him to use explosives, and when he was provided a fake passport to leave the country, did Odeh know that his colleagues were about to set off a bomb? Of course, the best person to answer that question was Odeh himself. According to his attorneys, Odeh wanted very much to testify on his own behalf. His attorneys also believed that, by virtue of his high intelligence and articulate expression, he could persuasively demonstrate his rejection of violence against innocents and his commitment to protect the country he had grown to love. Defense attorneys rarely want their clients to take the stand, but, after initial reservations, they agreed that Odeh might as well present his views.

The prospect that Odeh might testify alarmed the other defense teams. The specter of a committed al Qaeda member trotting out in detail the organization's activities, particularly its illegal acts, would only hurt their clients. According to Odeh's attorneys, jailhouse solidarity—particularly Odeh's concern to protect K.K. Mohamed, who faced the death penalty—kept him from testifying on his own behalf. Given his counsels' representations in court, Odeh most likely would have argued that al Qaeda's attack on the Nairobi embassy was Islamically incorrect,[22] a perspective that contrasted with that of al-'Owhali. Odeh might even have characterized his behavior as resistance to the group's faulty ideology. For al-'Owhali, if your leader orders you to kill, and the act is justifiable under Islam, then you must obey. Under this logic, the Nairobi bombing would have been "Islamically correct killing" undertaken at a leader's direction in a time of war. Al-'Owhali's defense counsel would have a lot of work to do in the closing arguments, and the penalty phase (if we got that far), to convince the jury that such a war existed and that bin Laden was legitimately leading the battle.[23]

In my view there was simply no way that the phrase "Islamically correct killing" could describe Jamal's death. What possible justification could there be for a plan to kill Kenyans, Tanzanians, Americans, or anyone else who had died in the East African bombings? All the discussion of killing and whether it could ever be justified—in war or peace, at the hands of terrorists or governments—brought me back, again and again, to my own views on the death penalty. My gut opposition still strong, my reasoning had become clearer. The U.S. government's power to investigate and prosecute the embassy bombings case was undeniable, as was the government's desire to make an example of these defendants and an unequivocal statement about terrorism. Experiencing that power up close, and sensing the strong temptation to use it in any way that would achieve those goals, convinced me that such tremendous power must always remain carefully guarded, deployed judiciously, and only for the most important purposes. Killing an individual already in state custody and no longer a threat to others seemed a needless deployment of such power, even trivializing the act of killing itself. Regardless of whether due process had been followed to the letter, using the government's power to kill an individual would, it seemed to me, always constitute a misuse. My position allowed for the state to engage in some kinds of killing, including in an unavoidable war or a justifiable defense of the population; but only a very few instances of state killing could pass muster as correct. As I became more settled on the justifications for my position, new questions arose: Given that I objected so strongly to the government's support for execution, did I have the obligation to resist? Did the admonition against being an ostrich also apply to me?

At first I had hesitated to ask Jamal's family about testifying in the penalty phase. I was concerned that assisting the prosecution by lining up witnesses for the penalty phase would offer more support for capital punishment than my oppositional stance allowed. I suspended my ethical reservations and focused on solving potential communication problems. My Kiswahili-English dictionaries yielded translations for "death penalty" and "execution." The word for the latter derives from the Kiswahili verb *kunyonga*, meaning "to twist," as in "to twist the neck" or "to throttle." Over time the verb came to mean "to hang," including to hang pictures or to hang criminals, the most common method of execution in colonial times in East Africa, and the only remaining one. Given the linguistic complexity, I opted for the verb *ku-ua*, "to kill," without specifying a method and hoped that I would not be called on to describe lethal injection in Kiswahili.

My call to Jamal's sister, Fauzia, gave her the opportunity to chide me for our less frequent contact in recent months, but she accepted my explanation that attending the trial had made my life terribly hectic. When I alerted her that my call was to raise a grave question, she softly murmured, "Bismillah," the invocation pronounced in order to begin any significant action "in the name of Allah." I explained that the U.S. government wanted the family to consider certain questions. I separated the two issues, asking first that family members decide whether the defendants, if found guilty, should be given life in prison or be killed. Fauzia questioned me about the trial's progress and asked whether I thought these men were guilty. I told her that I thought so but the trial was not over yet. She berated them for their terrible acts and for throwing away their lives. Then I broached the possibility that two family members could come to the United States to represent the family by testifying at the case. I mentioned that the government wanted Jamal's nephew to be one of the two. We agreed that the family would meet to determine its responses. Then Fauzia spoke in a hushed, intent voice, "What I want, what would really, really make me happy, are you listening, Susan? What I want is for *you* to tell us what *you* think and that will be *our* answer, too. We want to do what *you* think. Do you understand?" My heart sank. Deciding whether the family should participate was exactly what I had tried to avoid. But in that moment I realized that I could not remove myself from their decision. Fauzia accepted my point that we might have different views, and that the government knew this and had trusted me to relay *their* opinions, not mine. Acknowledging this as understandable, Fauzia secured my agreement that, if I disagreed with their position, I would at least tell them.

When I called a week later, Fauzia passed the phone to Jamal's brother, Sufyan, who conveyed the family's decision. He told me first that they had chosen two people to represent the family, if requested. They agreed with the suggestion that our nephew, Mohamed Jelani, was a good choice, because of his youth and strong bond with Jamal. But they wanted him to be chaperoned by an older, more worldly relative, a man named Saidi, who had worked for years in the tourism business and was comfortable talking with foreigners. Saidi had also been one of Jamal's many

best friends. As Sufyan began to address the issue of punishment, it was clear that the family's view of the death penalty,
which differed from mine, bore the complexities both of Kenya's
plural legal system and the trial's location in the United States.
In principle, they accepted that, as sanctioned by Islamic law,
the death penalty could, in some cases, be the appropriate punishment for murder. Sufyan sought my agreement here, but I implored him to tell me their views first. "After all," he said, justi-
fying their perspective, "if they're guilty, this is not a small thing
that they've done." Yet the family felt that, because the trial was
neither before a Muslim judge nor in Africa, their opinions with
respect to punishment had no standing. "It's *your* government
that is doing this, so we cannot say anything about what should
happen." But he quickly added that, if requested by the U.S.
government to represent Jamal in court, they would certainly do
so. When Fauzia took the phone, she asked if I endorsed their
decision, and I told her I did. Their felt marginalization suggested to me that they would not have to feel responsible for a
death verdict or at least not as responsible as I, a U.S. citizen,
would feel.

Sufyan got back on the line, and I asked him a question that
had troubled me for some time: "What if I had been killed? What
would Jamal think about the death penalty?" Silent at first, Sufyan ventured, "You don't know the answer to that?" "I think I
know, but I wanted to ask you and the family." Sufyan relayed the
question to the relatives standing around the phone, and I heard
guffaws, cries of surprise, and a burst of indecipherable opinions.
Sufyan finally answered, "Jamal had a temper, right? If you were
killed, he would have been furious. He would have killed them
himself." In the background, good-natured agreement and some
protest erupted. The call had gone on too long. I said good-bye
and was left alone to sort through the implications.

Would Jamal have killed? By saying that he would have, Sufyan not only pointed to his brother's notorious but rarely unleashed temper but also, I realized, to the family's understanding of his love for me. At once grateful for recognition of our
bond, I was also troubled that Jamal's love for me would consti-

tute a reason for killing. Sufyan's view could also be understood as a statement about Jamal's determination to put matters right himself, to refuse to leave justice for others, including any government.[24] Yet, how can we know that he would have killed? So much evidence to the contrary made me doubt that he would have committed the act, although he might have wanted to—at least initially, at least in theory. I thought of a story I'd been told about his father, whom Jamal had tried to emulate. Jiddi refused to kill any living being, including the tiny ants that annoyingly establish their colonies in Kenyan homes and routinely troop in long lines across floors, walls, furniture, and unsuspecting sleepers. For Jamal's father, even ants were living creatures to be preserved. As Jamal told me once, the smallness of ants should bring out human humility not the arrogance that fuels random or concerted acts of killing.

One of the deep and enduring sadnesses following the loss of loved ones is that lost with them is any certainty about their views on new situations. Turning to bits of evidence from a loved one's life, those left behind can piece together a course of action that he or she may have taken. Stories of acts performed in the past are fodder both for remembering loved ones and for projecting their perspectives. But these stories are always subject to interpretation in the present by those who remain. Although difficult to admit, I will never know for certain what Jamal would have done had the bomb killed me, or how he would have responded to other moral challenges. But drawing on his life and words, and positing approaches he might have taken, are, for me, important acts of remembering him and also extending his contribution to my life. While he lives on through those of us who turn to his example, we have to acknowledge that we interpret and thus reinvent his perspectives in a new time, one that he cannot share. At first this idea was chilling to me. It admitted the finality of losing Jamal and precluded ever gaining his "true" perspective. But then I realized that this approach refused to freeze Jamal, or his views, at the moment of his death. It acknowledged my role in re-creating Jamal's perspective, in using his life as a flexible, not frozen, guide. At the same time I had to be willing to take responsibility for what I claimed to do in his name, that is, to stand behind my actions regardless of the authorities I invoked to justify them.

The prosecution took three days to make its closing arguments, even though only a few claims against the defendants seemed debatable. Prosecutor Ken Karas patiently reviewed the evidence, plainly filling out the chronology of al Qaeda activities. For instance, a decoded conversation between Haroun and Odeh revealed their interest in el Hage's welfare on a trip to Afghanistan. El Hage returned from that trip with a policy from bin Laden that shifted the East African cell from business ventures to military planning and gave new duties to Haroun and Odeh. Prosecutor Karas had focused more on el Hage than the others in his closing. He argued: "And it is tragic. It is tragic, ladies and gentlemen, because it robbed the United States of an opportunity to investigate and crack the bin Laden cell nearly 11 months before the embassies are bombed" (p. 5263). Wadih el Hage's defense attorneys continued to contest the representations made against their client, especially the evidence of perjury.

In his closing statement on Odeh's behalf, Tony Ricco emphasized the government's reliance on guilt by association, as evidenced by Odeh's flight with the other cell members just before the bombing. Predictably Ricco used the example of the witness Kherchtou, present in Nairobi at the time of the bombing, to make the point of how easy it is for mere association to determine guilt. His strongest argument was that other cell members were more directly involved than Odeh, who appeared not to have had any influence over others nor a definitive role in the planning and execution of the Nairobi bombing. He offered positive images of Odeh as a committed soldier, a purist driven out of the organization by young hotheads, and, curiously enough, a humanitarian who had tried to stop the suffering of Muslims. Ricco took a break while his co-counsel, Ed Wilford, dissected the limited physical evidence against Odeh, focusing on the purported sketch of the Nairobi embassy found in Odeh's Witu home. Wilford pressed the point that the fingerprint found on the notebook containing the drawing was not Odeh's, and then opined, "And this blast cone? I don't know if it's a snow cone, a fishing net hanging off the back of a boat to catch fish. It can be whatever you want it to be" (p. 5790). Ricco's famed rhetorical style emerged as he returned for the final minutes of the closing. Invoking a standard approach in defense closings, he urged jurors to look closely at all the evidence and to strive to do justice. He referred to Martin Luther King's "arc of justice" turning "slowly, slowly, slowly" toward the truth and then, laying it on a bit thick, compared Odeh to the protagonist of the movie *Amistad*, popular at the time, about an African who "represented a very unpopular cause" and nonetheless "stood up in a courtroom, manacled, and in his own way said, 'Give us free' " (pp. 5806–7).

In their closing statement, we finally heard al-'Owhali's attorneys' theory of the case. They painted a picture of a war involving the United States and al Qaeda. Their approach, grim and provocative, did not sit well with the victims observing the proceedings that day. K. K. Mohamed's attorneys made the most humble presentation, not contesting his guilt.

I should have known that the closing arguments would be partisan, but still I was taken aback by the prosecution's final rebuttal. Pat Fitzgerald's vehemence in condemning the defendants struck me as crossing a line into personal rage, against el Hage in particular. His presentation made me so uncomfortable with my previous connections to the prosecution, that, after a break, I sat with the journalists rather than on the victims' side. I wanted to distance myself from the anger in the push toward conviction, even though guilty verdicts seemed warranted.

In charging the jury, Judge Sand returned equanimity to the discourse. The kind of painstaking care the court displayed to lay out the jurors' tasks in deliberating and to incorporate the requests of all parties revealed the other side of the government's power, namely, the law itself as a bedrock foundation to guide jurors.

With breaks for emergency dental work and a house closing, jury deliberation extended well beyond the predictions of a decision after several days. As the days of waiting dragged on, the courtroom atmosphere turned carnivalesque. Opponents crossed the bright lines of the bar and the center aisle seeking company and diversion. In the front row, usually occupied by security men wearing wires, a court reporter sat chatting with a federal marshal. In the interpreter's booth, one of the Swahili speakers helped the court clerk practice the pronounciation of East African names in preparation for reading them during the verdict. Laughter rang out from the few journalists valiantly waiting along with the rest of us; one of them brought brownies to share. On the far side of the court, the *New York Times* reporter scribbled furiously as a defense attorney grimly answered questions. The few of us who came daily were grateful for anything that interrupted the waiting, such as when the jurors asked, repeatedly, for Judge Sand to explain the meaning of "aid and abet."

Sitting in court with victims whom I knew would testify in the penalty phases, I felt more silenced than ever and frustrated that, despite all the gains of the victims' rights movement, I seemed to have lost or rejected my place at the trial. At the same time as I hoped for guilty verdicts for three of the defendants (still uncertain in my mind about Odeh's role), I dreaded the penalty phases that would follow. Arrangements were already being made for Jamal's family to travel to the United States. The tension was more than I could bear—the specter of the ostrich haunted me—and I decided to act. First, I agreed to be interviewed by a radio journalist who would highlight my anti–death penalty stance if the trial moved to penalty phases. And then I sent a letter to U.S. Attorney Mary Jo White to ensure that the prosecution understood my opposition. My letter praised her office "for the skillful and professional manner" in which it had pursued the case and described the comfort I would find in knowing "definitively the role that these defendants played in these terrible acts and . . . that they will be punished." I went on to express the basis for my opposition to the death penalty generally and, in particular, the reasons why I believed it was inappropriate in the case of K. K. Mohamed: "Mohamed's functionary role in a larger conspiracy and the possibility that Mohamed might provide additional information that could lead to the capture of suspects still at large, and the convincing arguments by terrorism experts that state executions have little or no deterrent effect on future acts of terrorism." I ended with this: "In my opinion, a sentence of life imprisonment instead of the death penalty for Khalfan Khamis Mohamed would not be an act of mercy; it would be an act of justice." I must have assumed from their tenacious pursuit of the case that granting mercy would be unthinkable to the prosecutors. Mercy seemed to me an emotion held by individuals rather than institutions or state officials, even though governments issue pardons, which are thought to symbolize mercy. I had assumed that prosecutors would want to be above sentiment, operating in the more detached realm of justice where due process and fairness controlled decisions.

When, after two weeks of jury deliberations, the court clerk threw open the door beside the judge's bench and nodded conspiratorially that the verdict was in, I felt a cold sweat break out. As the jury's foreperson replied "guilty, guilty, guilty" to all the major charges, a mixture of relief and trepidation washed over me. Al-'Owhali's penalty phase would begin the next week.

CHAPTER SEVEN
Dramatic Exposures

THE PROSECUTION'S miscalculation of how long the jury would deliberate meant that witnesses for the al-'Owhali penalty phase had already been in New York for several days when the verdict came in on May 29. Despite strong protests from al-'Owhali's attorneys, who wanted at least a week to prepare, Judge Sand ruled that the weekend plus two days would suffice, given that further delay would inconvenience the many people, including U.S. officials and victims, who had traveled from Africa and venues across the United States. Although victims welcomed the guilty verdict, they were tense from having waited so long and eager to testify. Just before the verdict came in, one of the American victims of the Kenyan bombing asked me if I would be testifying in K. K. Mohamed's penalty phase, which was scheduled to begin a week after jurors had finished deciding al-'Owhali's fate. I said no without elaborating, not wanting to seem disrespectful of those who had chosen to do so. When I asked about his own participation in al-'Owhali's penalty phase, he said, "Yeah, I want to tell those bastards to their faces what they've done to me and my family."

The majority opinion in the Supreme Court case *Payne v. Tennessee*, which established the constitutionality of victim impact evidence in capital cases, emphasized the jury's need to appreciate the human consequences of a crime.[1] The *Payne* decision meant that witnesses would be permitted to recount the horror of the attack, the pain of injuries, the loss of loved ones, and the financial and emotional impact of the crime on them as living victims.[2] Their narrated lives would become evidence of the crime's gravity. Juxtaposing depictions of their lives prior to the crime against the difficulties and sadness afterward had the potential to influence jurors, and anyone else in court.

With the *Payne* decision in 1991 the inclusion of victim impact testimony in capital cases became a matter of settled law, but its volatile history reflected the strong opinions still surrounding it. Several years before *Payne*, the Supreme Court had expressed reservations about allowing victims to speak at penalty phases in *Booth v. Maryland*.[3] The justification in *Booth* and other cases, and in the dissents from the *Payne* majority, was that the highly emotional nature of victims' testimony could lead jurors to abandon rational thinking about the crime and its punishment. Scholars, activists, and others who applaud the expansion of victims' rights in legal processes embrace the role offered to victims in capital trials and point to the positive, therapeutic value of testifying. Prosecutors and victims' rights advocates depict the participation of victims and their families in the penalty phase as offering an important experience of agency that other parts of the trial—even eyewitness testimony in the guilt phase—cannot provide. For victims, who face the struggle daily to regain control over their lives after the tragedy, telling their stories in court can be an important milestone toward reclaiming a sense of stability.[4] Some hope to confront the convicted defendant with the horror of his crime. Other victims seek public acknowledgment of their pain or loss. Still others feel a solemn obligation to make a public representation of a dead loved one, to make sure that the dead victim is "present" and recognized in the legal proceeding.

Even though my opposition to capital punishment precluded me from testifying in the penalty phase, the desire for recognition for my loss, and for Jamal, remained strong. When Mike from the FBI asked me for a picture of Jamal, and explained that they were "making a collage for the penalty phase," I said I would think about it. I wondered whether this representation— which sounded like a kid's art project—would satisfy my desire for recognition. Mike was persistent, calling twice more to ask whether I had sent a photo. "It can be anything," he urged, "even a passport photo. Even one that's old or damaged. We can work with it." I wondered why he thought I would use a passport picture to represent my husband. If Jamal's picture was to be shown in public, in court, wouldn't I choose a beautiful photo?

When we lived in Dar es Salaam, Jamal bought a vinyl, pink-flowered album and filled it with photos of us smiling for the camera at our home and on trips. After the bombing, friends and family in Kenya and the States passed the album around. Remembering Jamal, they cried for all we had lost. I had looked at it only once since his death, and then with difficulty. I sat down with it after a call from Mike and, turning its heavy pages, considered many attractive options. The first one I chose caught Jamal straight on, with just the right light highlighting his smile. But he shared the photo with someone we hardly knew, a controversial politician named Haji from Pemba, Tanzania, which happened to be the island birthplace of defendant K. K. Mohamed. About a year after we had met him, Haji sought political asylum in Kenya. Rather than face questions from the FBI later, I cut Haji off with scissors. In the other photo I chose we looked so joyous that I had sent copies to friends when we announced our marriage. I was not entirely pleased with sending Mike a picture that included me, since I had refused to participate in the penalty phase, but I couldn't bring myself to cut us apart. I sent both photos. If the FBI did not want me, then they could cut me off.

The prospect that the photo might be altered to suit the prosecution's needs reminded me that every representation made in court, whether through photos or victims' words describing the unique characteristics of a loved one, as the *Payne* decision allowed, would be managed by the prosecution. Photos and statements would emerge as part of testimony guided by a prosecutor and subject to defense objections. Scholarship in this area reveals that victims' participation in the penalty phase is a double-edged opportunity. The state's goals shape victims' stories; the prosecution must keep a victim focused not on what had the most impact for the victim but what will have the most impact in convincing a jury to impose the harshest penalty. Many victims who tell their stories in a trial's penalty phase express surprise when faced with time limits and requests to control their emotions. They are urged to avoid outbursts and asked not to cry. Others are steered by prosecutors' questions to areas they might not have wanted to speak about, such as personal emotional trauma, household intimacies, or their financial circumstances. By law, victims are not permitted to discuss their views of the death penalty and whether the jury should impose it or any other specific punishment. Because some victims are less aware of, or interested in, the legal purposes behind the penalty phase and the conventions of testifying in that part of the trial, their attempts to tell their stories sometimes clash with the goals of the prosecutors or judge.

I thought that my decision not to offer impact evidence meant that I would experience neither the gratification of representing myself and Jamal in court nor the frustration of losing control of our stories. But because my East African family elected to participate, and because prosecutors chose to represent me despite my silence, I participated in ways that allowed me to experience how the penalty phase promises agency to victims but often delivers something quite different. This experience made me distrustful of claims about the importance of the penalty phase for victims' recovery and to wonder whether victims should participate in this part of the trial at all. I also became more aware of what the state gains by including victims' testimony. Alone among the other forms of testimony and argument, victim impact statements voice the "sacred name of pain"[5] that reminds everyone of a crime's human toll. Some would argue that victims' voices, and the pain they express, are entirely appropriate in the courtroom context. Yet the reverential treatment of victims' stories of pain can operate to dehumanize the defendants and thereby undermine the fairness of the trial. As I participated in the embassy bombings trial, I became aware of new dimensions of these concerns that emerged precisely because it was a capital case involving terrorism.

In mid-May, while we were waiting for verdicts in the guilt phase, defense attorneys moved to block the prosecution's planned use of certain photos in the penalty phases. On behalf of defendant al-'Owhali, attorney Fred Cohn argued that the photos were extremely gory and to show them would be more prejudicial than relevant, the latter being the legal requirement. Judge Sand scheduled a hearing where I watched as attorneys for both al-'Owhali and K. K. Mohamed argued vehemently against the photos. With the photos visible only to the judge and the attorneys, Cohn held that to display them risked overwhelming the jurors' reason with emotion, another contentious issue that had long concerned jurists. K. K. Mohamed's attorney expressed similar concerns:

Ruhnke: I lodge an objection to the second photograph, which depicts a charred and disfigured corpse lying on the ground—[looking up] they are in different order? There is a photograph among the five of a charred corpse.

Sand: With burned out automobiles in the background.

Ruhnke: Yes, and the embassy fence in the background. (p. 6351)

Ruhnke went on to argue that the photo was not relevant enough to the prosecution's case to warrant display: "All this photograph does is show a horribly disfigured body of somebody who was killed in the bombing. It does not prove or move forward any of the aggravating factors alleged by the government that are not already in this case." He also objected to a photograph of "what I can only describe as a pile of human corpses on the floor, it appears probably of some morgue in downtown Dar es Salaam, Tanzania." He urged Judge Sand to exclude both photos because the danger that they would prejudice jurors substantially outweighed their probative value (p. 6352).

Interrupting Ruhnke, Judge Sand contended that the jurors, who were in their second week of deliberation and had not had a "knee-jerk reaction to the magnitude of the losses," were sensible enough not to overreact to the photos (p. 6350). Responding to Ruhnke, prosecutor Mike Garcia reminded the court that the prosecution had the burden of proving the aggravating factor that multiple killings occurred. To justify use of the lone corpse, he moved to the somewhat different argument of the impact of such an image on survivors present at the bombing.[6] Judge Sand decided that all the photos could be used. In making a similar ruling in the al-'Owhali phase, he had emphasized that the Nairobi bombing was not bloodless and the prosecution had a duty to show the event and the agony experienced by families.

Ruhnke's graphic descriptions of the photos had come without warning. Thinking about a pile of bodies in the Dar morgue sickened me. Still suffering from post-traumatic stress syndrome, I was afraid of seeing any image with blood or body parts. And I was conscious of a cold, growing fear that Jamal could be depicted in one of the photos. In the hallway outside court, a prosecutor and several FBI agents listened sympathetically to my concern that the photos might upset me when shown in court. Each said he would check on the images they planned to show and get back to me.

A week later I inquired again about the photos. As one prosecutor nodded in agreement, the other assured me that they were willing to do whatever I wanted with regard to displaying the photos. They could show me the photos beforehand to prepare me for the public display. They could alert me, and anyone else, so that we could leave the courtroom if something upsetting was about to be shown. He told me to think about it. As we returned to court, Mike from the FBI pulled me aside to say that if I would like he could describe what each photo actually depicted. He suggested that knowing more about them might help me make a decision. With the jury still out, we retreated to the back corner of the court. Slowly and evenly he described each picture as he remembered it. "There is one of a security guard. There's another of a dead body, not a security guard. It's hard to tell. There is another looking at the crowd and the smoke. You're actually in that one, but most people wouldn't notice you. I don't even think the prosecutors noticed, but I knew it was you. There's one—you can hardly see it—of bodies kinda piled up, in the morgue." I asked, "The one of the body, is it the gardener?" "No," Mike said slowly. "I'm not sure about that one." Mike's virtue in this situation was that he treated the conversation as though it were really hard for both of us, which it was, and really important. But the problem remained that he wasn't sure who was depicted in the photos.

Again I focused on the lone corpse. What was most upsetting was that no one had considered that it might be Jamal. Seeing the photo in open court, what would I do? Would I turn away as I had from the images of cars burning outside the Dar embassy? Would I lean forward, looking for signs of life or of suffering or of final peace? Would I become hysterical? That night I decided that I needed to know if Jamal's body would be shown. My reasons were initially self-protective. I should not have to face photos of my personal horror in the public space of the court. Yet also motivating me was the conviction that, to the extent possible, the government should know the identity of any body they planned to display.

The next day I told Mike I would look at the photos and try to identify the bodies if they would agree to substitute different photos for any that depicted Jamal. In his most solicitous voice he said that he saw no problem with that. When I encountered him a few days later, he handed me a big manila envelope. "Thanks for the pictures," he said. "Check this out." Later I opened the envelope and pulled out a blowup of the wedding photo I had provided for the victims' collage. My reward for giving us to the government.

On the first day of Mohamed al-'Owhali's penalty phase, Judge Sand admitted that, because this was the first penalty phase in recent years in the Southern District of New York, the court had little experience with this kind of proceeding. But he conveyed with certainty the responsibility facing the jurors who would have to "make a unique individualized judgment about the appropriateness of sentencing another human being to death. This is not a mechanical process. Neither is the decision determined by raw numbers" (p. 6672). Their decision would require weighing the aggravating factors presented by the government against the mitigators offered by the defense.

In an opening statement the government mentioned standard aggravating factors such as al-'Owhali's lack of remorse and the future danger he posed. But, as prosecutor Pat Fitzgerald insisted, the impact of the crime on the victims was the most important aggravating factor. Fitzgerald began by reminding the jurors of "Rose," a woman killed in the Nairobi blast who had been mentioned in the opening statement, saying, "she was not just a name, not just a count in the indictment, but a person, a human being with a family and a personality, with hopes and with dreams" (p. 6674). Fitzgerald also mentioned several Americans who would testify later that day, previewing what their accounts would offer and warning the jury neither to resent hearing their painful stories nor to base their decision on emotion. In the defense opening, David Baugh conceded that every person who died was "an innocent," and he read the entire list of names of those killed in the bombings. His comment that jurors should "remember the human beings that were killed, the human beings that have been maimed and injured," turned into a dig when he added, "not just the Americans who there has been testimony about" (p. 6692).

The impact on the victims was portrayed through photos, testimony from twenty-nine people, and a videotape profiling the twelve Americans who had been killed while working at the Nairobi embassy. Among those testifying was a Kenyan nurse who had helped the injured after the bombing, who then read a poem depicting her horrifying experience. A doctor described treating burns, eye wounds, and other injuries. Some of the most agonizing testimony came from those who had been injured, many having endured months of painful recuperation. The videotape, a dignified and patriotic portrayal, presented the American victims as individuals with vibrant careers and loving families. Mention of their hobbies and habits made it easier to remember each as an individual. Julian and Jay Bartley—father and son—stood out. Julian was the highest-ranking diplomat killed in Nairobi, and Jay, his son, had been an intern at the embassy on his summer break from college. Sue Bartley was the first witness to testify. She had attended court almost every day of the trial and, like other family members of deceased victims, looked to this moment to obtain proper recognition for her husband and son, and attention to the suffering she and her daughter had endured. She read from a prepared statement. Others spoke more haltingly. Depending on the question the prosecutor asked, many began by trying to describe the person they had lost and their life before the tragedy.

> While Julian walked with dignitaries and heads of state, throughout his brief tenure on this earth he held fast to the belief that regardless of your economic status, job title or position, everyone should be treated with respect and dignity. As the first African American consul general to Nairobi, Julian brought a new sensitivity to consular work that had been missing.
> —Sue Bartley, who lost her husband, Julian, and son Jay (p. 6715)

When I first met Wilson, first of all, he was a very handsome man. He was very charismatic. He was very intelligent. I met him in college. He was in his second year, doing his stadia in biology. He was a very kind man. When we got married, he appeared to me as a very good father, a very good husband. One thing, in our tradition, most of the time men are not supposed to take part in the bringing of babies, things like changing nappies. It wasn't a man's job. But this was a man who would change nappies and even feed the babies.
—Doreen Ruto, whose husband, Wilson Kipkorir Mutani, an employee of the Teachers Service Commission, was killed while attending a meeting in the Cooperative Bank (p. 6781)

He was 27 years old. He was a young rising star in his job. He's athletic and energetic, and he was always bringing people home for dinner. . . . He just had this heart for people, and was so kind, and considerate. And I always called him a knight. He reminded me of like the old code of knighthood.
—Deborah Hobson, a U.S. Embassy employee, who lost her husband Kenneth Ray Hobson, an Army attaché to the embassy (p. 6756)

We woke up in the morning and my husband made a rather unusual request. There is a T-shirt I bought for him as a present, one of many memorable occasions. It was a white T-shirt and it had a message across, "I'm a Catholic, and Jesus loves me." He requested that I give that shirt to him to wear that morning. The T-shirt had been washed the previous night. It was not dry, and he insisted he wanted to wear it. I did not argue with him because I never wanted to enter into arguments.
—Mary Kahenzi, an employee at Cooperative House, who lost her husband, Thomas Kahenzi, a restaurant manager in a building nearby (p. 6724)

She worked for the State Department for 20 years and 22 days. However, she was a mother first and she absolutely adored her daughters
—Howard Kavaler, an American employed at the embassy, who lost his wife, Prahbi, who was also working there (p. 6845)

Howard Kavaler had also attended much of the trial. Like me, he had faced the horror of searching for his spouse after the explosion. It was the jurors' second time to hear stories about those moments of chaos, as the stories victims told in the penalty phase resembled those offered by eyewitnesses in the guilt phase of the trial.

> I went back to the front of the embassy, trying to get back in, and there were security people preventing people from returning. I went to the administrative consular who is a very close friend of ours, Steven Nolan, and I said "Steve I have to get back in to find Prabhi." I rushed back into the embassy. I went to where her office was. I never found her. Her office was—there was a great deal of rubble, a lot of debris. I never found her.
> —Howard Kavaler, whose wife's body was later recovered (p. 6847)

> Through the darkness I made my way out of [the Ufundi house]. I knew which way to go. As I got out of the building I saw people running from the direction of the embassy in the opposite way. They were bleeding and crying. Nobody was able to explain what had happened. I went down on my knees and prayed again. I thanked God for saving my life. I did not know that I was praying for my husband. I did not know that moment in time that he was dead.
> —Mary Kahenzi, whose husband was standing outside the Ufundi house when it fell (pp. 6725–26)

Almost everyone who testified described the moment of finding out that a loved one had been killed. That wounding instant— burned into memory—was itself a significant element of the impact on victims of a violent death.

> I handed all of my supplies I brought and just waited, and just I was dumbfounded, and I asked people as they were coming out "Have you seen, Ken? Have you seen Ken?" I know if he was alive he'd be helping people. And I guess some people knew but they couldn't tell me. And Ken's boss came out of the embassy and told me that he had died, and then I was escorted home and I handed over the keys to my jeep so they could use it for transportation for people.

—Deborah Hobson, who had been at home with her daughter when the bomb went off (p. 6758)

We looked through the names that were there [at the police station], and we could not get much from the list because they kept indicating an unknown African male. I remember I was really annoyed and angry about it because I kept thinking that someone should know where Wilson is, he is not any unknown African male, he is my husband, someone should find him.
—Doreen Ruto who lost her husband, Wilson Kipkorir Mutani (pp. 6784–85)

I got the message that the body has been found when I was in church, and I went down to the mortuary, not knowing what to expect. I found him laying on the mortuary floor. The T-shirt he had insisted on wearing was my means of identifying him. Yes, he was wearing, "I am a Catholic and Jesus loves me."
—Mary Kahenzi (p. 6726)

Despite the images of carnage depicted in victims' descriptions of what they endured as they searched for relatives in the rubble left by the bomb and in the overcrowded morgues and hospitals, it was just as difficult to listen to their stories of life after their loved one's death.

The teacher told [my daughter] that the night of the show, tell your mother prior to the show to dress you in a certain way. She had to tell her that her mother was killed.
—Howard Kavaler (p. 6850)

After his death it was like we lost direction. It was not having a sense of direction. I lost a mentor. I lost somebody, my best friend. His family missed him, too. Up till now my two children have not been able to cope with his death. Every time I leave home it's like, Mommy, are you going to come back or are you just going to leave and go where daddy went?
—Doreen Ruto (p. 6786)

Our lives have been catalogued in photo albums. Julian loved to take photographs. He used to photograph each of our moves to the next country. He used to photograph everything, from our parties to holidays and trips. Our entire lives in the Foreign Service, including when our children were infants, are documented. Last week our daughter graduated from law school. Although it was a joyous occasion, it was also sad. Julian was not there to photograph and document the moment.
—Sue Bartley (p. 6716)

The first day built to a crescendo with the appearance of Ellen Bomer, an American assigned to the embassy's commercial section. She described regaining consciousness after the bombing and, when she realized she was unable to see, praying that her sight would be spared. Years later, after many surgeries, she still had hope that she might one day regain her vision.

And I guess really—even to this day I don't know that I accept the fact that I am blind. I keep thinking I'm going to see, I'm going to see, I'm not going to give up. My Lord is not going to take both eyes, he might take one but he isn't going to take both, because I didn't do any of this. I was innocent. I was doing my job, and I was supposed to leave Nairobi on the 6th of August, but Secretary Daley was bringing a delegation of 13 businessmen to Nairobi to increase trade exports, so he asked if I would stay another two weeks. And I said OK, I would. It was just one of those things, you're in the wrong place at the wrong time. (pp. 6799–6800)

As Ellen Bomer finished her story, nerves were raw and eyes tearful all around the courtroom.

Later that afternoon, out of the jury's presence, defense attorney Fred Cohn objected to the prosecution's plan for a second full day of victim impact testimony. Following the same line of argument advanced in the earlier hearings, Cohn asserted that the Supreme Court decision in a case brought on behalf of Timothy McVeigh, convicted of bombing the Murrah Federal building in Oklahoma City and sentenced to death, warned against the cumulative effect on the jury of graphic testimony from multiple victims. With great emotion, he said, "Seventeen more witnesses is beyond the pale. I don't care whether it is another day or another hour. Ms. Bomer is enough to make anybody, make a stone weak. It's enough." To which Judge Sand replied, "I think you have made your point" (p. 6810). In another interchange Judge Sand had warned the defense that if the court followed the formula endorsed in the *McVeigh* decision—the same proportion of victims testifying to victims killed or injured—then victim testimony would last well beyond the two days planned.

Countering the defense claim that the first day of testimony in al-'Owhali's penalty phase had been overly emotional, prosecutor Pat Fitzgerald defended the number of victims and their comportment: "The witnesses that have spoken have carried themselves with great dignity and restraint. They have made an effort not to cry and I have nothing but respect for how they have conducted themselves. They have gone out of their way to fight back emotion and restrain themselves" (pp. 6810–11). The restraint required of victims and praised by prosecutors exacerbated the hard task of describing the impact of the crime.[7] The assumption that emotion can be detached, even temporarily, from an account of the incident does not adequately reflect some victims' experiences, and contrasted markedly with victims' behavior elsewhere. The jury did not see the Kenyan woman who collapsed in hysterical sobs in a stairwell as some of us were headed to the restrooms during a break. We crowded around to help; I sat down on the step behind to hold her head. Her reaction seemed to me a true expression of the bombing's impact: the utter inability to hold back the rush of tears. Victims' logic makes some of us mere shells of formerly strong selves. In public you are reminded of the tragedy, you cannot bear up under the pressure of thinking and speaking about it, you fear complete loss of control, you are undone by the bombing once again.

On the second day of testimony in al-'Owhali's penalty phase, the court was packed yet quiet. With his late wife's picture displayed on screens around the courtroom, Lawrence Ndugire testified about the bombing's impact on him and their three children. Lawrence's story was well known in Kenya. In the chaos after the bombing, the nation's attention focused on his wife, Rose Wanjiku Mwangi, who lay buried but alive in the rubble of the building that had stood next to the embassy. For the better part of four days Rose waited to be rescued. At intervals, rescue teams and other victims trapped near Rose heard her voice, but when the debris finally was cleared, she was dead. On the stand, Lawrence's brief answers to prosecutors' questions told Rose's story without embellishment and without conveying how, even in the midst of hundreds dead and thousands injured, Rose's protracted death was a horrifying loss for the whole nation, which had dubbed her "Candle in the Wind." Instead, Lawrence described the impact of Rose's death on their young daughter, Diana, who still "cannot understand how or who caused her mother's death, because they used to be so close" (p. 6860). As his testimony concluded, another photo was displayed. Taken shortly after Rose's death, this one showed Diana and her brother looking solemn with grief as they held up a picture of their mother. This photo, shown for just a few seconds at the New York trial, had made all the Kenyan newspapers in 1998.

Listening to Lawrence, I craned my neck to see a photo of his Rose, smartly dressed and smiling in life before the bombing. For victim after victim, it took only a few moments to be wrenched from an image as pleasing as Rose's picture to the attack, the chilling uncertainty, the frantic search, and then the devastating pain of loss. The progression toward the finality of death played out in a rhythm that had become familiar to those of us listening, and I found that I eagerly anticipated the photos of happy, healthy individuals, not yet victims, as momentary respite from the dreadful monotony of narratives that always turned tragic. I was not alone; each photo set off a soft chorus of "oh" and "tsk" and the "ahh" of sighs as these images made real the pleasure of life before the chaos. Most often a victim's smiling photo was displayed first, just as the loved one began the account. But prosecutors varied their routine, and by the end of some stories I found myself craving a concrete image of the deceased in that happier time. We had all become uneasy voyeurs of happy lives lost.

As the second day of testimony continued, prosecutors limited most victims' accounts. They jumped efficiently from the display of the initial happy photo to the question, "What has been the impact on you emotionally?" Few victims were asked to recount the whole story. When the prosecutor clarified what he was leaving out—"we won't ask you about what happened on the 7th"—we listeners were grateful for the lack of detail. A few witnesses looked startled at the abrupt shift from the story and needed to be thanked by the judge and dismissed. As testimony became more clipped and rote, victims were harder to distinguish from one another; their stories began to sound repetitive.

The prosecution ended with the poignant testimony of Clara Aliganga, an American mother whose son was a marine security guard on duty at the embassy and killed by the blast. Picture after picture of her smiling son, Nathan, illustrated her stories of the close, happy family that celebrated Christmas, weddings, and Nathan's homecomings from duty. Her testimony revealed the complex identity of a young man who went by a nickname, lost fifty pounds to join the marines, and loved to lay his head in his mother's lap. Many of us wept as we viewed the last photo—four young, grim marines carrying Nathan's flag-draped body out of the embassy.

After dismissing the jury for the day, Judge Sand held a hearing to determine which photos could be shown by al-'Owhali's defense attorneys in that portion of the penalty phase. The prosecution had lodged an objection against the plan to use photos of deformed Iraqi babies to illustrate the consequences of U.S. foreign policy targeting Sadaam Hussein, which allegedly had motivated al-'Owhali. Judge Sand refused to allow "gore for the sake of gore" (p. 6907). David Baugh responded:

Baugh: I have trouble accepting that the concern is subjecting the jury to gore. This jury, when Mrs. Aliganga testified today, I cried. When Mr. Fitzgerald asked her that last question—

Sand: He cried—

Baugh: —he cried. And further, when he asked the question about what—

Sand: So you're in a contest as to who can cry more and people who
cry over pictures of deformed babies?

Baugh: No, your honor, I am not in a contest. Actually I am challenging
you by saying, having heard that testimony, how can you say that
those pictures cause you to be concerned about these jurors being
subjected—they were subjected to gut-wrenching pain and suffering today and you said it wasn't prejudicial. (pp. 6912–13)

Judge Sand sustained the prosecution's objection; no photos of
dead Iraqi babies would be displayed. At the end of that day,
which seemed longer than most, prosecutor Pat Fitzgerald read
the following point into the record: "When [Clara Aliganga] testified, she had wanted to put in pictures of her son and the way
he looked when he returned to America with his face blown off.
And we agreed with her to limit that so that we did not show
that. I just want to put that on the record in terms of showing,
not trying to put in her gory photographs" (p. 6961).

Afterward, I shyly commended Mrs. Aliganga and others for
testifying with such strength. They were almost radiant, having
shouldered the tremendous burden of presenting a dead loved
one to the public. But the toll of the burden showed. One witness, hours after her testimony, still clutched a Bible and wiped
away an unceasing flow of tears.

The defense case in the al-'Owhali penalty phase took less than
two days. Even with Judge Sand's offer to issue subpoenas, the
defense had failed to convince expert witnesses to participate.
Each had begged off, citing both fear of reprisals and strong sentiment against assisting convicted terrorists. Al-'Owhali's defense
team had wanted academics or government officials to educate
jurors about the history of U.S. involvement in Iraq, Afghanistan,
Bosnia, and the Middle East in order to demonstrate that aggressive or even illegal acts had ignited al-'Owhali's commitment to
fight the United States. In arguing that he should be permitted to
subpoena the former secretary of state Madeleine Albright, David
Baugh laid out the defense strategy: As the U.S. ambassador to
the United Nations in 1996, Madeleine Albright had enforced the

sanctions that resulted in the starvation of many Iraqis and, as Baugh alleged, could be equated to genocide. If she had undertaken those acts, knowing that they violated the U.S. Code and the Geneva Convention, then U.S. government actions and al Qaeda actions could be viewed as similarly criminal. Judge Sand found Baugh's reasoning "totally unpersuasive" and recommended using other witnesses or documents to illustrate the situations that may have led al-'Owhali to participate in the bombing and to have no regrets (p. 6272). The prosecution had been largely effective in using an entirely different logic to depict the relationship between the U.S. government and al Qaeda as one between a sovereign nation and a nongovernmental entity. Under this rubric, violent acts that were deemed appropriate for a sovereign nation became criminal when pursued by al Qaeda or other such entities. Similar issues arose again when Baugh sought to play videotapes presenting U.S. foreign policy as genocidal and Judge Sand tried to dissuade him. Baugh's response, which implied that his strategy came at his client's request, heightened the tension that was building between Baugh and Sand. Several hours of tapes would eventually be played, including an interview with Secretary Albright, originally broadcast on *60 Minutes*, but "Miss Albright" as Baugh referred to her, would not appear in person.

The lone defense witness was Ramsey Clark, the former attorney general and a longtime critic of U.S. foreign policy. He described how U.S. support for bombing and sanctions campaigns directed at Iraq in the 1990s had had the devastating effects of polluting the water supply, destroying farms, and thereby lowering Iraq's standard of living and increasing infant mortality. Many people worldwide, especially Muslims, found the situation highly disturbing and condemned the United States. After an aggressive cross-examination by Pat Fitzgerald, David Baugh pursued damage control by asking Clark: "Do you in some way consider yourself to be un-American because you question your government?" Clark replied, "I think an American has an obligation to question our government if she loves it, because she wants her government to be good and do right" (p. 7060). Pat Fitzgerald sat fuming.

In the government's closing statement, prosecutor Michael Garcia reminded the jurors that their own verdict had definitively established the gateway and the statutory aggravating factors that had to be weighed against any defense mitigators.[8] It looked bad for al-'Owhali, especially when Garcia displayed a photo of the defendant taken shortly after his capture. He was smiling, almost triumphantly, his fist punching upward. Garcia urged the jury to see that "champ photograph" as evidence of al-'Owhali's lack of remorse. Acknowledging the pain of the Iraq situation, Garcia argued that al-'Owhali had never mentioned Iraq in his statements to authorities and that the political history outlined by the defense simply "[had] no place here, not in this penalty proceeding, where the focus and the purpose must be on the appropriate penalty for this defendant and for the crimes he committed" (p. 7171–72). Garcia concluded that the bombing was "not a military operation, as [al-'Owhali] would say, it's murder. It's a crime and he's responsible" (p. 7173).

In his closing statement for the defense, David Baugh vowed again that he would not try to justify the bombing but then linked the killings in Iraq to the deaths of the embassy bombings victims. Touching on politics, U.S.-related crimes abroad, and the jurors' own task of sentencing, Baugh drew the lesson that killing "only makes more killing, period" (p. 7182). At first I applauded Baugh's attempts to persuade jurors not to apply the death penalty. The point that "it doesn't make sense to pour any more blood on all that which has already been spilled" seemed fitting. But I recoiled from other remarks, namely, when he told the jury that "when you put Juror No. 1 or Juror No. 2 on that [verdict] form, it's going be like firing the bullet" (p. 7189) and he even went further, saying that the jurors would be "killers" if they signed the form.

Out of the jury's hearing Pat Fitzgerald complained about Baugh's insensitive tactics. Baugh rose to defend himself and somehow in the discussion he accused Judge Sand first of putting words into his mouth and second of painting all the defendants with the same broad brush simply because they were Arabs. We held our breaths as the ordinarily even-tempered judge came down hard, saying, "Do not accuse me of being a racist, because there is no justification for that, and for you to say that I reach any conclusion because a defendant is an Arab is unspeakable." To which Baugh replied, "Your Honor, to me, it is not unspeakable and I don't mind saying it. If it offended you, well—However, we are concerned about it."

Judge Sand made a harsher ruling than he might have on the complaints lodged by Fitzgerald and promptly called a lunch break. In the cafeteria everyone gossiped about the confrontation. One court employee said, in astonished anger, "Judge Sand was responsible for desegregating the Yonkers schools. If anybody's above racism, it's him." When we returned to court, the tension lingered. Sand entered frowning. Baugh slumped petulantly. He had made some tactical errors, but only the other defense attorneys could imagine the pressure he must have felt, fighting for a man's life. Letting his emotions get the best of him in court only made him as human as the rest of us.

None of the defendant's family members had come from Saudi Arabia to attest to al-'Owhali's character or to plead for his life. This situation, which David Baugh told the jury deviated from most penalty phases where people speak on behalf of a convicted defendant, raised the empirical question of whether a defendant with no visible supporters is more likely to get the death penalty than someone with family and friends, and also the ethical question of whether that is fair. Similar questions arise in relation to victim impact testimony: What of the irascible victim whose family holds no interest in avenging the death through law or in seeking recognition in court? Scholars point to this possibility as yet another problem with the inclusion of victim impact testimony in a trial's penalty phase. Relatedly, witnesses' stories pointed to the impertinent question of whether every life depicted had, in fact, been a happy one and all the victims positive forces for those around them. The unspoken rule that seemed to compel every witness to portray the deceased victims as kind, nonviolent, happy, and loving risked re-creating larger-than-life ideals. The human face of a crime victim depicted in court must be a happy one, rather than the more complex personas that most of us inhabit. Critics of victim impact statements have argued that those testifying are in a difficult position when the lives with their loved ones before the crime were a mixture of pleasure, pain, and routine as most lives are and the personal qualities of the deceased less perfect than the testimony would indicate.[9] For surviving victims, maintaining integrity while reproducing the humanity—the real individual qualities—of a dead victim can be a terribly difficult task.

During the week of waiting for a decision on al-'Owhali's fate, I asked prosecutors once again about the photos they planned to show in K. K. Mohamed's penalty phase. In a conference call they told me that the ones I might object to had already been through litigation, so changes were impossible. Knowing that the prosecution had dropped several planned witnesses during al-'Owhali's penalty phase, I felt manipulated by their answer and reminded them that I had willingly provided a beautiful photo of Jamal and myself that they were welcome to display. They explained that photos of victims before the bombing would show the impact of my loss, and photos of dead bodies would attest to the horror of the crime scene. Legally, they had to make both points.

With little to say in response, I forced myself to face the possibility that the prosecution might display a photo of Jamal's dead body. The prosecution's claim that Mrs. Aliganga had been prepared to show photos of her son's damaged body confronted me with my own weakness. But if Mrs. Aliganga had been willing to endure the pain of displaying the photos, she must have seen and believed in a purpose that, despite my soul-searching, I did not share. Relatives of victims can bear tremendous pain in the service of a righteous goal. My friend, Ashraf Rushdy, has written about the bravery of Mamie Till Bradley, who insisted on showing the lynched and broken body of her son Emmett Till and allowing it to be photographed. The published photos galvanized an African American movement against white supremacy. In an elegant essay, Rushdy argues that this strategy could be useful to combat the hatred beneath current, racially motivated crimes such as the murder by dragging of James Byrd. Photos of Byrd, displayed in the jury trial, were never published.

While acknowledging that published pictures of Byrd might have wounded the Byrd family, Rushdy advocates using photos of racist attacks to prevent future violence: "The past teaches us that images of terror—used responsibly—can foster a climate in which terror is no longer tolerated. I suggest that we aspire to the courageous example of Mamie Till Bradley, not the cautious compromises of newspaper editors who fear to offend their readerships. A citizenry alert to the horror of hate crimes would be compensation enough."[10] I admire those who would be willing to bear the pain of displaying images of their dead relatives, in court or even more publicly. Yet the political struggles in which the Till and Byrd families were engaged perhaps defined more clearly what positive goals could be achieved by displaying those graphic images.

While I knew that the embassy bombings had caused terrible suffering, I came to believe that I did not share the prosecution's goal of demonstrating terrorism's horror through displaying the bodies of my husband and other African victims. I could not apply Rushdy's justification for showing photos of lynching victims in this case. Jamal was not brutally disfigured because he was African, or Muslim. Quite the contrary, the criminal intent—at least by the prosecution's submission—was to kill Americans. Would showing Jamal's body do the work of sensitizing the citizenry? Which citizenry? Or would he provide a physical example full of irony? What other meanings would his body convey to the jury and to other Americans?

The condemnation of terrorism was but one of several frames for viewing photos of the embassy bombing victims. For me, the role of victims' photos in impugning terrorism was partly eclipsed by another political struggle involving photos of Africans. In courts and in the media, photos of unidentified African bodies in the wake of crime or disaster illustrate an Africa that is "chaotic" compared to a "civilized" West and offer no explanation of the global hierarchies that devalue African lives. Moreover, the use of depersonalized photos, even for the important goal of showing the seriousness of a crime, robs individuals of personal identity. That the prosecution seemed unconcerned that a body had not been identified, despite the fact that eleven people—rather than hundreds—had died in Dar, seemed an indefensible consequence. I was sure that the body of a white person would not be left anonymous and would not have been shown in court in that dehumanized state. That the prosecution wanted to use these photos to encourage jurors to favor the death penalty became, for me, an especially repugnant goal. Although grateful for the competence and dedication of the prosecutors, by the time the penalty phases began, I came to believe that anyone can be brought low by the relentless pursuit of a death sentence.

In my final meeting with prosecutors, Abby from the FBI once again described the photos. She began methodically, "There's someone injured being carried but that's a security guard." I interrupted, "I was told there was another single body, not a security guard." Abby stared at prosecutor Mike Garcia for confirmation, "There was a picture that had—but they were supposed to crop that body out of it." He stared back at her. I looked down at my hands spread flat on the table. Cropping bodies out? Maybe hearing this was worse than keeping quiet about the whole thing. I took a deep breath and said, "It seems to me that a body lying outside the embassy that has not been identified could be my husband. I'd just like to know." Abby and Mike Garcia left briefly, and, when Abby returned, she admitted that she had been mistaken; the body had not been cropped out. Her description of the lone corpse convinced me it was Jamal. I urged them not to use the photo, and Pat responded: "We don't want to put you through the pain of looking at the photo. But if you saw it and it was someone else, then this problem would go away." Technically, I thought, that's not true. They still wouldn't know whose body they were using. "But if you look at it, we can't say we won't use it," he added. My face must have shown so much anger, or pain, that, as I left, he said they would do "some more homework" and get back to me with a final decision.

On their fifth day of deliberations, jurors requested a copy of the oath they had taken when sworn in as jurors. Attorneys speculated that the group was split. Soon after, we learned that they had reached a decision. Trembling at what it might feel like to hear a man sentenced to death, I steeled myself and stared down at the special verdict form. Quickly the clerk moved through the findings affirming that the government had proved its case, as well as several statutory aggravating factors. So far their findings pointed to death. Heads popped up as the jury foreperson announced the jury's rejection of the prosecution claim that al-'Owhali posed a future danger. More splits in the jurors' ranks emerged around the various mitigating factors, and this began to cast doubt on their ultimate conclusion. Then, the foreperson read a list of the jurors' own mitigating factors. Under the law, creating such a list was allowable but highly unusual. Several victims stiffened when the foreperson declared: "The next mitigating factor is that executing al-'Owhali may not necessarily alleviate the victims' or victims' families suffering and the number of jurors who so find is nine." The jurors' views of capital punishment must have come in for a good deal of discussion, as five of them agreed that "life in prison is a greater punishment since his freedom is severely curtailed," and four found that "lethal injection is very humane and the defendant will not suffer" (p. 7333). Weighing these and the other findings, the jury could not unanimously agree to impose the death sentence on al-'Owhali. They offered this verdict knowing that by default al-'Owhali would be sentenced to life imprisonment without the possibility of release.

I was limp with relief and found it hard to face the other victims, whose statements to the media expressed anger and frustration. Howard Kavaler condemned the jurors for their cowardice. His twelve-year-old daughter told the press: "I'm pretty angry and disappointed he wasn't given the death penalty. He deserved it. He killed so many people." I felt for Howard, his daughters, and all the others who believed that justice had not been done.

The jury, remarkable for its painstaking process, the added-on mitigators, and the ultimate split decision, had stunned us by accepting the defense claims that al-'Owhali's "sincere belief . . . mandated by his religion" had motivated him to commit the offenses and that he believed the embassies to be "legitimate military targets." Perhaps the notion that a soldier should not be punished as severely as a criminal motivated jurors to hold back from imposing the death penalty. Or perhaps they held back because, as ten of them believed, execution would make al-'Owhali a martyr.

The jurors' inability to agree on executing al-'Owhali appeared to me to seal K. K. Mohamed's fate. If they had failed to believe that al-'Owhali deserved death, how could they justify executing K.K., who had not gone to the bomb site and was responsible for fewer deaths? When I raised this with prosecutors, Pat Fitzgerald set me straight. "One date," he said, "November 1, 2000, makes all the difference." The prosecution planned to show that K.K. had participated in a brutal attack on a corrections officer assigned to guard his cell block. That attack would prove that his violent tendencies continued and, if incarcerated, he would pose a danger to others, including prison guards.

The prosecutors' attempt to persuade the jurors that K.K. would have to be executed rather than imprisoned would come later. As K.K.'s penalty phase began, we were all focused on the victims' testimony. Jamal's relatives arrived from Kenya and, in a brief interview with prosecutors, were hastily prepared to give testimony. The night before victim impact testimony was scheduled to begin, I left a message for an FBI agent asking if the disputed photo would be used. In the morning, as we hurried from the hotel into vans for the trip to court, an agent pulled me aside to say that the prosecution had decided not to display the photo. Coming at the last possible moment, this was a big relief.

The first witness for the prosecution was an American woman who had been trapped in her embassy office after the bombing. She described getting under her desk and then pounding on the door until colleagues came to free her. Her story was poignant, mentioning how she helped others—holding a friend's hand at the hospital—and how ordinary Tanzanians helped her—putting a hand on her shoulder and telling her "pole," which means "sorry." Her story returned several times to another American victim, who had been seriously injured. She described the depression this young woman continued to suffer and said that, with respect to the bombing, her friend "feels like she relives it a lot" (p. 7512). Under the loose rules of victim impact testimony, she and other witnesses described the impact on children and other victims who had chosen not to testify. They were not asked when they had last spoken to the victims they quoted or how they could know what another victim feels.

Wearing one of my brother's suits, my nephew, Mohamed Jelani, took the stand looking much younger than his twenty-eight years. He was shy, responding through the Swahili interpreter in one-word answers and volunteering little. Our wedding photo was displayed, and he was asked to identify us. Prosecutors wanted him to say "Jamal" or Jamal's full name, Abdurahman Abdalla, but out of respect Mohamed could say only "Uncle." Mohamed misremembered the ages of Jamal's sons. His description of Jamal's role in the community built him up larger than life. Jamal was a teacher, a healer, a preacher, a businessman, the pillar of the family. Was it Mohamed's desire to please or the interpreter's tendency to embellish? Yet I was proud that Jamal was depicted as important and influential, which he was, and that it was clear that family and community depended on him. The chance to tell this story in court, in the United States, was the reason why his relatives had agreed to participate, and they would appreciate this tribute.

Nonetheless, I imagined the story I could have told, a true and emotional one: as we neared the embassy that day, Jamal started skipping down the sidewalk, rejoicing that his visa had come through the month before. He laughed about being "legal," saying this word in English and then "tayari" meaning "ready" to leave in two weeks for the United States. Unspoken then and in court was the new life we had planned together. My story would have emphasized Jamal's connections to family and community. I could have told how his cousins borrowed a car, bribed border guards, and drove all night to help ensure his body would be returned to Kenya for burial. How hundreds of people turned up in the middle of the night for the funeral. How Mohamed Jelani had refused to eat for a week after Jamal was buried. My story would have partially concealed the financial difficulties faced by my in-laws after Jamal's death; the Swahili cultural imperative to conceal family problems might have led me—like

Mohamed Jelani—to gloss over this part. I crafted this story in my head, knowing that I wanted to tell it publicly but could never do so when the goal was to secure someone else's death.

I looked at our wedding photo displayed in court and came to appreciate that my motive for sending the pictures was not simply a desire to ensure Jamal's presence at the trial. I also hoped to send a message about our relationship. I was—no differently than other victims—using the trial as a public forum to make political and personal statements. While the bombings marked a severe rupture between some elements of the Islamic and Western worlds, I wanted our relationship to demonstrate the possibility of differences bridged.

Most of the victims and their family members who testified that day were ordinary Tanzanians, relatives of the security guards and drivers who were killed. Shabani Mtulia, whose wife, Mtendeje, was killed at her guard post in the embassy, described how his life "had been going like halfway" because he had lost Mtendeje's support, including for their two children. He mentioned that, on the day of the bombing, she had been scheduled to take the embassy's exam to qualify for a secretarial position and, in preparation, had brought along her school certificates and also a Koran. On the whole, the monosyllabic answers of the Tanzanian witnesses contrasted with the more vivid accounts given by the Kenyans and Americans in al-'Owhali's penalty phase. For some Tanzanians, the flat brevity of their testimony was an artifact of using an interpreter, but education, class, and culture operated to homogenize them into stereotypic depictions, and the prosecution seemed not to push them. Most of the Tanzanians testified about living in quite bleak circumstances, before and after the bombings. I wondered if jurors had a hard time relating to these victims in contrast to the middle-class Kenyans who told of dropping a loved one off at work in the city or watching the unfolding horror on television.

A rumor made its way around the courtroom. K.K.'s defense team had traveled to Tanzania to interview these witnesses about their attitudes toward the death penalty, and to a person they had all expressed their opposition to capital punishment. A few

weeks earlier, out of our hearing, the defense had made the crafty
move of requesting to play the tape in court pending review by
Judge Sand and the prosecutors. Once Fitzgerald's team had seen
the witnesses express their religious and ethical opposition to the
death penalty, prosecutors could no longer make the argument—
as they had in the al-'Owhali penalty phase—that only a sentence
of death would satisfy the victims. As defense counsel knew, the
tape of victims' views of the death penalty did not have to be
played in open court to influence the trial.

Prosecutors looked grim all day. These stories could not possibly convince the jury to impose the death penalty when more
vivid accounts had failed to do so for al-'Owhali. In late afternoon I went to the prosecutors' chamber to pick up my relatives.
Mike from the FBI had a look of dismay. To be polite I asked,
"How do you think it went?" "Okay," Mike said. "People did
their best." "Mohamed Jelani was nervous," I said, knowing that
his clipped answers were probably not what Mike and others
had wanted from our story. "It's hard," I added. "Yeah," Mike
said. "We ask victims to do really hard things."

At the end of the day four of us sat at South Street Seaport waiting for orders of fish and chips. Mary Porter and I shared the
headphones of my small radio to hear me on the National Public
Radio report I had taped previously with Melissa Block, who
had covered the trial. It was fitting for me to speak out on the
very day I would have testified. Noting with appreciation the
"definitive answer" offered by the guilty verdict, I expressed my
frustration that, as a death penalty opponent, there was "no
space for me in the trial."

I listened to my statements about the terror I experienced in
the bombing, my views of the trial, and my reasons for refusing
to testify; I felt that I had made the public statement of my views
that was not possible in the courtroom. For victims, every telling
of the tragedy can mean some loss of control over the story; I
am grateful that Melissa captured this dilemma and yet let me
conclude with what was really at stake for me. "In the end we
will none of us get what we really want, and that's to have the
people we loved back, to have our lives back, to have the plans

that we'd made that we thought we would be able to enact in our lives back. That's not going to come from a judicial process. It's not going to come from a particular form of punishment. And for that I'm sorry for myself and for everyone."[11]

As we ate, I told Mary and my relatives that the Kiswahili interpreter said he wanted to cry when he saw our wedding photo displayed in court and that the other interpreter had to take over for him. Then Mohamed Jelani looked at me sideways and asked if I had seen "that other picture." Thinking that he meant the other one I'd sent to the FBI, I said, "The one where he's smiling?" "No," he said, and glanced at Saidi and then down. He looked terrible. "The one at the bombing." My hair stood on end. "They showed you a picture of him after the bombing?" He nodded. Saidi told me, "The lawyer put it in front of him and he looked and he just cried. Then they started to ask him questions."

"I just turned it over," Mohamed said.

I railed against the prosecutors; they should never have shown him that photo. Then it dawned on me that they had shown him the photo for a simple reason: to make this vulnerable, sensitive young man angry enough to want K. K. Mohamed put to death and to tell a story to achieve that end.

On a break during closing statements the next week, I followed Mike from the FBI out of court. In front of the elevators, I confronted him: "How could you have shown Mohamed Jelani that photo?" "We wanted to spare you," he told me. I choked back "bullshit" as my response, because I knew it would come out too loud. I insisted that they had done something very wrong. Did he realize that Mohamed would bear this sadness so far away from his home and family? That he would return to Kenya where no one would understand what he had gone through? That, as far as I could tell, no one could say for certain that his testimony—or any victim's—was worth all this pain?

The following week we were standing in Mary's kitchen, and Saidi looked at the photo display of friends and family on her refrigerator. His eyes teared up. In a fluid motion he lifted our tiny wedding photo from under the magnet, brought it to his lips, kissed Jamal, and gently secured us back in our place, an intimate and heartfelt expression of reverence for dead and living victims.

CHAPTER EIGHT
Representing the Defendant

THROUGHOUT THE embassy bombings trial, another terror case repeatedly captured national attention. More than a year before, Timothy McVeigh had been convicted of bombing the Murrah Federal Building in Oklahoma City, and, as deliberations in al-'Owhali's penalty phase proceeded, he faced execution by lethal injection. Defense attorneys complained that jurors could hardly avoid the nonstop media coverage. Hoping against hope not to hear a death sentence pronounced, I felt myself fast-forwarding to a moment when embassy bombing victims, like the victims of Oklahoma City, might be faced with the executions of those who had harmed them. I listened to the Oklahoma City victims with a desperate sense that their views of McVeigh's execution might guide me should I find myself in similar circumstances. Their perspectives ranged widely—from heated calls for revenge, to clear-eyed acknowledgment that retribution was only fair, to faith-filled forgiveness, to adamant refusals to allow McVeigh, or his punishment, to have any effect on them. Ultimately they would handle McVeigh's execution in different ways. Some would attend the event itself. Others who had planned to go would not, in the end, show up. Still others would stand outside in protest, perhaps in prayer. I had no idea what I would do in their circumstances and hoped I would never face the choices they had.

It stuck in my mind that many harmed in Oklahoma City portrayed the execution as a welcome and appropriate means of silencing Timothy McVeigh, of "shutting him up" once and for all. Victims complained that through publicity and the trial itself they had already heard enough from McVeigh, and about him; they looked forward to the time when execution would render him unable to speak ever again. And many were stunned when, before his execution, McVeigh himself would "speak" through last words read on his behalf. Quoting the poem "Invictus" confirmed both his continuing defiance of authority and his lack of remorse. He asked no forgiveness, thus denying those victims with the impulse to forgive the chance to do so and hardening the resolve of others who simply wanted him gone. It is a common view that convicted criminals, especially terrorists, should be given no platform for expressing themselves. So often victims and their families want to be shielded from hearing from those who have harmed them, and, when they do, through choice or chance, the experience can be painful and yet, in rare cases, satisfying. Anyone who had been waiting for McVeigh's execution so as to gain, from his last words, anything that victims routinely crave to hear from the condemned—such as remorse, regret, confusion, or even terror in the face of punishment—found his words a grave disappointment. My heart went out to the victims, and it was hard not to agree when many charged that, with his last chance to speak, he had harmed them yet again and thereby proved he had nothing of value to say.

Sentiments expressed by the Oklahoma City victims, and the anguish wrought by the execution itself, challenged me to interrogate my persistent sense that, despite the long embassy bombings trial, I had yet to hear enough from those found guilty. I could not endorse silencing the defendants, particularly K.K., for the simple reason that I still felt we had more to learn about the bombings, especially in Dar es Salaam, and that somehow K.K. could enlighten us. My interest rose when rumors flew around court that K.K. would take the stand during the penalty phase. Just before the defense presented its side, Mike from the FBI called to remind me that K.K. might testify. He urged, "You should be sure to come. It's the chance of a lifetime." "Yeah," I thought, "*K.K.'s* lifetime." Speaking on his own behalf might be the best chance K.K. had to save himself. Yet it was hard to imagine how he could ever explain what he had done. I realized I was both intensely eager to hear K.K. and absolutely terrified. Would he finally answer my "why" questions? Why did he participate in the bombings? Why did he turn away from the values of his family and society? Why did he believe in al Qaeda's message and tactics? But looking to K.K. for answers was a gamble. If he expressed pride in his deeds, it might be better to have heard nothing, as in al-'Owhali's penalty phase. Conversely, what if he was able to explain how he had become caught up in the crime in a way that sounded rational? Would it be even more distressing if he were able to persuade me to empathize with his perspective? Or what if K.K. simply expressed profound remorse? I felt a mixture of fear and desire at the prospect of hearing him speak. And yet, if I sincerely wanted to understand why the bombings had occurred, why K.K. had helped to carry them out, then I needed to listen, even to K.K., and to anyone who chose to speak on his behalf.

Judge Sand counseled jurors to treat this penalty phase separately from al-'Owhali's. He acknowledged the similarity of the procedures and of the gateway and statutory aggravating factors. When the judge read the list of mitigators that jurors would consider as they weighed evidence offered by each side, differences between the two defendants began to emerge. K.K.'s attorneys would try to show that, in contrast to al-'Owhali, their client had been recruited as an "expendable member of the conspiracy," had tried to help authorities after his capture, was remorseful for his actions, "would not participate in such a crime in the future," and, if executed, would cause his family much grief.

The most important contrast between the two penalty phases lay with the following non-statutory aggravating factor that the prosecution would try to prove: K.K. was a future danger, and the evidence was his involvement in a violent attack on a corrections guard named Officer Pepe at the Metropolitan Correctional Center (MCC) where he had been incarcerated before the trial. Media accounts of the brutal attack, which irreparably damaged the guard's vision and brain, had all attributed it to Mamdouh Mohamed Salim, another embassy bombings defendant who had also been awaiting trial at the MCC. For his role in the attack—it was alleged that he had stabbed Officer Pepe in the eye using a sharpened comb—Salim was charged with assault, and his trial for conspiracy related to the bombings severed from that of the other defendants.

More people than I had expected filled the courtroom in the first days of the penalty phase. Victims and other observers from Tanzania, along with my family from Kenya and the United States, took up most of the seats on one side of the courtroom. A large contingent of journalists crowded together across the aisle. Sitting in front of us, in rows often reserved for law enforcement or dignitaries, were a dozen corrections guards and several members of Officer Pepe's family.

Prosecutor Michael Garcia opened for the government. To simplify, he told the jury that three dates were important. Obviously the first was August 7, 1998, the day of the bombings. The second was October 5, 1999, when K.K. was apprehended in South Africa. Characterizing K.K.'s callous attitude at the time of his arrest, Garcia began to build an image of K.K. as a ruthless killer: "And on October 5th, Khalfan Mohamed talks to the FBI agents and he shows no remorse for his horrific crimes. No remorse, although it's a year later and he has had time to learn that the 11 victims of his crime were Tanzanians. They were his countrymen. They were mostly Muslims. He's had time to learn all that, and he shows no remorse" (p. 7447).

I was dumbstruck. Jamal was Kenyan, not Tanzanian, not K.K.'s countryman. Why were they so carelessly lumping the African victims together? Ben Weiser, reporting daily on the trial for the *New York Times*, caught my eye from across the aisle; I had recently called to admonish him when one of his articles reported that everyone killed in Dar es Salaam was Tanzanian. But Garcia's account of what happened on the third date, November 1, 2000, troubled me even more, as he narrated: "[Salim] lured [Officer Pepe] back to that cell where [K.K. Mohamed] was waiting. Officer Pepe opened the door, stepped in, and was viciously attacked" (p. 7449). As he uttered the words, "was viciously attacked," Garcia turned around and pointed right at K.K. Despite this ringing accusation, my trained ears had heard him use the passive. I thought, why is he pointing at K.K. and yet not naming him? He promised evidence to show that K.K., along with Salim, had attacked Officer Pepe.

In his opening statement, defense counsel David Ruhnke accused Garcia of playing "fast and loose with the facts" in depicting K.K.'s involvement in the assault on Officer Pepe, allowing that "perhaps that is the kindest, most non-accusatory way to say it [is] that there is a failure of proof as to what occurred" (p. 7473). K.K. had not confessed to playing any role in the attack, and Ruhnke insisted that evidence would show that he had not been involved.

The stark contrast between the opening statements indicated that we were about to witness a hard-fought trial within a trial. The ultimate outcome would be grim. Either K.K. would die through execution, with all the moral complexities of that punishment, or he would die having lived the rest of his life in prison, a sad waste, or a dangerous time bomb, if the prosecution's view of him proved correct. As the penalty phase began, I had the sense that we would witness a titanic battle quite different from the guilt phase of the trial.

Paul McAlister was the prosecution's first witness concerning the attack. He had been one of Salim's attorneys. As McAlister testified, on the morning of November 1, 2000, he had gone to the 10 South wing of the MCC to meet with Salim, something he had done many times before. Officer Pepe—the only guard on duty—let him onto the floor. When his co-counsel, Charles Adler, arrived, Pepe locked the two into one side of a small room and went to get Salim, who had yet to decide whether he wanted to see his attorneys that day. From the beginning Salim had been a tough client. He had asked for new counsel, saying at a magistrate's hearing that McAlister and Adler were not representing him well. That request had been denied about a week earlier.[1] Salim had sat down across from his attorneys and began searching intently on the computer. He complained about the machine, which was old and had no disk drive or Internet access. Growing increasingly agitated, he called Officer Pepe over and demanded to return to his cell to retrieve more documents. McAlister recounted that, before leaving, Salim removed his orange prison jumpsuit and held it against a folder he carried in front of him. In McAlister's recollection, Officer Pepe did not handcuff Salim. On exiting, Salim started down the hallway, to the left. He assumed that Salim and Pepe continued around to the other side of the U-shaped hallway heading toward Salim's cell at the end, number 6.

A lot of time passed. McAlister and Adler wondered aloud whether Salim intended to return. He had sometimes ended their meetings abruptly. The phone at the guards' desk rang and rang. McAlister glanced out the window of the locked conference room and saw frantic activity on the closed-circuit video monitors just behind the unoccupied guard's desk. The screens flashed images of corrections officers running down hallways on 9 South, the floor just below, and of guards gathered behind the door to 10 South, clearly trying to get in. The attorneys became concerned as the guards entered the floor and began checking doors, including theirs, to be sure they were locked. Next, McAlister was stunned to see several guards come down the hall dragging an inert body, which they dropped right in front of the door. It looked like Salim, and McAlister thought he might be unconscious, or dead. He and Adler watched as one guard stood over him, took out a key, and jabbed it near the man's eye. Blood spurted up. In fact, there was already blood on the floor in long waves from where the body had been dragged. And then as the guard raised his hand to jab the key again, another guard noticed Adler and McAlister watching through the window and screamed at them, "Don't look. Turn around." Salim was immediately pulled farther down the corridor, out of sight of his attorneys.

The horror McAlister and Adler were witnessing continued as Officer Pepe came into view. He was walking slowly down the hallway, supported by guards. A large object protruded from his left eye; blood soaked his clothes. He, too, was quickly removed from their view. Much later that day, McAlister and Adler were released from 10 South. Because they were in the position to be witnesses to the events of November 1, 2000, they were no longer able to represent Salim who faced an indictment for attempted murder and other charges. Officer Pepe's condition worsened in the days after the attack, as the stabbing had impaired his vision, speech, and nerve function.

McAlister's account, although vivid, clear, and largely confirmed by Charles Adler who testified later for the defense, cov-

ered only a small part of what had happened. The attorneys'
vantage point allowed them to see down just one hallway of the
cell block, but Officer Pepe was not attacked there. And the precise location of the attack was crucial. Did Salim stab the officer
at the bottom of the U-shaped hallway (just after turning the
corner) or in the hallway closer to his cell, or did he wait until
he reentered cell 6, as Garcia had alleged. If it were the latter,
did Salim have help from his cellmate, K. K. Mohamed?

We learned some versions of what might have happened from
the MCC employees who had come on the scene after Officer
Pepe's body alarm went off.[2] And with their testimony, from my
view, the penalty phase of the trial took a perverse turn, as they
contradicted one another on several key issues. For instance,
Roderick Jenkins, the first MCC employee to testify, told us that
he was also the first of fifteen to twenty other officers to enter
10 South. He testified that, as he headed toward cell 6, K. K. Mohamed "lunged at me with a substance, a bottled substance,
squirting something on my person." Just as he was struggling
to hold K.K., Salim burst out of his cell, squirting at him with
one hand and holding something with the other. In his action-
packed account, Jenkins single-handedly held off the two opponents. If Jenkins's recollection that K.K. had lunged at him, and
then resisted handcuffs, were true, K.K.'s defense team would
have a tough time countering the future dangerousness argument. But officers who came in just behind Jenkins, and who
testified after him, remembered things differently. In Lance
Maiden's recollection, K.K. did not lunge but assumed a "fighting stance" back in the corner. On cross-examination, defense
attorney David Stern asked, "Now, you were able to see Mr. Mohamed's hands, you said, right?" "Yes." "And they were
clenched, is that fair to say?" "Yes." (p. 7714). "Shit," hissed a
prosecutor sitting just behind me. I glanced around and saw him
shaking his head. Clenched fists held up to fight, or clutching a
bottle? When Jenkins mentioned that K.K. had squirted something, Garcia asked him about the container used, and the officer
responded, "It's a commissary item that [inmates] purchase. It's
a honey bottle shaped [as] a bear with the yellow cap" (p. 7668).
Mary Porter and I looked at each other in surprise, struck by

how ludicrous it sounded: innocent honey bears deployed as jailhouse weapons.

On several issues, including whether K.K. had had "blood on his hands," the accounts were too confusing and contradictory to establish whether and how K.K. had been involved. Some of the confusion, but not all, was attributable to the frantic pace of the incident. Lightning quick reactions might be hard to recall or explain in hindsight. Given that the stakes were high for the officers' testimony—any one account could make the difference between the jury finding K.K. a future danger or not—witnesses could have been nervous or could have been trying to help the prosecution. These accounts contrasted with the trial's guilt phase, when the testimony of prosecution witnesses snapped into place critical pieces of evidence that ultimately revealed a plausible account of the bombings. In this phase the facts were contested; pieces were missing or distorted. I was not alone in my frustration that we would never know what happened; others—from all sides—had trouble hiding their annoyance.

If K.K. had run from cell 6, refusing to be part of the attack on Officer Pepe, then it would have been a lucky break that stationary video cameras mounted in the halls and cells of 10 South continuously recorded activity, displaying it on monitors at the guards' desk area. For many months K.K.'s defense team had been trying to obtain the videotape made in the cell at the time of the attack, but the MCC insisted, at various times, that the tape had never been made, that it had been copied over, or that it had been lost. Of all the inconsistencies heard during K.K.'s penalty phase, the stories of the videotape were the strangest. They left me feeling that perhaps there had been a cover-up. Maybe K.K. had run out of the cell and thus the tape would exonerate him. But if a cover-up existed, it was more likely that the segments taped over would have shown police officers beating up the defendants. Or perhaps the VCR simply did not work, and this security lapse required a cover-up. I felt that time was being wasted as we dragged through details and, in the end, were left with no idea of what had happened to the tape if it even existed.

Lieutenant Carrino was the first of several people to testify that, after the attack, Officer Pepe repeatedly uttered some version of the following: "I gave them a fight." Carrino claimed to be "99 percent sure" that Pepe said these words as personnel tried to stabilize him for the trip to the hospital. But in the FBI's written report, Carrino had repeated Pepe's utterance that day as, "They slipped the cuffs, and I fought back." Elise Santulli, an MCC employee who rode in the ambulance with Officer Pepe, insisted that he had said, "I gave them a fight," as he was being whisked along New York streets. Later, under treatment at the hospital attended by a physician's assistant (PA) unaffiliated with the MCC, Officer Pepe allegedly said it again, "I gave them a fight." But neither the PA's medical report nor Santuli's FBI debriefing memo mentioned the statement. Through tears, Santulli testified that she had visited Officer Pepe every day for months. At that moment I thought she indeed believed that the officer had said, "I gave them a fight." But I no longer believed that I would learn what truly was said. The defense zeroed in on the utterance, knowing that it implicated K.K. and thus had to be countered. Their alternative story was that K.K. had left the cell when Salim brought Officer Pepe in; probably he had already been stabbed. K.K. then crouched in the back corner of the hallway until the officers came. They depicted any resistance on K.K.'s part as self-defense. In his closing statement David Stern repeated these sentences over and over: "I gave 'im a fight. I gave them a fight. I gave 'em a fight. I gave him a fight" (p. 8663). In Stern's nasally New York accent, they were indistinguishable.[3]

Physical evidence collected in and around the cell left no doubt that the attack had been prepared in advance. But it was Mamdouh Salim's fingerprints, not K.K.'s, that were found on chilling notes about hostage scenarios. Comments from attorneys and media accounts depicted Salim as belligerent and ruthless. His unreconstructed opposition to the United States was evident in comments he made when speaking out in court during pretrial hearings. Observing that Salim seemed consumed by rage, one court employee admitted feeling scared to be in the same courtroom with him, despite the security.

Two honey bears were found outside cell 6. Of the three found inside, one was filled with detergent and another with water. Several belonged to K.K. In his closing statement, David Stern admitted that K.K. had a "sweet tooth" and routinely ordered honey. During the afternoon break, Judge Sand looked down at the evidence table and asked, "Can I see a honey bear jar?" Consumed with some emotion that made me shake, I just put my head down not knowing if was tears or laughter or some mixture erupting out of the tension built over days of gruesome testimony. My eyes teared from trying not to laugh, and I told myself it simply was not funny, not at all. It was grisly and grim. Whatever rose up in me became harder to contain as Judge Sand next asked, "Do we have an exhibit of a Keffe's Louisiana Hot Sauce?" I took deep breaths and, after a while, finally looked up. If I laughed it was because it all made too much sense to me: raised on the Swahili coast, K.K. no doubt liked his tea sweet and his food spicy.

Shortly after the attack, an MCC employee had grabbed a handheld video camera to record the crime scene. One segment showed K.K. Mohamed naked, strapped face down to a gurney. The cameraman circled him and shot in smooth, slow motion, while K.K. remained totally inert. Each eyewitness from the MCC was asked by defense attorneys if K.K. had fallen hard, been punched, or battered by the shield. "No," came the universal reply; no one had used excessive force, even though K.K. had punched at least one of the guards, and other guards had sustained minor injuries. Hospital reports confirmed that both K.K. and Salim had been badly injured. At some point, K.K.'s nose and eye socket had been fractured.

Watching this in a New York courtroom it was hard not to think of the assault on Abner Louima and other instances when law enforcement officers turned violent. Both sides addressed the issue in their closing statements. Prosecutor Pat Fitzgerald, conceding that Salim had been injured with a key, minimized the effects, saying: "It must have happened. Adler and McAllis-

ter are telling you the truth. I submit to you under the stress of
the situation it wasn't as bad an injury as they thought."[4] The
potential for violence in jails and prisons—by inmates or those
who guard them—was an important issue during the "trial
within a trial." Arguing that K.K. had participated in the attack
on Officer Pepe, the prosecution asserted that his violent nature
could never be controlled, even in a maximum security prison.
For their part the defense not only argued against this view of
K.K.'s character but also pointed out that the purview of prisons—the job they do well—is controlling inmate violence.[5] The
prosecution's closing statement detailed the many ways that
prisoners routinely violate institutional rules, undermine procedures, and manage to use violence, especially against prison
guards. The idea that convicted prisoners, including terrorists,
cannot be controlled is terribly worrisome for victims, who want
certainty that an offender can never do violence again. To admit
defeat in this task called into question the foundational assumption that the government should use its vast resources and
power to incarcerate the dangerous, while protecting those who
guard them. Of course, human error, technological failure, or
other unforeseen circumstances could disrupt even the most me-
ticulous arrangements. Yet the inert body of K.K., and his shackled body in court, stood as proof of what we needed to believe
in: the state's ability to control violent offenders.

The crudely shot image of K.K. strapped to the gurney haunted
me for days. The reduction of a human to a mere body—one that
can be subdued, examined, regulated, and transported—is always striking and humbling. In this instance the violence that
had clearly been effected on that body was a reminder that any
body can also be damaged or killed, easily crushed, like an ant.
A body bruised and frightened under the control of the state begs
for mercy and, seeing K.K.'s body in this condition, drew out my
own feelings of pity. I resented that the trial had made me pity
K.K. Moreover, the parallel between the image of K.K. strapped
to the gurney and that of the condemned man, strapped down,
awaiting a lethal injection was undeniable. I wanted the state to
manage K.K.'s body, as it would any convicted criminal deserving punishment. I wanted the state to do this fairly and compe-

tently, to handle K.K. as a person, so that my thoughts need not dwell on K.K.'s body again.

In mounting their case, K.K.'s defense team had to focus on convincing the jury that the proposed mitigators outweighed the testimony from survivors and victims' family members, the evidence about the guard attack, and their own finding that K.K. had committed the crimes as charged. The defense attorneys identified factors that might have led K.K. to participate in the bombings, including his limited education, the loss of his father at a young age, and his intensive religious training and ideological indoctrination. They also planned to prove a classic mitigator: in hindsight, K.K. regretted his actions. At the same time K.K.'s lawyers would try to humanize their client by explaining his background, including his East African home and family. To vote for a sentence of life and not death, jurors would need to see K.K. as a person, perhaps even to develop empathy for him. Despite the prosecution's allegations that K.K. had a deeply violent nature, defense attorneys tried their best to depict their client as mild-mannered, pious, and nonviolent, a dupe caught up in a violent organization.

The defense turned first to Professor Jerrold Post, an expert on the psychology of terrorism, who, at their request, had interviewed K.K. for more than eleven hours on several different occasions in the weeks just prior to the penalty phase. In his testimony Post identified several incidents in K.K.'s background which he believed had led the defendant to participate in the bombings. First and foremost, K.K., when still a child, had lost his father, a mitigator that the defense hoped the jury would find persuasive. Post insisted that this event compelled "young Khalfan" to seek out alternative authority figures. He found them at the mosque in Zanzibar where he diligently studied the Koran, in his older brother who persuaded him to leave secondary school a year shy of graduation and relocate to Dar es Salaam to work in the family's retail shop, and in various charismatic Muslim leaders, especially those preaching in the mosque he attended in the city. Through lectures and casual encounters at mosques, K.K. learned about the suffering of Bosnian and

Chechen Muslims and became "consumed" with the idea that he should do something to help them. Post noted that K.K.—always a bit of a loner—relished feeling connected to a worldwide Muslim community. He longed for the training that, as promised in videos, would prepare him to serve as a uniformed soldier fighting alongside other Muslim men. As everyone in court knew, in the mid-1990s K.K. left Tanzania for the first time, headed for a military camp in Afghanistan, and, with Post's testimony, we finally learned more about why.

K.K.'s past included many of the standard experiences of a young Muslim man trained by al Qaeda operatives in Afghanistan, but the main thrust of Post's testimony was that K.K. differed from others who went on to become terrorists.[6] For one, his motivations began with the desire to help others, not to hurt anyone. To distinguish him from well-known terrorists such as Ramzi Yousef, and from al Qaeda members, Post carefully outlined K.K.'s subordinate roles during training and then in the bombing. To confirm K.K.'s lowly position, Post had also interviewed defendant Mohamed Sadeek Odeh, and that conversation allowed him to describe al Qaeda's unique approach to their personnel. In contrast to other terrorist organizations, they relied on nonmembers, like K.K., for logistical assistance. By virtue of al Qaeda's "tiered organization," those of lower rank or nonmembers (e.g., K.K.) were rarely informed about plans and strategies. As Post put it provocatively, "Khalfan Mohamed was distinctly not a member of al Qaeda. He was recruited to help with logistics. He falls into the classification of what they did strategically, of taking individuals committed to help Islam, to help the struggling Muslims around the world, and in effect brought him in in that role—distinctly not a member of the al Qaeda, distinctly not an Islamic fundamentalist terrorist indeed" (p. 8320).

Not an Islamic fundamentalist terrorist? Well aware of Post's training and long career profiling terrorists for the CIA, I tempered my initial reaction, which was to dismiss this conclusion as totally off the mark. Wasn't K.K. more than just a hired lackey? Hadn't he justified his political commitments through religion? I wanted to know more about K.K.'s motivations. For me, watching videos in the mosque (however inflammatory), and being susceptible to authority figures (however charismatic), failed to account for what seemed monumental decisions for an unsophisticated, uneducated young Zanzibari man. Yet, on rereading the trial transcript, I had to admit that Post's testimony backed up his outlandish conclusion. According to Post, K.K. contrasted himself with the Pakistani trainees he had encountered at the Afghan camps, noting that his comrades had "fire in their eyes." It may have been K.K.'s inability to understand the lectures on the group's ideology (which were delivered in Urdu, a Pakistani language K.K. did not understand) that accounted for him feeling, as Post put it, less "inflamed." Post built the impression that K.K. never understood some important messages, such as Osama bin Laden's role in the camps, al Qaeda's future plans, and its anti-Americanism, a position developed after K.K. had left Afghanistan. Still, as Post noted, K.K. was gravely disappointed when, upon finishing two training courses, camp leaders told him that he would not be needed for combat, and so he had no choice but to return to his job as a clerk in the family's Dar es Salaam shop.[7] At that moment, it seemed, K.K. had failed to establish himself as a credible Islamic fundamentalist terrorist.

Another difference between K.K. and al Qaeda members like Odeh or Salim was that K.K. was a follower. At the training camps in Somalia, and then later in Dar es Salaam, K.K. encountered many strong leaders, including Hussein who had recruited him for the jihad job that led to the bombing. As Post recounted, Hussein's request came not long after K.K. learned that his older brother was planning to close the family shop and leave for England to seek a better life. Desperate to follow his brother, yet unable to obtain a visa because he had dropped out of school, K.K. felt abandoned. Hussein's charisma drew K.K., the consummate follower, to accept the option in front of him: go to work for the Dar es Salaam cell.

But Post told us little about what K.K. was thinking when he agreed to do the jihad job. Maybe he was just following orders from Hussein, a persuasive leader. But a vignette Post related suggested that K.K. was not entirely passive. When dynamite was brought to the house that K.K. had procured for the group,

K.K. asked about the target, assuming it would be in Somalia. In a sharp tone, Hussein told him not to ask questions and to get him a soda. As K.K. told Post, he did what he was told—he brought Hussein the soda and stopped asking questions—but the pained look on his face indicated to Post how disappointed he was to discover his low standing in the group. Although it seemed that K.K. might have thought for himself at times, Post made a good case that, in general, he was a follower.

Post's testimony fascinated me. I was grateful to hear about K.K. from someone who had actually spoken to him and was neither his defense counsel nor a government representative. Although it took until their third interview, K.K. had eventually opened up to Post, even about incriminating topics. I suppose I valued Post's testimony, in part, because of his training as a social scientist, a psychiatrist no less, which meant that he interviewed and analyzed in ways more familiar and congenial to me than, for example, FBI interrogators, whose overt partisanship was inevitable. Interestingly, Post began with a typically anthropological impulse, saying that, in an interview, "I always try to put myself in the other person's shoes" (p. 8333). Post's effort to see K.K.'s world from the young man's perspective paid off; K.K. opened up. And, although I doubted that Post sympathized with K.K. or his position, his expression of empathy had resulted in a portrayal that was less scathing and less crowded with stereotypic assumptions about terrorist motivation than others drawn during the trial.

Yet I was so jaded by this point that I found it hard to accept at face value anything anyone said. As I thought more about Post's testimony, and listened to him negotiate Pat Fitzgerald's tough and contemptuous cross-examination, I was aware that, even though a professional, Post could not escape the partisan label that applied to most witnesses. He had a vested interest in supporting the approach he had developed as a terrorism expert. Crafty geniuses bent on ruthless violence (e.g., Ramzi Yousef or Salim) were one kind of terrorist, whereas K.K. was another altogether. Yet Post's accomplishment was impressive. Despite my own training and the value I placed on getting inside a person's world, I would never have been able to sit across from K.K. and interview him with the empathy needed to draw out the revelations Post's testimony described.

On cross-examination, Post made another crucial point: once K.K. had seen pictures of the bombings, especially of the dead victims, he regretted his participation, and, when he expressed remorse, had tears in his eyes.[8] Having been told that a defendant's remorse can facilitate a victim's healing, I listened carefully. As a counter to the reasonable assumption that a convicted capital defendant might say anything in order to save his own life, Post offered a clever twist: "I . . . said to him, 'Well, if you had the chance again would you still participate in jihad?' And to my total astonishment, he said, 'yes'. I was a bit taken aback. He said, 'I am a committed Muslim. I am committed to the cause for the suffering Muslims around the world. But there are many ways of doing jihad. Their jihad is not my jihad' " (pp. 8336–37). Post went on to explain that K.K.'s jihad would include starting schools, teaching Koran, opening clinics. Again paraphrasing K.K., Post illuminated yet another way in which K.K.'s thinking diverged from that of his al Qaeda trainers: "He said, 'My understanding of the Koran is that . . . there are no circumstances that justify taking innocent victims, and had I asked questions or thought, I now regret that I did not ask more questions about what they were doing' " (p. 8336–37).

Hearing that K.K. regretted the bombings took my breath away. Even more surprising, however, was the rush of sheer anger that inflamed me. For the very first time I was furious at K.K. Questions bubbled up: How could he have been so unthinking, so unquestioning, so irresponsible? How could he have had so little regard for his own community? K.K.'s remorse had humanized him for me. It had made him into a person, and that flawed Swahili man could finally be the subject of my expectations, my deep disappointment, and my sizzling fury. For a moment I was afraid that the rage his remorse brought out in me was destructive and vengeful. Testing my commitments again, I was grateful that I still could not wish that death would be K.K.'s punishment. Knowing that K.K. understood and accepted the depravity of his crime, I realized that he would inflict on himself an even harsher punishment than execution. For the rest of his life he would have a jihad job—jihad in the sense of individual struggle against internal temptation and evil. I thought this not out of satisfaction or pity but instead with resignation and a sick, plaintive feeling of frustration that maybe it all could have been avoided.

In the end, we knew K.K.'s perspective only from moments of desperation—under interrogation in South Africa and during the trial for his life—when he conveyed his remorse, or lack thereof, and always from the mouths of others. Thinking about those brief glimpses, I was persuaded that K.K. had thought about his actions, had felt regret (especially during the long months of his incarceration), and had changed his views. How the jury viewed these snapshots would determine their conclusion about the defense mitigator that "Khalfan Mohamed is remorseful for the deaths, injuries and other consequences of the bombing of the embassy and would not participate in such a crime in the future" (p. 8739).

The FBI had led me to believe that none of K.K.'s relatives would attend the trial, because they were all furious with him. When the group walked into court one afternoon, about fifteen in all, and took seats across the aisle, I was shocked not only because they had come but also because the atmosphere became unusually charged, as court marshals moved forward and stood abreast in the front and middle aisles. K.K. did not immediately realize that his family had entered, and once they were seated, the marshals blocked his view of them entirely. The relatives—standing and straining to see him—were quietly ordered to stay seated. When a Swahili interpreter who had been helping the family went partway up the aisle to get K.K.'s attention, a marshal angrily threatened to throw her out of court. Even K.K.'s attorney was rebuffed when he asked the marshals to sit so that K.K. could see his mother. Later on, when the marshals moved along and family members met eyes with K.K., faces initially lit up and then dissolved into tears.

Several times that day I glanced across surreptitiously, noting that, despite K.K.'s notoriety, his relatives looked to be members of a modest East African coastal family much like any other—and more like Jamal's family in cultural background, language, religion, dress, history, and ethnicity than any other Africans who had come to the trial. My relative, Saidi, looked across the aisle, shook his head, and said, "He has really dishonored them." His face reflected the mixture of anger and pity that none of us spoke of openly.

The first of six witnesses from among K.K.'s family and friends was a member of the "adopted" family for whom he had worked after escaping to South Africa. Shahima Dalvie, a young mother, had come on behalf of her relatives to stand up for the man they had known as "Nassor." As she explained, when Nassor came looking for a job at their Burger World restaurant, they hired him as a chef. His work and demeanor so impressed them that they invited him to live at their home. As Shahima testified, "We just felt that he was a good guy, that we needed to take him in and take care of him" (p. 8411). In her description, K.K. had led a simple life in South Africa. He worked. He taught the Koran to Shahima's mother and son. He prayed with her father-in-law. Unabashedly enamored of K.K., Shahima said, "We went as far as saying that Nassor is the kind of guy that we would marry to our daughters. That's how much we think of Nassor" (p. 8412). Shahima concluded by saying in response to Stern's question, "And have your feelings about him changed?" "Not at all. It will never change" (p. 8413). For Shahima, Nassor had to remain that helpful, pious young man who had needed and justified their charity and trust. Knowing that the jury had already convicted K.K., I wondered how they felt about the assertion of another Dalvie family member who testified on videotape that the Nassor they had known "wouldn't hurt an ant."

As Shahima spoke, K.K. convulsed with sobs, big tears raining one after another onto his shirt. He had cried like this just a week before, when attorney David Ruhnke described the conditions under which K.K. would be imprisoned for life, if the jury voted against the death penalty. Ruhnke had slowly spun out a haunting scenario that first asked the jurors to imagine having to live in a hotel room—"like a Holiday Inn"—for the rest of their lives, acknowledging that it might not be so bad, that they'd get

used to it, and then asking them to imagine being confined only
to the bathroom, with no TV or telephone, and then being
watched twenty-four hours a day and coming to realize that they
would never see their loved ones again. As K.K. cried under
Shahima's warm, sad gaze, was he comparing the image of life
in prison to the good life he had lived with the Dalvies—a decent
job, a nice family atmosphere, time to pray, respect for his religious knowledge? He could have been crying out of self-pity,
fear, shame, or remorse. Each time he broke down, one of his attorneys put a hand on his shoulder to steady him.

Beginning with one of his brothers, we heard from five of
K.K.'s relatives. Those who testified were asked simple, uncon-
troversial questions about K.K.'s childhood and character. Their
brief answers indicated the similarity between K.K.'s early life
and that of many Swahili boys who had grown up in the small
towns and villages on Zanzibar Island. His siblings acknowledged that K.K. had outdone the rest of them in school, sports,
and religious learning, and his unfailing kindness and mild
manner were mentioned repeatedly. Each family member or
friend who testified on K.K.'s behalf was asked a version of the
following question: If K.K. is executed, how will it affect you
and your family? Their replies resembled that offered by K.K.'s
twin sister Fatuma: "It will affect me badly." K.K.'s mother testified last. She struggled to remain composed as she talked of her
son as a "good child" and lamented that during their brief visit
at the jail a window had prevented her from touching him. Her
answer to the question of how K.K.'s execution would affect her
was predictable: "It will hurt me. He is my son." Her words and
tears underscored that family members shoulder a horrific burden when asked to come to a foreign country to plead for the
life of a relative, to be given very little time to do so, and to be
restricted in what they could say. And yet K.K.'s family members were permitted to express their opposition to K.K.'s execution. On the one hand, I believed that the accused should be able
to use any tactic whatsoever to fight a death sentence. On the
other, I believed that, just as my love for Jamal as his wife was
no reflection on the gravity of the crime, K.K.'s mother's love
for him should not bear on the severity of his punishment.

Whether the mother was still capable of loving a convicted murderer was as much a reflection on her, and on their relationship, as on the son's crime. Making families of the accused a party to determining the penalty places a huge responsibility on them in a moment when they are struggling mightily to sort through strong emotions.

Perhaps it was my sense of the burden faced by K.K.'s family that drew me to them. I found myself constantly aware of their presence just a few feet away. I wondered what they were thinking about the proceedings, how they were managing in these strange, bitter circumstances. My strong desire to connect, and my even stronger reflex to hold back, puzzled me then and now. K.K.'s family represented another opportunity to learn more about K.K. and his motivations beyond the clipped answers they had given on the witness stand. I wanted to blurt out to them: "Why did he do this? What did you know about it? How can we persuade other young men not to take the same path?" My questions would not be meant as accusations but rather as sincere starting points for engaging with them. I shared my ambivalence with friends; most urged me to protect myself. They warned that in a situation of so much pain on all sides little could come from such an exchange. In the courtroom, so far from coastal East Africa, our shared connection with Swahili culture certainly influenced my interest. But the courtroom context made acting on that sentiment unthinkable. Defense attorneys would have tried to protect the defendant's family from a victim's harangue. Prosecutors would have wanted to prevent any pretense of sympathy on my part or any action that might jeopardize the appearance of a fair trial. No one saw the divide between us as a chasm that could or should be breached.

The tension around my decision not to speak with K.K.'s family came to a head one afternoon when an interpreter who had been assisting them asked Mary Porter and I where K.K.'s relatives could get halal food, that is, food prepared according to Muslim dietary restrictions. Mary offered directions to the two restaurants we had been frequenting with Jamal's relatives and then, realizing that both families might end up eating in the same place, politely asked the interpreter to take the group elsewhere if they saw we were already there. The interpreter reacted swiftly, "We can eat there. It's a free country." Later that week we were sitting in the back of a tiny halal restaurant as several of K.K.'s family members walked in. We all tensed up. As we passed by them on our way out, I half nodded to K.K.'s sister. She smiled. Afterward, I realized that she had no idea who I was.

If things had gone a bit differently for K.K. in South Africa, he might not have faced the death penalty at all. After apprehending K.K. on a visa violation in October 1999, South African authorities granted the U.S. government's request to take custody of him. Together with local legal aid lawyers and the Dalvie family, K.K.'s defense team—funded by the U.S. federal court—filed claims in South African courts charging that K.K. should have gone through extradition proceedings before being handed over to U.S. officials. They argued that during an extradition process South African officials might have asked the United States to guarantee that K.K. would not face the death penalty.[9] South Africa's new Constitution had eliminated the death penalty and set into motion procedures to block extradition in cases where a suspect might face it. A lower court in South Africa upheld the constitutionality of K.K.'s treatment, but in mid-May 2001, as we were waiting for the guilt verdict in the embassy bombings case, South Africa's newly formed Constitutional Court issued a reversal. The Court held that K.K.'s "deportation"—it could not be called an extradition because the proper procedures had not been followed—violated South African statutes and also the constitutionally guaranteed protection of K.K.'s fundamental human rights.

Judge Sand ruled on the matter in a hearing on June 12. He began by praising South Africa's Constitutional Court and the quality of its jurists. He expressed his personal hopes for the country's future. But, with a firm tone, he held that the Court's opinion, although a plausible interpretation of South African law, had no relevance to the embassy bombings trial where U.S. law governed unequivocally. His reasoning was that, as a matter of law, once a defendant appeared in a U.S. court, how he got there no longer mattered. That said, the South African decision provided K.K.'s defense a bit of leverage. The following would be included with the other mitigators: "As a matter of South African law, Khalfan Mohamed should not have been released to American officials without assurances that he would not face the death penalty in the United States."

In their closing arguments the prosecution tried to convince jurors that K.K. had actively participated in the attack on Officer Pepe and thus posed a future danger in any prison population. Predictably defense counsel emphasized that the government simply had neither the witnesses nor the physical evidence to prove that K.K. played an active role. Each side painted portraits of K.K., and the depictions of his character could not have been more starkly opposite. Pat Fitzgerald held nothing back in depicting K.K. as ruthless and unremorseful for those killed. Fitzgerald hit on a brilliant image, arguing that K.K. was dangerous *not* because he has "the fire in the eyes" that other terrorists have but because he has "the ice in the veins, and he can play Mr. Nice Guy, but he sits there waiting to kill again." The "ice in the veins" was mentioned several more times as Fitzgerald went about depicting K.K. as a cold-blooded killer, a timebomb, and, finally, in another inspired stroke of rhetoric, Fitzgerald declared that K.K. "is a bullet that ripped through these 11 people and hasn't stopped" (p. 8560). The toll on the victims was mentioned repeatedly, including how Officer Pepe had been robbed of his human dignity. Officer Pepe's reputation for showing kindness to the defendants established him as especially humane in contrast to his attacker(s).

The defense grabbed this last chance to encourage jurors' empathy for their client. As he began his summation, David Stern insisted that despite the huge cultural gulf between K.K., who was raised sitting on school benches made out of coconut palms and breathing the Indian Ocean breeze, and the American jurors, who were raised on corn flakes and color TV, they all shared a basic humanity. As Stern argued, K.K. had demonstrated his humanity: he loved his family, and they would grieve for him. In the defense accounts, he became once again the "little guy from Pemba," humble, poor, and unsophisticated.

Such starkly different accounts of the attack, and such divergent images of K.K., were, for me, just more disturbing evidence
of the extremely partisan nature of this portion of the trial. For
victims who opposed the death penalty and thus saw no need
for a trial within a trial, sitting through the indeterminacy and
distortions of the penalty phase was a frustrating waste of time.
Did the jury resent as much as I did the desperate yanking on
our emotions? The penalty phase demonstrated that the extreme
nature of a capital prosecution called at times for the lowest tactics of lawyering, and everyone sunk to the occasion.

Jurors deliberated for three days. They failed to agree either to
sentence K.K. Mohamed to death or to life imprisonment. By default, he would spend the rest of his life in prison without the
possibility of parole. When we learned in court that the jury rejected the non-statutory aggravating factor that depicted K.K. as
a continuing and serious threat to others, it was clear that the
trial within a trial mounted to demonstrate this point had been
unpersuasive. Yet jurors' perspectives on K.K.'s character were
mixed. A clear majority voted for mitigating factors that might
have swayed some toward a life sentence (e.g., the fact that others of greater culpability would not face the death penalty and
that K.K. had acted out of religious belief). The jury was deeply
divided; one juror frowned and shook his head as their verdict
was read. Later interviews with the jurors would reveal some of
the contours of their differences, but at that moment their decision followed the logic of the al-'Owhali verdict and at the same
time rebuked the prosecution's attempt to prove K.K.'s involvement in the assault on Officer Pepe. One of the two mitigators
that jurors themselves added conveyed this directly: "Khalfan
Mohamed's last psychological report . . . judged his potential of
harm to others to be low."

Judge Sand thanked the jurors for their half a year of service
and noted that they had proved wrong those who had said that
"a case of this type could not receive a fair trial before an American jury" (p. 8760). He shook hands with each juror as the
panel filed out of the court's back door for the last time. After
a few remarks on logistical arrangements, Judge Sand ad-

journed the proceedings until September 19, 2001, the scheduled date for sentencing. I left the courthouse in a daze and
crossed the street to sit on a park bench. I had agreed to speak
with Ben Weiser, the *New York Times* reporter who had meticu-
lously covered the trial and would go on to interview the jurors.
When Ben phoned, I read him a statement that thanked everyone involved, especially the jurors, and expressed my sympathies to the victims and their families. I made the point that East
African victims still suffered economically as a result of an attack on U.S. interests that had nothing to do with their lives.
Then I admitted that, as an opponent of the death penalty, the
verdict in the K.K. Mohamed case was a "profound relief." In
a lofty tone I concluded: "Rather than seeking vengeance, I urge
anyone who is outraged or grieving to put their energies into
working for more justice and equality in the world and working
against violence in all forms."

Feeling tired, I left the park and boarded a subway headed to
Penn Station. Just as the doors closed, Tony Ricco ducked in. As
a defense attorney for Mohamed Sadeek Odeh, Ricco had had
no reason to come to court during either penalty phase. On
seeing him it hit me that finally the trial was over, and the bright
line between victims and the defense no longer held the same
meaning. He smiled when I said his name, and then became
more sober as I explained who I was. As he offered his sympathies for my loss, I reassured him that I appreciated what he had
done to ensure a fair trial. I told him about the K.K. verdict, and
he shook his head saying, "You know that's really the tragedy.
If you watch K.K. and listen to him, he's a nice guy. Polite, soft-
spoken. It's tragic that he got mixed up in this." I ventured that
K.K. seemed different from some of the others, and Ricco was
quick to agree, insisting that he would not have defended someone as unpredictable as Salim or others who were still "in denial." It cheered Ricco to learn that I had opposed the death penalty. We reached his stop, and he clasped my hand firmly before
stepping out.

Ricco's description of K.K.—nice, polite, soft-spoken—were the
same words used by several FBI agents I had questioned about
K.K. early on in the trial. "Mild-mannered," said one. "He didn't

Figure 9. Courtroom sketch of K. K. Mohamed and Judge Sand. Credit: Christine Cornell

even need to be cuffed on the plane from South Africa." After all the evidence I had heard and gathered, the basic questions remained: Who was K.K.? The simple, polite young pawn? Mr. Nice Guy with ice in his veins? An innocent honey bear filled with hot sauce? The Dalvies' eligible young bachelor who would never hurt an ant? Uncertain about how a trial could ever establish which of these might be the most true, another image came to mind: the food grinder used to pulverize the TNT that made up the bomb. K.K. had given the grinder to his nephew, telling him to be sure to have it thoroughly cleaned as it had been used for "impure" purposes. We would never know whether K.K. intended for the cleaning to destroy any traces of evidence or whether he simply wanted to be sure that a valuable household object would become useful again. No matter K.K.'s intentions, to me the grinder symbolized the possibility of rehabilitation.

K.K.'s character, and how it might change over time, will remain a mystery. With the jury's verdict, K.K. was destined to live, but he would suffer a social death. The Special Administrative

Measures (SAMS) under which he would be incarcerated prohibited any public communications. If his position against Americans hardened, or if he denounced Osama bin Laden, I would never be told. Only if the SAMS were lifted would I, as a victim, learn more about his character, his condition, why he had committed the crime, and what he thought about it all in hindsight.[10]

But hadn't we already heard enough about K.K.? By the end of the penalty phase I found myself seized with the feeling commonly expressed by victims that the trial was "about the defendant" and neither about those harmed nor about the causes of the crime. At the outset of the book *Eichmann in Jerusalem: A Report on the Banality of Evil*, based on the author's reporting of Adolph Eichmann's capital trial, Hannah Arendt noted the limits on the purview of a criminal court even in so extraordinary a case: "Justice demands that the accused be prosecuted, defended, and judged, and that all the other questions of seemingly greater import—of 'How could it happen?' and 'Why did it happen?', of 'Why the Jews?' and 'Why the Germans?', of . . .—be left in abeyance. . . . On trial are his deeds, not the sufferings of the Jews, not the German people or mankind, not even anti-semitism and racism."[11] So many who observed the proceedings, or who followed Arendt's dispatches in the *New Yorker* magazine, were incensed at these limits.

Although offering a definitive verdict, trials inevitably fail to satisfy the desire of victims and the public for answers to broader questions. Even recognizing beforehand that the trial's mission necessitated a focus on the defendants, I continued to believe that ignoring certain other topics hindered the development of a coherent explanation. Still asking "why" at the trial's end, I realized that this small question had multiple dimensions. At its broadest, the question expanded to other questions such as why a group like al Qaeda exists and why is the group attacking U.S. interests. The trial offered the answer regarding al Qaeda's own ideology, expressed in its documents and videos: al Qaeda had organized in response to U.S. policies in Iraq and the Middle East, including the presence of American troops in Saudi Arabia, and with the goal of establishing Islamic governance, possibly worldwide. Left unresolved after the trial were whether other reasons existed such as the involvement of another government or unsettled scores between the United States and the mujaheddin—and perhaps other parties—after the Soviet campaign. Other than bin Laden, depicted as a megalomaniacal fanatic, the composition of al Qaeda leadership, and their motivations, were relatively unelaborated. At that point experts had just begun studying al Qaeda, and yet many had the sense that it was a new type of terrorist organization. Some members were very well trained, and their goals were long term. I was not particularly motivated to delve more deeply into explanations at this global level, especially because the trial had shown me that considerable information about the higher echelon of the organization and its history was still concealed by its members and those trying to stop them.

The penalty phase had addressed the "why" question at the other end of the spectrum: why did one individual, namely, K. K. Mohamed, join al Qaeda and participate in the bombing? Yet I was frustrated that Professor Post's analysis of K.K.'s motivations focused primarily on individual psychology, especially on the effect of K.K. losing his father. As an anthropologist with interests in East Africa, and as a victim seeking explanations, getting into K.K.'s social world was of more interest to me than getting into his head. From my perspective, explanations had to lie at the nexus where individual psyche and global ideology meet in real-life social, political, and economic circumstances. Pursuing a middle-range "why" question intrigued me no doubt because of anthropology's tendency to focus on context. Although Post had filled in some activities of the military camp where K.K. had trained, and a social history of K.K.'s family prepared by a defense consultant offered more detail about the places where he had lived, I needed to know more about the environment that had shaped his views on the ground, in Dar es Salaam, at the mosques he attended, through the neighbors who patronized his brother's store. This young man had not lived in a vacuum, and I wanted to know who or what supported him and his choices. During the trial we had learned little about the Dar es Salaam of the early 1990s, where K.K. had somehow become radicalized.

The politics of that and other local settings, including Zanzibar and Kenya, remained a vague background in the defense portrayal. Given my connections to the region, and my presence during the time when K.K. had made these choices while other young men had chosen differently, I wanted to reexamine this place I knew so well to understand why K.K. had been pulled into religiously motivated violence.

We learned at the trial that a Dar es Salaam mosque had been the site of K.K.'s personal transformation into someone seeking to join a global movement to help Muslims. Throughout East Africa, mosques have long been centers of community interaction and thus formative contexts for young men in particular. Although my own experience in mosques was limited, I knew that they had also been sites of controversy, where different forms of Islam converged and factional struggles over religious interpretation and authority ensued. Various factions—whether passing through from abroad or having grown up from the grassroots—have used mosques to champion a reformist perspective of one kind or another. Some have advocated various fundamentalist beliefs. Although these efforts at reform sometimes led to bitter factional struggles in mosques and surrounding communities, they never seemed to overwhelm local perspectives, and beliefs that threatened to silence others had been met with opposition. Even Wahhabbist discourses, although strongly represented and well funded, constituted minority perspectives kept in check by a local ethic of tolerance. K.K. had made the point to one of his interviewers that recruitment to al Qaeda operations always happened *outside* mosques, albeit by people he had met inside. The struggle over forms of Islam in East Africa in the years leading up to the bombings begged questions about the ideologies that had been circulating and whether extremist perspectives had begun to make inroads against local, more tolerant practices. Were these ideologies accompanied by political projects that urged Muslims as a community to oppose other populations seen as oppressors, including the United States or Russia? I had never encountered significant anti-Americanism in East Africa, but was I looking in the wrong places? Or overemphasizing coastal Islam's pluralistic tendencies? Or ignoring what might have been right in front of me? If such discourses had been right in front of K.K., what effect had they made on his choices and on the choices of others around him?

I thought about these questions in relation to an incident that had occurred five months before the embassy bombings. Jamal and I had just returned to Dar es Salaam from a trip to Zanzibar. We had trouble getting a taxi from the ferry dock downtown out to the university. When we finally found a driver, he told us he would take us the long way around as there had been trouble on the main road. A prominent mosque was the site of a riot involving young men, and a Tanzanian military unit, called the FFU (Field Force Unit), had been brought in to subdue them. Jamal joked in Kiswahili, "FFU—Fanya Fujo, Uone," which translates as "Make Trouble, You'll See." News accounts showed the trouble that the young people, mostly male, had made as they emerged from the mosque to smash kiosks, destroy merchandise, and throw debris in the street. Accounts also described the FFU beating the rioters. Several participants and bystanders were killed, and hundreds of people, primarily Muslims, were arrested. Later, when some of those arrested made accusations of having been beaten as well as suffering torture and sexual assault while in custody, authorities refused to investigate. From across the religious spectrum, Tanzanians viewed the incident as a terrible abuse of authority by the secular state, even as they condemned the rioters' violence. Media accounts insisted that radical elements in the mosque had incited the youth. Aryeh Oded, a scholar who analyzed the incident, explained that the mosque had been under virtual siege by the Tanzanian government, which accused mosque officials of harboring preachers who had delivered anti-Christian sermons. Government demands to turn over the preachers had led to a buildup of tension, which erupted into the violent street protest. The incident heightened the already grave concern over religious politics and its putative links to broader fundamentalist beliefs and calls for violence in the name of Islam. The mosque appeared to be the site of both outside and local influence that plunged a wide range of Muslims into a struggle against the government and the surrounding non-Muslim community.

As I thought back over the 1990s there was no shortage of incidents involving violence between East African Muslim communities and either the secular state or a non-Muslim population. Dar es Salaam had seen riots over shops selling pork. Zanzibar had witnessed political marches turned violent, especially in relation to local elections where discourses of Islam were used to unite voters. Kenya had struggled with violent protest during the rise and eventual fall of the Islamic Party of Kenya in the early 1990s. In many instances governments brought control through the use of significant force. In these incidents rhetorics of politicized Islam were expressed and contested by many parties. Further exploration of the dynamics might reveal the influences on K.K. and his co-conspirators, on other East Africans who had chosen violent tactics, and on the broader population, some of whom participated in violent incidents and many others who rejected violence. I sought to understand the individual–local community–global nexus of ideology and experience that brings people to violence in the name of politicized religion. Such an analysis would illuminate the nature and strength of globally circulating ideologies that counsel violence in the name of Islam and the on-the-ground experiences that sometimes produce adherents. It would also interrogate local perspectives that had always valued and appreciated the humanity in others and the need to avoid violence for that reason.

The anthropologist David Parkin, with long experience in East Africa, cautions analysts to take great care in interpreting political activity undertaken in the name of Islam. He makes this point in a brilliant analysis of a rally and march that he witnessed in the mid-1990s in Zanzibar. Many of the young male participants carried banners that called for Zanzibar to join the Organization of Islamic Conferences (OIC), despite opposition from Tanzania's central government. During the march they damaged tourist bureaus and curio shops that lined Zanzibar's streets and served the island's thousands of visitors. In analyzing the incident Parkin questions the easily drawn connection between the march and a global fundamentalist movement.

Even though the banners expressed political positions circulating globally, such as political unity through the OIC and the de-
nunciation of Western nations, Parkin sees in the hands of the
young men "blank banners," that is, signs conveying something
more and something other than the words written on them.
They reflected the young men's inchoate desires to resist against
their particular local conditions. Among these were the experience of tourism as altering their lives ("consuming them," in
Parkin's view) and offering them little in return. These young
men were frustrated as well by another economic problem: the
skyrocketing inflation of payments made to potential brides
prior to marriage. The inability of many young men to raise sufficient "bridewealth" had resulted in delayed marriages and the
sexual frustration that can ensue in a gender-segregated society.
A final issue of contention was the Tanzanian government's increasing control over political expression, especially politicized
religion. This mixed bag of sentiments—impossible for the
young men to articulate concisely—was expressed through
proclamations in the rhetoric traveling globally at the time. No
doubt some in the crowd knew exactly what the signs said, but
others may have had less interest in the words than in harnessing the power of the international to protest the local.

Believing anthropology to be a "great irritant" to sweeping
generalizations about the reach and strength of global movements, Parkin argues that "looking closely and intensively at a
particular, local Islamic movement, such as in Zanzibar, we find
so much at the level of explanation that simply does not fit the
global rhetoric."[12] Parkin's approach helps to make sense of similar incidents of protest using political Islam launched in East
Africa in the 1990s.[13] Certain globally circulating ideologies
might have been opaque to the youth involved, yet the harsh
effects of the global economy on their lives were all too real. By
the mid-1990s tourism had begun to be a grave disappointment
in Zanzibar and other parts of the coast. The region was generally suffering from marginalization in the global economy, and
young people found few employment opportunities as the neo-
liberal age took hold. Hopelessness and demoralization extended even to those who had been well educated and especially

to those in the disproportionally undereducated Muslim community. Young men, in particular, felt they had been bypassed by the global economy. Migration from the region, another effect of the global economy, had multiple impacts. For some it was a ticket to economic stability. For those unable to obtain visas (e.g., to the United States or Western Europe), it heightened alienation. Those who migrated to work in Saudi Arabia and the Gulf States were exposed to varieties of Islam, including fundamentalist perspectives which some brought back home. In Kenya and Tanzania the sense among many Muslims that they faced discrimination by the government fueled both despair and opposition. Charges were routinely made that the state denied Muslims services (e.g., education, passports, and other documents) and curtailed their political expression. The use of police and other armed forces to quell protest became a rallying point for those who sought to counter governmental oppression and justify their own use of violence.

By directing attention to the economic and political factors behind some acts of violence in the name of religion, I do not mean to excuse K.K. or anyone else who might, out of feelings of humiliation, anger, or hopelessness, choose to ally with a strong oppositional ideology that promises a new regime whether on earth or in heaven. Rather, my intention is to highlight the complex set of conditions under which potential followers might be cultivated. Ignoring the local complexities of economy and politics leaves only simplistic images of holy wars declared by ruthless leaders and blindly followed by faceless adherents. Such images explain little and impugn whole populations. They also miss the fierce dynamics of local struggles and thus offer little insight into reducing the power of those ideologies. Many communities in East Africa have been embroiled in struggles involving fundamentalist discourses and projects, calls for violence and deployments of it, discrimination and government repression, and community discontent and factionalism. And yet, from what I could tell, the region had produced only a few K.K.'s and a shallow pool of supporters of violence in the name of Islam. Despite the embassy bombings having occurred on East African soil and that incidents of violence occurred throughout the 1990s, it seemed that the influence of a global politicized Islam had been some-what contained. Repressive tactics by the state accounted in part for holding radical viewpoints in check but also stimulating them. It would not surprise me, however, if the ideologies es-poused by these minority Muslim populations, which had al-ways managed diversity in religious practice and politics, also played a role in sustaining a pluralistic context and controlling those who sought to silence others, especially with violence.

My continued quest to fill in the local background, to know what the young men around K.K. were saying, many of whom had not joined radical groups or acted on their beliefs with vio-lence, came partly out of a sense of guilt that I had been only vaguely aware of the conflict brewing at the time and the heavy pressures on young Muslim men, including our family members, our neighbors, and my students. In hindsight, I can see that my question had begun to shift from why K.K. had signed on to a violent movement to why more people around him did not join in. In the midst of framing these issues, just two months after the verdict in the embassy bombings trial, the attacks of September 11 put my quest to know why in a very different light.

CONCLUSION

At a time when everything has been globalized, from capital to communications to production, what about justice, what about its globalization? In an age when humanity is being redefined and unified across
frontiers, who speaks in humanity's name, who judges and punishes in
the name of that humanity?
—Ariel Dorfman, *Exorcising Terror*

In the aftermath of September 11, 2001, the term "jihad" is all too familiar to most people. To both the Muslim fanatic and Muslim-hating
xenophobe, jihad is simply "holy war" declared by Muslims against
Westerners. For the Muslim apologist, jihad is instead purely the inner
struggle against one's own selfish tendencies. Neither interpretation
takes into consideration the possibility of engaging and transforming
the social order and the environment in a just and pluralistic fashion
that affirms the humanity of us all.
—Omid Safi, *Progressive Muslims*

IN THAT INSTANT on the morning of September 11, 2001, when
smoke and fire heralded a massive attack on the United States,
the East African embassy bombings turned into a precursor, a
wake-up call. Pundits asked whether that call had gone unanswered or had those few officials who had been working frantically to address the threat been ignored or stymied in their efforts or had flawed intelligence and institutional jealousies stood
in the way of an effective response. Despite several commission
reports and a dozen best-sellers on the topic, the question of
why the embassy bombings—and other warning signs—failed
to stimulate a response to prevent the attacks of September 11
will never be answered to anyone's satisfaction.

The 9/11 attacks also changed the meaning of the embassy
bombings trial. Speculation erupted almost immediately over
whether the trial might have caused the attacks; two of the planes
hit just blocks from the federal courthouse where the convicted
embassy bombers still awaited sentencing.[1] Terrorism experts
rushed to point out that an attack of such scale and strategic complexity must have been developed too far in advance to have an-

ticipated the timing of the trial. On another point, prosecutors aggressively disputed charges that the trial had publicized information used by al Qaeda operatives to avoid detection as they planned the 9/11 attacks; they insisted that no classified material had been made public at the trial.[2] Still other critics maintained that the trial and, in general, the criminal justice approach to terrorism constituted diversions from more effective responses. In their view, had President Clinton followed up the missile strikes in August 1998 with additional military action, particularly in Afghanistan, 9/11 might never have taken place.[3]

These criticisms minimized the accomplishments of the embassy bombings trial, as if to assert that, once the United States was attacked on its own territory, the painstaking search for justice through the legal system was no longer the best response. At the same time journalists and commentators turned eagerly to the trial transcript and scrutinized its pages to learn more about the organization, ideology, and operations of the group behind the latest attack. The evidence presented at the trial constituted the most significant public record about al Qaeda. It troubled me, however, that those who mined the transcript drew on evidence without questioning its validity. They reproduced statements that had been challenged in court and quoted liberally witnesses whose character was impugned by their al Qaeda affiliation. It was as if the jury's guilty verdict had rendered truthful everything presented, including the words of the prosecution's star witness Jamal al Fadl and other al Qaeda operatives. Given the trial's many flaws and drawbacks, including documents censored, hearings sealed, the defense largely silent, and so much effort focused on achieving or preventing a death sentence, the process could hardly be viewed as an open forum for producing the truth about al Qaeda terrorism.

The creation of a public record of terrorist activity—despite its flaws—was an important accomplishment of the embassy bombings trial. The trial also succeeded in providing recognition to victims for our suffering and losses. These factors, combined with the trial's role in explaining how the bombings came about and in responding definitively through the verdict and sentences, were important to me and, I venture to say, to the public.

Throughout this book I have contended that the embassy bombings trial—as an open terror trial—was invaluable because it provided these elements of justice. And yet it was inherently imperfect. Any criminal prosecution raises concerns about fairness, and a terror trial that prosecutes an attack on government interests is even more prone to the abuse of state power. I was grateful for all that the embassy bombings trial had offered and accomplished but, afterward, remained concerned that the state's massive power had been deployed in ways that compromised the ideals behind the many invocations of justice at the trial.

Some might argue that, once 9/11 brought even more evidence of al Qaeda's destructive goals and capabilities, abuses of power through the response of the criminal justice system were hardly worth noting. Yet, in addition to providing the elements of justice mentioned above, the embassy bombings trial—similar to any open terror trial—also offered an opportunity to showcase the American legal system and the values at its core. To an extent that surprised skeptics (including myself) who, from the outset, wondered whether the embassy bombings defendants would get a fair trial, the U.S. government rose to the challenge, particularly by appointing talented defense counsel and meeting virtually every expense request made by all parties. Judge Sand's careful consideration of thorny issues at the heart of judicial fairness (e.g., the conditions of interrogations conducted abroad) served to highlight the commitment to justice of the U.S. legal system. After 9/11 it seemed to me even more important to retain and display this commitment. Yet the official responses to 9/11 largely bypassed legal remedies by focusing on military actions. Also, the intensification of security measures domestically and internationally restricted freedom of movement and invited racial profiling. New legal and extra-legal procedures for questioning and detaining suspected terrorists also led critics to charge that the growing war on terror included significant compromises of civil liberties.

My experience at the sentencing of the embassy bombings defendants, held on October 18, 2001, confirmed both my support for open trials and also my reservations about their provision of justice. For me, the trial was flawed not, as some have argued, because it diverted the U.S. government from more extensive military responses but, among other reasons, because it failed to ask the deeper questions that might have begun to illuminate why violence was directed against U.S. government interests in the first place. What drew these attacks and plunged the U.S. into a war of terror and, eventually, a war on terror? Why had these and other young men become involved? I am not so naïve as to imagine that pursuing answers to such questions might have prevented 9/11 or al Qaeda's other attacks. Nor do such inquiries replace trials or investigations. Rather, the pursuit constitutes a quest for justice in another form, beyond the law, and is crucial to understanding the threat posed by terrorists and the even more challenging project of preventing terrorism in the long run. My own attempts to develop greater knowledge of the dynamics through which extremist ideologies gain adherents in local venues, as outlined in the previous chapter, are but one approach. Fundamentalist beliefs and unilateralist actions are the clearly articulated twin symptoms of the problem in those contexts, especially when these perspectives advocate a disregard for the value of human life in all its diversity and for the dignity of individuals. When this disregard is also reflected and reinforced in the surrounding political and economic conditions, quite extreme perspectives can readily gain influence. Reaching across differences to explore the dynamics of those contexts—however frightening and distasteful a project—is itself an act that runs counter to a unilateralist reaction, which would assume the superiority and validity of one's own perspective. The kind of pluralism that would recognize and foster human dignity must be given a role in working against terrorism. Reaching across differences to develop more precise analyses does not imply acceptance or tolerance of every ideology, group, or individual. Rather, it repudiates fundamentalism by recognizing that at the very root of fundamentalism lies its most dangerous weapon: the closing down of inquiry, especially across differences.

Security at the sentencing of the convicted embassy bombers was more elaborate than it had been during the trial, and the courtroom was packed. With the death penalty no longer a possibility, I accepted the offer to address the court. No doubt I was swayed by the same powerful motivations that had led other victims to participate in the trial's earlier phases: the desire to tell my story and Jamal's, to reach empathetic listeners, to represent those who could not be present, and to achieve recognition as a victim. I was the first to take the stand. No one had given directions on what to say, and I was grateful for the freedom to tell my story—uninterrupted and unguided—in a manner of my own choosing. I began by saying that, until the death penalty had been ruled out, I had felt unable to participate in the trial. That was my message to the prosecution and the judge. I then described the terror of the bombing and the frightening aftermath but did not dwell on that horror, as I knew that the telling might overwhelm me. My intention was to draw a sharp contrast with the defendants' stated beliefs when I said: "Jamal was a deeply religious Muslim, in the most admirable sense. His life was guided by the ideals of kindness, charity, faith, mercy, and respect for life." At the words—respect for life—I looked straight at K. K. Mohamed; he stared back and then looked down. In mentioning what had been lost through Jamal's death—such as his pivotal role in the family and community, and the guidance, especially religious, that he had provided his sons—my goal was for the defendants to comprehend that they had cut short the life of someone committed to promoting and fostering Islamic values. It was to the broader public that I spoke when I mentioned several collaborative projects—charitable, intellectual, and commercial—that Jamal and I had been pursuing between his Kenyan community and my own in the United States.

Several victims spoke after me. One young woman read a poem about missing her mother's love and then asked the judge to pronounce the sentence so that "justice will come our way." An American man injured in Tanzania made reference to the possible involvement of Iran in the embassy bombings and wondered why the U.S. government had not pursued this connection. Several who spoke used strong language to condemn the defendants and made no effort to hide their disappointment that the jury had not voted to execute al-'Owhali and K. K. Mohamed. Their words expressed the double anger of vengeance thwarted.

Any plans to bring victims or other observers from overseas to attend the sentencing were rendered impossible by the security measures adopted after the attacks of 9/11. Letters from East Africans were likely among the many sent to Judge Sand expressing views about the appropriate punishment. Similar to the Americans, they would no doubt have recognized their lost loved ones and spoken of their own grief or injury. Some may have broached the question of financial assistance, given that so many in East Africa continued to suffer economically.[4] About a year later I gained some insight into their perspectives about punishment when I viewed the videotape of interviews with Tanzanian victims that had played a role in the trial's penalty phase. K. K. Mohamed's defense team had arranged for the victims to be interviewed one-on-one by an East African man trained in mediation. In Swahili he asked each victim to narrate his or her experiences related to the bombing. After stories that depicted their shock, loss, and grief, most victims described their continued difficulties and mentioned that they had received only minimal assistance, what is locally called "something to wipe the tears." Then, after warning that a "hard question" was coming, the mediator asked each what punishment they thought K.K. should receive, and every victim indicated a preference for life imprisonment over the death penalty. Their wide-ranging justifications included religious beliefs and a concern that K.K. had been used by superiors who would escape punishment. Several victims asserted that life imprisonment punishes harshly because it separates a prisoner from his family. This deprivation seemed to be both an especially important indicator of the severity of imprisonment and an appreciation of the fundamental humanity of the prisoner, whose continued interest in family was assumed. None of the Tanzanians expressed a desire for the defendants to suffer physically, although they did say that imprisonment would and should force K.K. to contemplate his crime for the rest of his life.

But the more I examined the taped interviews for clues into how these victims felt about the death penalty, the more convinced I was that treating the videotape as a factual record of their views was inappropriate. It was not that victims had been untruthful but rather that their responses were clearly shaped by the odd context, that is, a conversation with representatives of the American defense team. The videotape confirmed that victims' views of capital punishment and their decisions about participating in a capital trial are rarely clear-cut or predictable. As victims anticipate a prosecution, attend the trial (or watch from afar), and adjust to its aftermath, they have various reactions to capital punishment, and many repeatedly evaluate their beliefs and their own role in the trial. Trials test victims' abstract beliefs. The variety of our expressions at the sentencing displayed yet again the differences among us as victims. We had experienced the tragedy differently. We were treated in different ways by a legal system to which we had made mutually exclusive requests that reflected this diversity. No trial could have offered any of us or all of us everything that we might have asked for. I ended my statement by mentioning the evolution of my views as an explanation for why I refused to speak about the emotional impact of losing Jamal, saying, "I need not tell you [about that impact], because I have come to believe that there is nothing that you, as the judge or the state, could do to these individuals that would sooth the sorrow that haunts me, having lost Jamal." I told the court that I would look elsewhere for solace but would look to them for "justice" and for the guarantee that those convicted would be prevented from injuring others and would lose their liberty as punishment.

Through my own experience at the sentencing, I came to appreciate that victims can benefit tremendously by appearing in court to tell their stories. Speaking straight to the judge, the public, and the convicted bombers gave me a rush of emotional satisfaction. And yet I was grateful that the punishment the defendants received did not depend on my words alone or on whether I had been articulate enough for the judge to appreciate the depth of my sorrow. It would also have been unwise for me to treat my participation in the trial as a prerequisite for personal healing. Given that the prosecutors are fickle as to how they include victims in trials, and given, too, that victims' needs are so varied, trials hold out unrealistic promises despite the rhetoric of the victims' rights movement. For some victims, financial assistance might have soothed what the trial left still raw. But many, especially if their material needs are not acute, find money an empty panacea. One victim told me, a year after the trial, that all he had really wanted after the bombings was a signed letter of apology from a high-ranking U.S. government official, not a document that could be scrutinized to reveal an admission of criminal liability but a sincerely stated recognition of the pain he had suffered in service to his country. Perhaps, like me, others wanted a serious inquiry into why these events had happened at all.

In his nonfiction book about the death penalty, the novelist Scott Turow highlights several "exceptionalities" that are routinely mentioned in debates over capital punishment. The first is that, as a punishment, "death is different," because it is irrevocable. This quality is frequently invoked in arguments against the death penalty. But balanced against this perspective is the contention that "murder is different" in comparison with other crimes and thus warrants an exceptional punishment. This argument relies on the sensibilities of the victims' families, as well as the irrevocable nature of death through murder, to justify its call for the death penalty for convicted murderers. After 9/11 another exception emerged: "terrorism is different." Surveys taken after the attacks found broad support for executing those responsible for 9/11. Even people who had previously opposed the death penalty expressed the view that terrorists deserved it.

In one respect, murder by terrorism is different because it is murder committed during an action against a government (or a group) for a purported political end. Without discounting the pain inflicted on those who lose a loved one through such an act, its horror also stems from the threat to the state and the disruption of the state's duty to protect those within its borders. Although every murder challenges state order, murder by terrorism positions the targeted government differently. The focal charge against the four defendants—conspiracy to kill Americans—implicated the state in the conceptualization of the crime.

But the emphasis on America as victim provided a counterpoint to the treatment of each individual as a murder victim in his or her own right. Repeatedly prosecutors referred to the murder of the individual victims to depict the real horror of the crime. They pursued this strategy in the guilt phase of the trial when they dismissed defense attorneys attempts to depict the embassy bombings as acts of war between the United States and al Qaeda, and again in the penalty phase when they justified the death penalty by emphasizing the harm caused to murder victims and their families. References to individual victims rather than to America were doubtless more effective for jurors. Undertaken in the name of political ends, and with states or other entities as its target, terrorism has a two-faced image that captures its harm to states and to individuals. The trial's tendency to vacillate from one face to the other depending on the tasks before the adversaries made it harder to appreciate that the real horror of terrorism comes because, in harming individuals, it also uses them for political ends. How to reflect this in a legal context, how to capture both faces at once, was a challenge unmet in the adversarial context of the embassy bombings trial where splitting the two faces of terrorism served tactical goals.

Attempts by the defense to depict the bombings and other al Qaeda activities as salvos in a war against the United States emerged for the final time when two of the four defendants—Mohamed Sadeek Odeh and Wadih el Hage—made statements at the sentencing. (The two others had allowed their counsel to speak for them briefly.) Before Odeh spoke, his defense attorneys asserted their client's disavowal of any responsibility for the bombings, his remorse for the deaths and destruction in East Africa, and yet his continued affirmation that he had participated actively in the military branch of al Qaeda in an effort to "change oppressive circumstances." In his own remarks, Odeh asked the court why a trial had taken place when the United States had already punished Afghanistan and Sudan for the bombings through missile strikes in 1998 (p. 117–18). Next, Wadih el Hage read a rambling statement in which he asserted his innocence by arguing that he had never supported extreme acts, such as the bombings. The condemnation of U.S. foreign policy—the familiar litany against U.S. support for the embargo in Iraq and for Israel, and the presence of U.S. troops in Saudi Arabia—highlighted the notion of al Qaeda terrorism as war, where violence justifies violence in return.

Prosecutor Pat Fitzgerald's ears flamed as he stood to respond. He began by admitting that prosecutors rarely speak at sentencings and that he had not intended to do so. With barely controlled fury he reminded the court that el Hage had chosen to work for al Qaeda and, when asked, had refused to provide the U.S. government with information about the organization's criminal activities. Through that behavior, which included numerous lies, and his other work for al Qaeda, el Hage, according to Fitzgerald, "betrayed his country, he betrayed his religion, he betrayed humanity." Fitzgerald's depiction of el Hage as a traitor, as someone with merely the pretense of being an American citizen, again invoked the scenario of a war between the United States and al Qaeda and, curiously enough, the image of Fitzgerald and the other prosecutors as fighters positioned on the front lines.

If the notion of the American nation as a target of the embassy bombings lies behind the prosecution, then it is possible to view the embassy bombings trial itself as another salvo in that ongoing war. Perhaps the jurors realized this when they agreed with the mitigator that executing al-'Owhali would make him a martyr and thereby refused him an act that would play out another of al Qaeda's strategies.[5] The image of the trial as a weapon in a war contrasts with fundamental notions of law and prosecutions as offering a justice wholly separate from state violence. Such ambiguity in the trial was only heightened by the specter of the death penalty, which, in this rubric, could be interpreted as an act of violence in the ongoing war. Simply put, imposition of the death penalty would contribute to the confusion between punishment as an end product of justice and punishment as the next offensive. An ultimate punishment, one that is exceptional in that its physical violence results in death, blurs the line between the meting out of retributive justice and the tactics of war.

Arguments over the death penalty have often focused on what it symbolizes about a nation's underlying values. The embassy bombings trial displayed internationally U.S. support for the death penalty, which had been abandoned by so many other nations. The comparison was highlighted when Judge Sand dealt with the opinion of the South African Constitutional Court concerning K. K. Mohamed's deportation. Even though the nation was in the throes of severe economic inequality, a related high crime rate, and a history of oppression, the post-Apartheid government decided that the power to execute criminals was not one they needed. Perhaps those leaders—many of whom had experienced the wrath of the Apartheid government—rejected the tools of rule that displayed symbolically and materially the underlying values of the old regime. They knew too well the ease with which such tools could be used unjustly. Internationally, critics of the death penalty depict it as barbaric, as counter to an ethic of respect for human life, a conclusion that embarrasses me as an American.

Defenders of the death penalty insist that it can be viewed as an act of retribution—not of vengeance—and thus remain consistent with the concept of just punishment. Yet the argument becomes strained when the same government that prosecutes the crime and carries out the sentence is also positioned as the target of the attack. In such an instance, arguably the case with the embassy bombings, it becomes difficult to ensure that vengeance has not motivated the punishment. Tempering the power of any government always poses a challenge but becomes especially difficult when the state, as a victim, might choose the prerogative that individual victims sometimes claim when they act on vengeance. The state pursues vengeance more subtly by including victims' voices in the trial, which risks articulating the revenge that might readily grip individuals in pain but has no place in a quest for justice intended to serve broader goals of the public. In trying to make this point in a conversation with Pat Fitzgerald prior to the penalty phase, I asked him whether, as an undergraduate political science major at Amherst College, he had studied with Professor Austin Sarat, whose perspective on the American death penalty had influenced my own reasoning. I had hoped that Pat might have encountered Sarat's ideas, including his point that "state killing . . . both expresses sovereign prerogative and . . . satisfies public desires for vengeance by responding to the pain of the victims of crime. However, responding to those desires reveals both the weakness of the state and its strength, its dependence and its power. State killing co-opts the call for vengeance and the politics of resentment as much as it seems, at first, to express them."[6] The revenge that motivates individual victims, that society might want to express, and that Sarat argues can be co-opted by a state pursuing the death penalty might creep even more readily into the government's approach to prosecuting accused terrorists, when their crime—almost by definition—threatens state sovereignty. And yet acting on vengeful motives is precisely what weakens a nation's ability to pursue justice and to maintain its sovereignty unquestioned.

Controlling the urge to act with vengeance or the related urge to make use of victims' sentiments of vengeance became monumentally more difficult after 9/11. The prosecutors and their assistants, many FBI agents working on terrorism, and the federal court staff worked just blocks from ground zero in Manhattan. Knowing what they did about al Qaeda, and powerless to stop its harm, they felt keenly the impact of the attacks. When we gathered with prosecutors for the last time in the victim/witness lounge after the sentencing, Pat Fitzgerald told us about one of their own who had died when the World Trade Center collapsed. John O'Neill, a central figure in the FBI's investigations of terrorism, had resigned his government position to become head of security at the World Trade Center. A good buddy of Pat's, O'Neill had worked tirelessly to convince superiors in the FBI and other agencies that the U.S. was vulnerable to an al Qaeda attack. A documentary about O'Neill, produced after 9/11 by the Public Broadcasting System, called O'Neill "The Man Who Knew" and reported the distressing fact that his superiors in the Justice Department and in the FBI had dismissed his warnings. Pat, so hard-nosed throughout the trial, fought back tears as he asked us to remember O'Neill, his family, and his sacrifice in our prayers. I would never have wished for Pat to know personally what it felt like to be in the moment of greatest calamity—to lose a close friend and colleague—and to lose him through a political act that caused more terror. If Pat's harsh comments at the sentencing reflected sentiments ranging from grief to rage to futility to a desire for revenge, he could hardly be faulted. But the challenge of controlling those emotions, of tempering the urge to act rashly or with vengeance after such an attack, might be yet another reason to deny the government the power to deploy an ultimate, irrevocable punishment.

Similar to any ritual, the trial had a certain aesthetic in that it consisted of a sequence of actions followed through to a conclusion, the sentencing, itself a ritual with a beginning, progression, and end. Rituals move people through time to a new moment, transforming them from one status to another. The sentencing offered an end point to a process that, until then, had yielded what felt like unending pain. Although we all knew that legal appeals, further media coverage, and other unanticipated developments might follow the sentencing, we also knew that, when Judge Sand pronounced a definitive sentence for each defendant, the ordeal would be over. Many of us believed this despite our deep victims' knowledge that, after a tragedy, there is no "closure," something those who love us hope desperately we will find.

An earlier ritual had been another important marker of my own transition. Just four months after the embassy bombings, I had returned to Malindi, Kenya, for a ceremony to mark the end of my edda, the "waiting period" after Jamal's death. Never having attended such a ceremony, I followed the lead of Jamal's sisters, who had invited a couple dozen female guests. We softly chanted prayers, and then someone watching for the clock to reach the moment of Jamal's death said, "Now." Fauzia motioned for me to follow her to the bathroom. At her direction I showered and put on the attractive new dress and headscarf she provided. She sprayed me with perfume and held up a mirror while, with hand shaking, I put on bright lipstick. Two women led me back among the guests who came forward to greet me. Each shook my hand, kissed me on both cheeks, and handed me a wrapped gift. The packages came faster and faster, and soon I was overwhelmed by their generosity and rejuvenated by the whole experience.

Afterward it dawned on me that the ritual to end my edda resembled the ceremony that a Swahili bride participates in just prior to her wedding, when she is bathed and adorned by her close female relatives and friends. The anthropologist in me recognized it as a rite of passage marking a bride's transition on her way to a new status as a married woman. Purification achieved through bathing and the change in social status made evident through donning new clothes and makeup are central features of such rites. The anthropological interpretation was glaringly obvious: the ceremony constituted me as having left behind my status as a widow, including the seclusion and restrictions of edda, to rejoin the community of Swahili women.

After my return to the United States a few weeks later, I described my experience to my support group of other young widows. They enjoyed my description, but some looked puzzled and disappointed when I pointed out the connection between the ritual to end edda and the one that prepares a Swahili bride for marriage. Not hiding her skepticism, one group member asked if I had felt ready for such a major transformation. I was honest about my ambivalence. On the one hand, I still felt like a widow and certainly had no interest in remarrying so soon after my loss. On the other hand, the ceremony had felt positive. Another group member wondered if the ritual risked hurrying a woman out of widowhood when she might want or need more time. "Maybe," someone ventured, "a widow could ask for the ritual to be delayed until she felt ready?" "No, it doesn't work like that," I tried to explain. "It's a legal time period; it's not negotiable." Heads shook; looks of disappointment turned to disapproval. The group's facilitator intervened, "It's good that you got a lot out of being there and out of the ritual," she said. "But remember, *you* are in control. No one can force you to adjust too quickly or to feel anything, if you don't want to." Her point reflected the "if-that's-what-you-feel-that's-okay" approach to grief, which is assumed to empower a widow by putting her in charge of her emotions and entitling her to reject the attempts of others to control or judge her feelings. Yet that bedrock of contemporary grief counseling failed to capture something important about my experience in Kenya. It felt gratifying to be welcomed back into the community by women who recognized and paid tribute to my suffering as a widow. This point led the American widows' group to lament the rarity of community recognition for their plight. For me, the community's assertion of my changed status, and its expectation of changes in my behavior, allowed my emotional state to transform. Even though we all knew that I remained devastated by losing Jamal, his community—with no compulsion and no insistence—affirmed its understanding were I to feel or behave differently than I had in the first months after Jamal's death. I agreed with the young widows that no one could tell me what to feel. And yet the ritual, as a community intervention, allowed me to choose from a broader swath of the emotional spectrum and counteracted hesitancy or guilt if I experienced moments when my abject sorrow lifted, when I laughed or smiled or appreciated beauty once again.

That said, the transitions of status experienced by widows, and by victims, are delicate operations. As widows and victims travel paths of recovery toward fuller engagement as actors in the social world, their behavior garners scrutiny. Who decides when is it time to move beyond the role of victim? When it is appropriate for a victim to respond actively or aggressively to the harm that has occurred? Which actions, if pursued by a victim, might negate that very status? These questions apply to the "nation as victim" as well as to individuals. In the case of the United States, as one of the victims of the embassy bombings and subsequent attacks, the international community has watched with high expectations. I do not mean to draw too sharp a contrast between Western individualistic approaches to recovery from grief and ones where African communal norms might predominate but rather to highlight that the course of recovery for victims—whether individuals or nations—includes a role for a larger community. My own view is that attempts to stay within community norms can help in the transition toward recovery and effective response.

The U.S. government's odd position as a targeted victim of terrorism is one reason why a conventional adversarial trial falls short of achieving justice and why new approaches to justice might be warranted. Changes in terrorism itself also suggest that alternatives be pursued. Globalization has altered terrorism; its membership and operating sphere cross borders more routinely than in the past. As stateless entities, groups such as al Qaeda defy the conventional categories used to address acts of violence; thus it may make more sense to prosecute their crimes before an international body, such as the new International Criminal Court in the Hague or a special tribunal. An overarching international body, as representative of the global community, can perhaps raise questions that are beyond the purview of the victims, including the targeted nation, to address broader concerns. The U.S. government would likely have resisted such a prosecution at the time of the embassy bombings and has actively attempted to limit the jurisdiction of the International Criminal Court. Yet an international decision might have served everyone by offering a resounding condemnation of terrorism more relevant globally than a verdict from a U.S. court. Individual victims would face trade-offs in the difference between a trial in a national legal system and one overseen by an international body. For instance, American victims of the embassy bombings might have felt more removed from the proceeding at the same time as an international body might have provided a more satisfying response for those victims with ties to East Africa and concerns about the U.S. role in the prosecution.

Those who would design alternatives to prosecuting terrorist acts through national adversarial systems can examine other legal and quasi-legal institutions and processes for insight and strategies to consider. Truth and Reconciliation Commissions, forged in South Africa and then adopted elsewhere, operate by encouraging all parties to a conflict to come forward with claims against those who have harmed them or to explain their own wrongful behavior. Such forums are especially useful in situations where political violence has harmed parties on all sides, that is, where no one's hands are clean. Such forums emphasize the importance of airing multiple accounts of the tragedy and seeking some agreed-upon "truth" of what happened. The broad exploration of motives that takes place in such settings might produce a more complex picture of the origins of terrorism. Efforts also are made toward reconciliation when the parties are willing, although reconciling may be of less interest to parties who have suffered violence from an amorphous global network than, for example, those harmed in the genocide in Rwanda, where survivors and family members of victims must figure out how to continue their lives side by side. Creative thinking about how to address the multiple needs of victims, the public, and nation-states, and to do so at an international level, might lead to innovative and productive responses that serve a wider array of people. For instance, individual victims might also benefit from a different type of setting or additional venues for publicizing the incident. For me, a broader forum, where multiple accounts could be presented and a wider range of issues pursued, might have served my interests in learning more about why the bombings happened.

After 9/11 the U.S. government's responses to terrorism indicated little interest in broader forms of inquiry. In fact, the role of the justice system in responding to terrorism was subordinated to that of the military through the invasion of Afghanistan. Several key al Qaeda operatives were killed in that war, including at least one high-ranking member indicted for the embassy bombings, and others responsible were targeted. Others captured in Afghanistan or Pakistan or in raids in other nations and transported to Guantanamo Bay detention facilities or interrogation sites might have been involved in the embassy bombings, perhaps even among the indicted, but secrecy surrounds these detentions. The whereabouts of some individuals taken into custody remains unknown,[7] including Ahmed Khalfan Ghailani, a Tanzanian indicted for the embassy bombings and captured in Pakistan in 2004, and rendition to third countries has been a key means of handling suspects. The conditions under which all these detainees are held and the techniques of interrogation generally mean that information gained from them will be unacceptable in U.S. courts. The effort to bring trials has bumped up against the desire to keep information classified, particularly concerning sources of intelligence and the details of U.S. operations in the war on terror.[8] It is hard not to draw the broad conclusion that, in the post-9/11 climate, the U.S. government's power has been used to cordon off inquiry into terrorist activities and to limit the presentation of such material through the judicial system.

The events of 9/11 affected the punishment of embassy bombings defendants even after their trial concluded. Each defendant had intended to appeal his conviction. The defendants became concerned, however, after 9/11, when it seemed that anyone associated with al Qaeda would have great difficulty obtaining an impartial trial. It is no surprise that intervening events would influence a retrial; however, the great likelihood that they would operate retroactively to turn a life sentence into one of death, and after only a short period of time, is evidence of the death penalty's arbitrary application. Wadih el Hage's attorneys requested a retrial when they learned that videotapes of prosecutors interviewing the government's star witness, Jamal al Fadl, had not been provided to them before the trial. In denying the request, Judge Kevin Duffy (who replaced Judge Sand) criticized the prosecution's "inaction, incompetence, and stonewalling," which he believed came close to jeopardizing el Hage's conviction.[9] Given the attitudes underpinning the war on terror, the Special Administrative Measures under which the embassy bombings defendants have been incarcerated are unlikely to be lifted. When I interviewed him a year after the embassy bombings trial ended, defense attorney Tony Ricco lamented the impact of the SAMS on his client, Mohamed Sadeek Odeh, and criticized the broader social implications: "I think there's a great deal that, as a nation, as a people, we can learn from listening to those who have taken their anger to another level and that when we silence them we ultimately do ourself a disservice down the line." I had to admire Ricco for his ability to imagine that he could learn from al Qaeda's discourse, given that we were sitting in his office just across the street from the gaping hole that had been the World Trade Center. Despite experiencing destruction up close, Ricco remained committed to asking hard questions including why al Qaeda's violence had come to his doorstep. Although I was sanguine about whether hearing more from any individual defendant would clarify why terrorism gains adherents, as a general principle the silencing brought about by the SAMS goes against my sense that our overall response to terrorism as a nation and as a global community must have inquiry at its heart, even as it protects, defends, and punishes. Uses and abuses of government power through imposing strategies of silencing, closing down, and shutting up, which have been pervasive in the war on terror, rankle the impulse in me that believes open inquiry to be the cornerstone of a just society.

Since 9/11, there have been no shortage of accounts by scholars, policymakers, and journalists relating the origins and effects of terrorism. Many have proffered answers to the "why" questions that I found so challenging. Most useful for me were those that explore the contexts where fundamentalist, unilateralist, and repressive ideologies have encountered other ways of thinking and the outcomes of such meetings. Less useful were scholarly ruminations that focus on identifying an inherent evil in certain Islamic ideologies. In these approaches attention is directed to how extremists draw on distorted versions of Islamic texts to convince followers to engage in violence. While carefully noting that these are extremist views, these commentators highlight the role of Islamic ideology as the prime motivating factor underlying terrorism and the key to its power. For instance, Jean Bethke Elshtain had little to say about the actual contexts in which these ideologies operate and discounts the importance of the political spheres in which they develop and gain strength.[10] This leads her to conclude that changes in American foreign policy are unlikely to stop radical Islamic ideology from its destructive path. Identifying a bad strain of Islam—one resistant to political influence—not only locates the problem in a disembodied religion but fails to account for how people become part of movements allied under an ideology. It also offers little insight into how Muslims and others counter these movements.

Opposing discourses have long met in complex arenas, where local, national, and global politics shape the influence of particular ideologies. Examining the economic and political dynamics that have afforded extremist views more sway is a strategy that refuses the premise that ideologies—and fundamentalist ideology in particular—can have an a priori power to garner supporters. The dynamics of these contexts vary considerably; however, noting similar patterns across contexts is a step toward building strategies to confront the interplay of ideology and contextual features that results in destructive campaigns. For instance, the presence of political oppression influences which ideologies (and their related movements) gain strength. Economic opportunity, or lack thereof, also figures importantly, as young men, in particular, search for the means to support themselves and construct meaningful lives. My familiarity with the Kenyan situation, where extremist ideologies had been countered in the past with moderate success, indicates that the interests of national governments in controlling violence are key in shaping the rise of ideologies. But state control cuts both ways. Depending on the tactics used, governmental power can contain or eliminate those voices advocating violence, and yet the use of tactics that disregard human rights can fuel the oppositional logic that leads disaffected individuals to join groups promising a new regime. Heavy involvement by repressive governments has meant that local negotiations are largely eclipsed or hijacked.

When the embassy bombings trial ended, I believed that continuing to examine such contexts for what they would reveal about terrorist violence would offer an approach to justice more satisfying than what I had experienced through the trial alone. But as the military responses to the 9/11 attacks mounted and the war on terror began in earnest, it became difficult to pursue the research that would lead to a fuller analysis. For one, the actions of those who justify violence through extremist ideology had become more deadly and more widespread. In November 2002 Kenya suffered another attack by extremists linked to al Qaeda who detonated a bomb at a seaside resort and attempted to shoot down an Israeli tourist jet. It may be the case that some of the violence in the post–9/11 period was long planned and carried out by militants already in position; however, new recruits also seemed to be signing on, even as al Qaeda membership was being depleted through military and policing action in many countries.

Research in East Africa has also been made more difficult by the war on terror. The Kenyan government's fight against actual and suspected terrorism has been fierce, garnering much local criticism. Kenyan officials have worked in concert with the United States and other governments to flush out suspected al Qaeda members, other religious extremists, and their sympathizers operating in East Africa. For their part, Muslim leaders in Kenya have insisted that terrorists from outside the nation have cruelly used their communities and that, as a result, the Kenyan state and the U.S. government have unfairly targeted them. In coastal Kenya feelings of anger, frustration, and humiliation have mounted. Muslim leaders, who initially pledged to work against terrorism, and with the Kenyan government and the FBI, have witnessed the negative effects and lament that the turmoil has created sympathizers of violence in their midst. Charges of police abuse, secret detentions, intimidation, and abusive interrogations have led to public demonstrations. It seems that Kenyan Muslims, who had previously welcomed and admired Americans—including tourists and naval personnel who dock at Mombasa's port—have been repositioned as another of America's Muslim enemies. Kenyan leaders point out that the attention to fighting terrorism has eclipsed donors' interests in addressing Kenya's pressing economic and political needs.[11]

Inquiry in the midst of such a strained situation is not impossible, but violence and its threat pose significant barriers. Those who would conduct research on such settings have to admit that, even without intending to, researchers can put those whom they study at risk. If it were possible to conduct effective and ethical research at this time, it would likely demonstrate that what has transpired in East Africa may have turned more hearts and minds against the messages that the United States has always championed in Kenya and elsewhere, such as democratic exchange, rule of law, and pluralistic values. In the future, the answer to the question of why the violence continues may be directly linked to the very factors that preclude research: vio-

lence and oppression by a national government heavily supported by the United States. Given the political situations in Pakistan, Iraq, Afghanistan, Egypt, Israel, and the West Bank, this
answer will likely apply well beyond the nations of East Africa.

In the years surrounding the turn of the century, violence in
many forms—political, religious, state-sponsored, ethnic—has
thrust millions of people into moments they experience as the
greatest calamity of their lives. As in the story Jamal told me
about his father's death, such moments test one's faith, as sensations of shock, fear, rage, and grief can lead a person to act with
abandon, to seek revenge, and to destroy those who caused the
harm. In the moment of greatest calamity—at the death of a
loved one or a trusted colleague—the instinctual reaction for
most is unilateral self-defense, whether closing in or lashing out;
sudden death through terrorism may make the latter option
more likely. In pursuing one's unilateral interests, including legitimate self-defense, it is easy to put aside even strongly felt
values, such as the need to treat others with humanity. Many
actions taken in that moment of calamity look like retaliation.
　　In urging patience at the moment of greatest calamity, the hadith Jamal espoused would have those who are plunged into
calamity create a self-imposed barrier to guard against rash or
unthinking reactions. For believing Muslims, the patience so difficult to find in oneself in such moments demonstrates individual faith. For everyone struggling with strong feelings of grief
or fear, patience offers a pragmatic pause, one that might ensure
responses based on sober contemplation. Relatedly, victims
often say that an overwhelming tragedy focuses perception. The
rattling teacup that Ambassador Prudence Bushnell remembered hearing just after the Nairobi bombing is evidence of the
clarity of victims' perceptions in the midst of chaos. Many victims also experience an ethical clarity. A calamity underlines the
superficiality of most everyday preoccupations and thereby
makes core values—"what is *really* important"—stand out in relief. However one names this process, realizing priorities or
gaining perspective taps into foundational values that are
needed to navigate a tragedy. In the moment of greatest calam-

ity, finding the patience to pause, to plan, to inquire, to remember, and to show respect for life before acting is an exceedingly difficult task that asks much of victims but ultimately offers its own reward. For a response to terrorism to have any chance of remaining defensible and projecting a path toward the future, that response cannot suspend the values of acting judiciously, wisely, and with mercy.

The negative consequences of an unthinking or violent response increase exponentially when the victim lashing out in revenge or retaliation is a powerful government. And when that government has more power than any other nation on earth, the consequences can be extreme. Such power used in retaliation will almost certainly stimulate a sense of oppression and, in the long run, will draw attacks on its power.

Another aspect of the exceptional nature of terrorism is that in producing moments of calamity it forces victims to live with the idea that the moment of greatest calamity has yet to occur. In an interview about the significance of 9/11, conducted in October 2001, the great literary critic Jacques Derrida opined that "the ordeal of the event has as its tragic correlate not what is presently happening or what has happened in the past but the precursory signs of what threatens to happen. . . . A weapon wounds and leaves forever open an unconscious scar; but this weapon is terrifying because it comes from the to-come, from the future. . . . Traumatism is produced by the future, by the to-come, by the threat of the worst to come, rather than by an aggression that is over and done with."[12] His point is that we live with the idea of massive acts of terror—the embassy bombings, 9/11, the bombings in Bali, Madrid, Tunis, and London—as precursors. They remind us that the worst still looms. Although I agree that fear of future attacks has been a pervasive reflex in the post–9/11 era, and many actions have been taken with that scenario in mind, I disagree that this perspective is the inevitable consequence of terrorist acts. Rather, the tendency to live in fear of future calamity makes necessary a new project that would counteract the shadow of impending horror. The critical task is to push aside the specter of that horror by focusing on what a more harmonious social existence might look like and how we might achieve it. From my view this would require imagining vibrant pluralistic contexts, where diverse groups interact in a dynamic coexistence of multiple beliefs and values. Imam Abdul Rauf articulates nicely the need to put scholarship and practice in service of such visions when he invokes Europe's grand pluralistic past: "We strive for a 'New Cordoba,' a time when Jews, Christians, Muslims, and all other faith traditions will live together in peace, enjoying a renewed vision of what the good society can look like. In this good society all religious voices are welcome and given maximum freedom, and no one religion (or even atheism) is allowed to inhibit any other. Toward this dream we aspire."[13] Having the patience to project that vision before us in the moment of greatest calamity, and to keep it prominent in our thoughts and goals in the aftermath, would guide us toward productive and just responses.

Acknowledgments

ALTHOUGH THEY CANNOT all be named here, I am grateful to the victims of the East African embassy bombings and their loved ones, whose willingness to face the future after such a tragedy gave me strength to illuminate our experiences for others. Some enriched this book by sharing their experiences, formally and informally, including Howard Kavaler, Sue and Edith Bartley, Patricia Waggoner, Sita Magua, Blue Blais, Dudley Sims, Connie and Andy Simoson, Henry Kessey, and Ken Mease.

I want to thank Ambassadors Prudence Bushnell, John Lange, and Charles Stith for their thoughtful reflections and their courage. My understanding of the trial deepened through interviews with prosecutors Ken Karas and Patrick Fitzgerald, who worked with unparalleled drive and talent. Dedicated FBI Special Agents Mike Forsee and Abigail Perkins answered my many questions, and I appreciated all their dedication. Conversations with defense attorneys David Ruhnke, Anthony Ricco, and Ed Wolford heightened my respect for their skill and revealed new dimensions of justice. My respect for Judge Sand was only heightened by a conversation in which he graciously offered his perspectives. Terrorism expert Jerrold Post contextualized the bombings and the trial. Excellent reporting by Melissa Block (National Public Radio), Benjamin Weiser (*New York Times*), Phil Hirshkorn (CNN), other journalists, and sketch artist Christine Cornell created a rich record. I am very grateful to Janice Sandt, always a steady and empathetic victims' advocate, and to Kendall Montgomery and her staff in the State Department's Office of Casualty Assistance.

Wesleyan University was among several institutions that sponsored my work. I am grateful to Wesleyan colleagues and dear friends who encouraged me from the project's beginning, including Paula Auclair, Douglas Bennet, Douglas Charles, Mary Ann Clawson, Robert Conn, Kehaulani Kauanui, Lincoln Keiser, Susan Lourie, Akos Ostor, Joanne Palmer, Kate Rushin, Jennifer Scott, Anu Sharma, and Elizabeth Traube, and, finally, student research assistants Sepideh Bajracharya, Sonia Silbert, and Monica Cuquoz.

The National Humanities Center, where I held the Hurford Family Fellowship, provided the perfect venue for writing. My thanks to Kent Mulliken and a wonderful staff, particularly Bernice Patterson. Joanne Rappaport and other colleagues in the Writing Group offered helpful comments, and I appreciated the company of Jenefer Robinson, Moshe Sluhovsky, and especially Helen Solterer whose sweet sense of words helped me avoid some early ponderous prose.

The book took shape during two stints as a Rockefeller Fellow at the Kluge Center in the Library of Congress. Many thanks to Director Prosser Gifford, Les Vogel, the Kluge Center staff, and Center fellows. Melhem Salman's friendship inspired me; his generous reading of many chapters helped me to realize what was really at stake in this book.

Colleagues at George Mason's Institute for Conflict Analysis and Resolution (ICAR) provided an engaging atmosphere as the project neared completion. ICAR Director Sara Cobb offered an early astute reading and invaluable support. Thanks also to research assistants Talha Kose, Min Zaw Oo, Julie Shedd, and Lisa Shaw.

My writing benefited from the comments of audience members at talks hosted by Yale, Duke, Georgetown, George Washington, George Mason, the U.S. Naval Academy, the Library of Congress, University of California at Santa Barbara and at Irvine, and the Institute for Policy Studies in Washington, D.C.

Comments from Austin Sarat, Lawrence Rosen, Richard Weisman, Mark Shire, Susan Coutin, and anonymous reviewers improved the manuscript. My "kin" in anthropology, Mack O'Barr, John Conley, Jan French, and Naomi Quinn, offered insightful suggestions and steady encouragement.

I am deeply grateful to Deb Chasman of the *Boston Review*, who helped me to find the voice that would do justice to my message. Many thanks to my agent, Wendy Strothman, for shaping the project and to her assistant, Madelyn Medeiros. Princeton University Press editor Fred Appel read the manuscript with care, and I greatly enjoyed working with him and the entire staff at the press. Thanks to Tad Slawecki for producing the map and to Rita Bernhard for careful copyediting.

I could not have undertaken this project without the encouragement of friends in and out of the academy, including Karen Bock, Susan Coutin, Betsy Geherin, Delna Ghandhi, Steven Gregory, Mindie Lazarus-Black, Sally Merry, Regina Schuller, and Susan Shapiro. Cynthia Horan and David Cameron offered advice and support at crucial moments. I turned often to my friend, Ashraf Rushdy, for encouragement and always was given the perfect suggestion of what I might read for motivation. For many years Alice Schumacher's patient advice has kept me moving forward. Although we met late in the writing process, Michael Sullivan's deep caring enabled me to finish, perhaps because he helped me to envision a bright future. I am overwhelmed with gratitude to Mary Porter for her support throughout, especially her willingness to revisit painful memories with the insight of an anthropologist and the sensitivity of a longtime friend.

Knowing I had the enduring support of family made this project possible. I have tried to honor my father's memory by weaving through the book his deep sense of justice. For inspiration and encouragement I owe much to my mother, Rena Hirsch; my brothers, Rubin and Kevan; my sisters-in-law, Leslie Bulion and Amy Hirsch; and my four accomplished nieces, Sally, Jen, Julia, and Isabel. I am also thankful for support from my Kenyan family, especially Fauzia, Mohamed Jelani, Saidi Athman, Shamsa Ali and her family, and to Jamal's sons Ali, Mohamed, and Iqbal. Asante sana.

Jamal's strong spirit still guides me; I can only hope that I have done justice to his memory and our commitments.

Notes

INTRODUCTION

1. Just a few days before the attacks Clinton had appeared before a grand jury to testify about his relationship with White House intern Monica Lewinsky.

2. The missile strikes were criticized by many governments, particularly in Africa and the Middle East.

3. Secretary of State Madeleine Albright, from an interview on CNN's *Larry King Live*, August 20, 1998. As reported on the Federation of American Scientists website at http://www.fas.org/man/dod-101/ops/docs/98082101_tpo.html (accessed July 2003).

4. On August 20, 1998, Senator John McCain (R–AZ) said, "Today's military action against Usama bin Laden's terrorist infrastructure in Afghanistan and Sudan is a welcome response to the August 7 terrorist attacks against the American Embassies in Kenya and Tanzania. I know I speak for all Americans in supporting the U.S. service members who took part in this operation, and in hoping that the strikes clearly signal our will to retaliate against terrorists who target American citizens abroad" (Federation of American Scientists website at http://www.fas.org/man/dod-101/ops/docs/98082802_ppo.html [accessed July 2003]).

5. The federal death penalty was extended to a wide variety of crimes through Pub. L. 103–322, 108 Stat. 1959 (1994).

CHAPTER 1

1. From Sahih Bukhari, vol. 2, book 23, no. 389. Narration by Anas (bin Malik?). A former chief kadhi of Kenya offers a similar quote: "Thawabu za kusubiri hupatikana kwa kusubiri pale anapofikwa na msiba" (The value of patience is obtained from being patient at the time of grief) (Sheikh Abdulla Saleh Farsy, *Mambo Anayofaniyiwa Maiti Bidaa Za Matanga Na Hukumu Za Eda* [Zanzibar: Mulla Karimjee Mulla Mohamedbhai, 1966], p. 4).

2. Years later Mary told me that, as we began the two hour drive from Mombasa to Malindi, I related the story of the bombing and the complicated logistics of getting from Tanzania to Kenya. She said that I spoke calmly and in great detail, for at least half an hour straight. Mary was the first person from my life in the United States whom I encountered face to face after the bombing. I must have needed to pour out my story to her, in English.

3. Farsy, *Mambo Anayofaniyiwa Maiti Bidaa Za Matanga Na Hukumu Za Eda*.

4. See John Middleton, *The World of the Swahili* (New Haven: Yale University Press, 1992).

5. Alamin Mazrui and Ibrahim Noor Shariff, *The Swahili: Idiom and Identity of an African People* (Trenton, N.J.: Africa World Press, 1994).

6. The percentage of Muslims in Kenya is a matter of dispute. Estimates range from 15 percent to 35 percent, with the Kenyan government insisting on the smaller percentage and Muslim leaders the higher.

7. The early days of mourning are called *matanga* after the large straw mats placed in the living room and bedroom for visitors to sit on.

8. Renato Rosaldo, "Grief and a Headhunter's Rage," in idem, *Culture and Truth: The Remaking of Social Analysis* (Boston: Beacon, 1989).

9. Susan Hirsch, *Pronouncing and Persevering: Gender and the Discourses of Disputing in an African Islamic Court* (Chicago: University of Chicago Press, 1998).

10. *Edda* is a waiting period following a death or divorce.

11. The edda of divorced women was often treated lightly. Stories abounded of divorcees in the edda period attending weddings and enjoying themselves in public. Whether divorced or widowed, men are not sanctioned by the Koran to wait before marrying again.

12. The struggle over how I was to be symbolized exposed a deeper tension: the widow, in a classic anthropological sense is betwixt and between. No longer a wife and not yet available for marriage—the two largest categories of women—a widow occupies a temporary and unstable position that is highly ritualized and often circumscribed from everyday activities. Writing about political widows in South Africa's apartheid period, Mamphela Ramphele notes, "Widowhood sweeps women into a liminal phase in which the woman's tie to the departed spouse is publicly reenacted. . . . The widow becomes the embodiment of loss and pain occasioned by the sting of death, and her body is turned into a focus of attention, as both subject and object of mourning rituals. The individual suffering of a widow is made social, and her body becomes a metaphor for suffering" ("Political Widowhood in South Africa: The Embodiment of Ambiguity," *Daedalus* 125, no. 1 [1996]: 99).

13. A prominent scholar of Islam highlights the emphasis on unity in Islamic spirituality: "Islamic spirituality is precisely this seeing the one, uttering the Name of the One, and knowing the One who is God in His absolute Reality beyond all manifestations and determinations, the One to whom the Quran refers as Allah" (Seyyed Hossein Nasr, ed., *Islamic Spirituality: Manifestations*, vol. 20, *World Spirituality: An Encyclopedic History of the Religious Quest* [New York: Crossroad, 1991], (p. xiii).

14. Jamal was known for his skill in harnessing spiritual power to help others, by guiding those in a trance or possessed by spirits who speak through them. Jamal engaged spirits, talking to the possessed person, teasing out from them hidden plans and desires, or even accusations released in the cathartic moment. In a small community such revelations ruptured, regulated, and renewed social relations, as reported by scholars of these practices including, among many others, Jeanne Bergman, Linda Giles, John Middleton, and David Parkin.

15. For instance, in a small　　　book outlining the proper behavior after a death and during t'e func　　　udge condemned as un-Islamic the practice of wailing after　　　.earing one's clothes.

16. Just a few years e. er a　:ismatic political leader—Sheikh Khalid Balala—had galvanized the support of young Muslim men who joined him in pursuit of a radical political agenda focused on ousting the existing local and national leaders affiliated with Kenya's ruling party. He had been educated outside Kenya and was thought to have returned with outside backing. Balala was harassed by the Kenyan government, jailed, and then released under questionable circumstances. Eventually the popularity of his brand of political Islam faded.

CHAPTER 2

1. In the weeks after the bombings, hundreds of highly motivated FBI agents descended on East Africa to mount the most massive investigation ever conducted by the U.S. outside its borders. For many agents, it was the first time to participate in a foreign investigation. Their wide-ranging tasks included establishing who was killed and how, collecting evidence from the bomb sites (e.g., explosives residue, human remains, and vehicle parts), conducting searches and raids on the perpetrators' suspected hideouts, following up on previous wiretap and surveillance investigations of suspected al Qaeda cells in the region, and chasing down leads stimulated by the rewards program.

2. At a joint press conference, Tanzania's Minister for Foreign Affairs and International Relations responded to what others might have been thinking about relations between Tanzania and the United States, given the charges of fellow East Africans that the U.S. had brought the bombing disaster on itself: "We are still friends. America is not the enemy. We know that the perpetrators of terrorism are the enemies. The Americans hate them as well as we do" (Lucas Lukumbo, "US-Tanzania Ties 'Unruffled'," *Daily News*, August 19, 1998, p. 1).

3. Watchman, "The Cutting Edge," *Daily Nation*, August 21, 1998, (p. 9).

4. Ibid., p. 86.

5. Madeleine Albright and Bill Woodward, *Madam Secretary* (New York: Miramax Books, 2003), p. 366.

6. Kenyans amassed a fund for bomb blast victims that provided assistance to some of those who were injured and their families.

7. Almost three years went by before funds allocated for educating the children of Tanzanian victims began to be disbursed.

8. The civil suit, *Odillia Mutaka Mwami et al. v. The United States of America et al.* CA 99–125 (CKK), filed in January 1999 by Washington, D.C., attorney Philip Musolino on behalf of forty Kenyans. The defendants were the United States of America, Usama bin Laden, al Qaeda, Sudan, and Afghanistan. The charges drew heavily on the Accountability Review Board report, which had criticized security at the embassy in Nairobi.

9. Although a few East Africans came to some events, most of the Africans injured, and their families—whose needs were generally greater than those of most American victims—were not invited. Some of them would attend separate sessions held later in Nairobi and Dar es Salaam.

10. David Kaplan and Stephan Lovgren, "On Terrorism's Trail," *U.S. News and World Report*, November 23, 1998, p. 30.

11. "FBI and Local Police Raid a Nairobi Hotel," *New York Times*, August 19, 1998, p. A6.

12. U.S. Says Suspect Does Not Admit Role in Bombings or Ties to Saudi," *New York Times*, August 18, 1998, p. 7.

13. Kenyan newspapers initially reported that Pakistani authorities permitted U.S. officials to fly Odeh to Nairobi, although controversy arose over when, precisely, U.S. officials gained access to and custody of Odeh, and they refused to comment on their involvement in his transport. Once back in Kenya, Odeh clammed up. The FBI admitted that he denied any role in the bombings, although they still suspected him. It may have been evidence brought from a raid on his coastal Kenyan home that convinced Odeh to speak more openly with the FBI. But more likely it was fear for his young, pregnant wife, who had been detained and brought to the very jail where he was being held.

14. Those in custody at that time included Mamdouh Mahmud Salim, Wadih el Hage, Mohamed Sadeek Odeh, and Mohamed Rashed Daoud al-'Owhali. Khalid Fawwaz was in custody in the United Kingdom.

15. Those indicted initially included Osama bin Laden, Muhammad Atef, Momdouh Mahmud Salim, Wadih el Hage, Fazul Abdullah Mohammed, Mohamed Sadeek Odeh, Mohamed Rashed Daoud al-'Owhali, Mustafa Mohamed Fadhil, Khalfan Khamis Mohamed, Ahmed Khalfan Ghailani, Fahid Mohamed Ally Msalam, and Sheikh Ahmed Salim Swedan. Superceding indictments included Ayman al Zawahiri, Khaled al Fawwaz, and Ali Mohamed.

16. Title 18 USC, Section 2332(a). Count 1 of the Superceding Indictment reads as follows: "It was a part and an object of said conspiracy that the defendants, and others known and unknown, would and did: (i) murder United States nationals anywhere in the world, including in the United States, (ii) kill United States nationals employed by the United States military who were serving in their official capacity in Somalia and on the Saudi Arabian peninsula; (iii) kill United States nationals employed at the United States Embassies in Nairobi, Kenya, and Dar es Salaam, Tanzania, including Internationally Protected Persons; and (iv) engage in conduct to conceal the activities and means and methods of the co-conspirators by, among other things, establishing front companies, providing false identity and travel documents, engaging in coded correspondence and providing false information to the authorities in various countries."

17. During the trial a ruling established that this law could apply to acts committed in the United States as part of the conspiracy *U.S. v. Bin Laden* 93 F. Supp 2d 484.

18. Count 1, Section e of original indictment, p. 10; Count 1, Sections t and v, p. 14; and Count 1, Section eee., p. 21, respectively.

19. Title 18, U.S. Code, Sections 844 (f) (1); and Title 18, U.S. Code, Section 844 (f) (3).

20. Count 2 of the superceding indictment. The charges of kidnapping and maiming were later dropped as per a ruling. Title 18, U.S. Code, Sections 956 (a) (1) and (a) (2) (A).

21. These charges, in Count 3 of the superceding indictment, refer to the killing of U.S. nationals, military personnel, and Internationally Protected Persons. Title 18, U.S. Code, Sections 1111, 1114, 1116, and 1117.

22. Count 4 of the superceding indictment. Title 18, U.S. Code, Sections 2332a(a) (1) and (a) (3); Count 5 of the superceding indictment. Title 18, U.S. Code, Sections 844(f) (1), (f) (3), and 844 (n); and Count 6 of the superceding indictment. Title 18, U.S. Code, Sections 2155(a) and (b).

23. *Maclean's* reports those arrested as six Iraqis, six Sudanese, a Somali, and a Turk. D'Arcy Jenish and William Lowther ("The Terror Trial: Investigators Hunt for Clues to East Africa's Bombings," *MacLean's*, August 24, 1998, p. 22).

24. It was thought that the water truck had visited a garage owned by Thomas Lymo earlier that day. Rumors also circulated that the bomb had been built at his garage (Obwogo Subiri, *The Bombs That Shook Nairobi and Dar: A Story of Pain and Betrayal* [Nairobi, Kenya: Obwago & Family Publishers, 1999], p. 69).

25. Investigators kept this quiet for a few days, hoping to encourage the perpetrators to correct the false story. Another rumor, reported in Kenya's newspapers, explained that three accomplices were killed in the Nairobi blast. Reports about the bomb being constructed in the tiny rooms at the Hilltop Hotel were similarly unsubstantiated. See Robert Frank, "FBI, Kenya Raid Hotel; Militants Vow Attacks," *Wall Street Journal*, August 20, 1998, p. 11.

26. Evarist Shija, "Cleared Dar Bomb Suspects Not Yet Released by Police," *The African*, August 19, 1998, p. 3.

27. In a trial held several years later in Tanzania, Hemed was acquitted of charges relating to the bombings.

28. A similar ceremony was held in Nairobi. Kenyan victims without embassy connections and the Kenyan public attended a large memorial service. Kenya named August 7 a national holiday.

29. Investigators soon found the small piece of metal containing a vehicle identification number from a Nissan refrigeration truck and traced the truck from its manufacture in Japan through five owners to someone assumed to be associated with the bombers.

30. Those killed were Yusuf Shamte Ndange, Abdallah Mohamed, Abbas William Mwila, Bakari Nyumbu, Mtendeje Rajabu, Mohamed Mahundi Ramadani, Elias Elisha, Doto Selemani, Saidi Rogath, Hassan Siad Halane, and Abdurahman Abdallah.

31. Martha Minow has written eloquently about the role of monuments in marking tragedy; see her *Between Vengeance and Forgiveness: Facing History after Genocide and Mass Violence* (Boston: Beacon, 1998). For a discussion of victims' disputes over memorializing Pan Am flight 103, see Allan Gerson and Jerry Adler, *The Price of Terror* (New York: Harper Collins, 2001).

32. "Islamist Group Urges Moslems to Reject US Reward for Bombing," *The African*, August 13, 1998, p. 18.

33. " 'Security Threat' NGOs Closed," *Daily Nation*, September 9, 1998, p. 1. The organizations closed initially were Help Africa People, Mercy Relief Inter-

national, the Al Haramain Foundation, the International Islamic Relief Organization, and Ibrahim bin Abdul Aziz al Ibrahim Foundation.

34. *Daily Nation*, "Muslims' Fury at NGOs Closure," Thursday, September 10, 1998, p. 1. This was the reaction of Prof. Abdulghafur el Busaidy of the Supreme Council of Kenyan Muslims.

35. Dr. Timothy Njoya, "Njoya: Leave Muslims Alone." *Daily Nation*, Monday, September 21, 1998, p. 1.

36. Paul Muite, a prominent lawyer and politician, and others condemned what they saw as political motivations behind the order. Several weeks prior to the ban, Daniel arap Moi, Kenya's president, had remarked that he was considering a ban on nongovernmental development organizations that engaged in national politics. Lawyers suspected that, with the excuse of "security," the government was making good on this threat. They were furious that the United States would collude in the government's attempt to weaken civil society and political opposition. In power for more than two decades, Moi's ruling party had a long history of political repression.

CHAPTER 3

1. Reporters from the *New York Times*, National Public Radio, Cable News Network, and Associated Press were routinely present.

2. The primary sketch artist was Christine Cornell, well known to New York courts.

3. "Transcript of *USA Vs. Osama bin Laden et. al.*," (2001), p. 20. Hereafter page numbers in the transcript will be cited parenthetically within the text.

4. Many excellent works have been written on stories in court, including works by Burns, Conley and O'Barr, Goldman, Matoesian, and Ewick and Silbey. Robert P. Burns, *A Theory of the Trial* (Princeton, N.J.: Princeton University Press, 1999); John M. Conley and William M. O'Barr, *Rules versus Relationships: The Ethnography of Legal Discourse*, Law and Legal Discourse series, ed. idem (Chicago: University of Chicago Press, 1990); idem, *Just Words: Law, Language, and Power*, Law and Legal Discourse series, ed., idem (Chicago: University of Chicago Press, 1998); Patricia Ewick and Susan Silbey, *The Common Place of Law: Stories from Everyday Life* (Chicago: University of Chicago Press, 1998); Laurence Goldman, *Talk Never Dies*: The Language of Huli Disputes (London: Tavistock, 1983); and Gregory Matoesian, *Law and the Language of Identity: Discourse in the William Kennedy Smith Trial* (Oxford: Oxford University Press, 2001).

5. Robert P. Burns, *A Theory of the Trial* (Princeton, N.J.: Princeton University Press, 1999).

6. According to Burns, "It is this double helix of narrative and argument that a lawyer calls 'my theory of the case.' . . . It omits much of the concreteness of what the trial will reveal; it is a 'cut' into the evidence. Good lawyers understand what 'cut' to make, which inspired simplification to pursue. They also understand that the trier of fact will come to understand that even the best 'factual theories' are rather too simple. The theory of the case is thus a simple, plausible, coherent, legally sufficient narrative that can easily be integrated

with a moral theme." (ibid., pp. 36–37). Burns goes on to argue that the jury's task of weighing the various theories of the case is an important aspect of trials, and justifies the jury system and the trial process despite their unwieldy and unpredictable aspects.

7. See Susan F. Hirsch, *Pronouncing and Persevering: Gender and the Discourses of Disputing in an African Islamic Court*, Law and Legal Discourse series, ed. William M. O'Barr and John Conley (Chicago: University of Chicago Press, 1998).

8. Under Muslim law, a husband is required to maintain his wife, which includes providing her with food, shelter, clothing, and other necessities.

9. Women tended to win for a number of reasons. First, they went to court only when their circumstances were dire. Also, the judges tried to discipline men in the community for political reasons. See Hirsch, *Pronouncing and Persevering*.

10. The scholarly field known as procedural justice has established that an ordinary person involved in a legal dispute can benefit from the opportunity to tell his or her side of the story to the judge, jury, and public. Even plaintiffs who lose a claim feel satisfaction from having participated. But satisfaction comes only if the process seemed fair, only if they feel that their problem received appropriate attention. Moreover, scholars have shown, at a fine level of detail, that litigants are most satisfied when they get the chance to tell their stories in court without interruption from objections or questions. See, for example, Conley and O'Barr, *Just Words*.

11. Mary Jo White, U.S. Attorney for New York's Southern District, had held that office during the earlier prosecution of the 1993 bombing of the World Trade Center. She very closely followed the embassy bombings case, sitting at the back of the court on some crucial days.

12. In fact, some of the deceased were citizens of nations other than these three, including Somalia and Eritrea.

13. Throughout most of the trial the defense teams included the following lead attorneys: for al-'Owhali—Fred Baugh, Fred Cohn, and Laura Gasiorowski; for Odeh—Anthony Ricco, Ed Wolford, Carl Herman, and Sandra Babcock; for Mohamed—David Ruhnke and David Stern; and for el Hage—Sam Schmidt and Joshua Dratel. Stern happened to be in court as a public defender the day K.K. was charged. Other than Stern and Ruhnke, everyone had been appointed to replace original counsel.

14. Anyone called for jury duty who had been listening to the radio or reading the newspapers in the days before jury selection might have been aware of the restraints on the defendants. In interviews conducted after the trial by the *New York Times* journalist Ben Weiser, jurors said that they had known about the shackles but felt that the many federal marshals standing in court, near the defendants, conveyed more directly the assumed danger they posed.

15. Schmidt argued in court: "Now, this case has often been called the embassy bombings, a shorthand term, because the government alleges this conspiracy ended up with the bombing of two embassies. Of course that was a great tragedy, but this case is more than that, because if it was just the embassy bombings I would not be here talking to you this morning, because Mr. el

Hage, and the government has conceded, was not involved in either of the embassy bombings" (p. 50).

16. Schneider did not remain on K.K.'s defense team.

17. Attorney Fred Baugh contested just one substantive issue when he cross-examined Staff Sergeant Briehl, who looked as though he could handle the pressure. Baugh asked him whether the gate to the embassy parking area had been open when he arrived. Swift objections stopped this line of questioning, which raised the issue of whether the embassy had had adequate protection before the bombing.

18. Less clear is whether victims of crime benefit similarly from narrating their stories in court. The philosopher Susan Brison, writing about her experience testifying in a French court against the man accused of raping her, concludes that it was difficult, but important, for her to tell her story. Immediately after her testimony she felt a "sudden unclenching" that allowed her to reposition the story of her trauma which she had been carrying around for so long. She conjectures: "Perhaps there is a psychological imperative, analogous to the legal imperative, to keep telling one's story until it is heard. After the story has been heard and acknowledged, one can let it go, or unfreeze it" (*Aftermath: Violence and the Remaking of the Self* [Princeton, N.J.: Princeton University Press, 2002], p. 110). As Brison acknowledges, her experience testifying was unusual. Many rape victims who face defense cross-examination in the American legal system routinely find themselves demeaned and their stories discredited, even after, as Gregory Matoesian showed with respect to the William Kennedy Smith trial, rape shield laws have been instituted to protect them. See Matoesian, *Law and the Language of Identity*. Nor can other crime victims assume that telling their stories in court will be a healing or even a positive experience. Hostile cross-examination, and fear of the formality and unfamiliar language, can make the experience profoundly alienating. Yet Brison's experience, which affirms that being heard, empathetically, helps victims move toward healing, holds out a tantalizing possibility at the same time as it sets up a risk of disappointment for those who testify in court.

CHAPTER 4

1. The Hart-Rudman Commission, as part of the U.S. Commission on National Security in the Twenty-first Century, issued a report in three phases. The final phase was published in late January 2001.

2. Among the authors writing about al Qaeda operations, Yossef Bodansky was virtually alone in emphasizing the connection between the group and Iran, negotiated largely through Sudan. See Yossef Bodansky, *Bin Laden: The Man Who Declared War on America* (Rocklin, Calif.: Forum, 2001).

3. In the post–9/11 literature on terrorism, some authors argue that the FBI seriously mishandled Ali Mohamed and probably failed to retrieve adequate information from him in a timely way (Lance Williams and Erin McCormick, "Al Qaeda Terrorist Worked with FBI; Ex-Silicon Valley Resident Plotted Embassy Attacks," *San Francisco Chronicle*, November 4, 2001). For an account of

his guilty plea, see Benjamin Weiser, "Bin Laden Linked to Embassy Blast by an Ex-Soldier," *New York Times*, October 21, 2000, A1.

4. The defendants were charged with four separate conspiracies: conspiracy to kill Americans, conspiracy to use weapons of mass destruction against American targets, conspiracy to kill officers and employees of the U.S. government, and conspiracy to destroy American buildings with explosives.

5. The use of conspiracy charges was similar to what had occurred during the trial of the 1993 bombing of the World Trade Center, as described by Robert E. Precht in *Defending Mohammad: Justice on Trial* (Ithaca, N.Y.: Cornell University Press, 2003). On criminal conspiracy generally, see Mia V. Carpiniello and Abigail Roberts, "Federal Criminal Conspiracy," *American Criminal Law Review* 37 (2000).

6. The mujaheddin were Muslim fighters recruited from many countries to drive the Soviets out of Afghanistan. Although not mentioned in al Fadl's testimony, they received funding and technical assistance from the U.S. government, largely through the CIA, during the 1980s. Accounts differ as to how and when the connection between the mujaheddin and the U.S. ended, with accusations made that the U.S. failed to keep promises to provide assistance after the war.

7. He identified these leaders as Osama bin Laden, Abu Ayoub al Iraqi, Abu Ubaidah al Banshiri, Abu Hafs al Masry, Dr. Ayman al Zawahiri, and Abu Hajer al Iraqi, among others.

8. Al Qaeda's media arm was supervised by an al Qaeda member with the fitting nickname of Abu Musa al Reuter.

9. This contested concept will be explored in chapter 6.

10. The NIF, which was the Sudanese government party, was unable to reimburse al Qaeda for a major road financed and built by the group. To pay off the debt, the NIF gave al Qaeda a tannery business. Al Qaeda had many businesses in Sudan but also bad loans and low productivity. When al Fadl questioned inefficient business practices, he was told that *jihad* (struggle), not business, was al Qaeda's central goal in Sudan.

11. Al Fadl was once sent with his family to Nairobi. When they embarked on the trip, they were told that they would live there permanently. After being picked up at the Nairobi airport by another al Qaeda operative, and providing this person with some documents from the organization, al Fadl was told that he and his family would not, in fact, be staying in Kenya. The next day they boarded a flight for Pakistan and were told to remain there until further notice. Al Fadl also testified that al Qaeda leadership could be insensitive and discriminatory with respect to ethnicity and nationality. African members had complained that Arabs, especially Egyptians, were being paid more and were trusted with superior positions. Al Fadl expressed disappointment that bin Laden, after listening to their complaints, responded by making those who had complained feel that they were undermining the group's broader goals. In his testimony al Fadl admitted that the discriminatory practices—particularly with respect to salary—had motivated him to steal.

12. Al Fadl tried to get attention from Saudi Arabia, which had interests in bin Laden's activities, and, as the defense pointed out, also Israel.

13. Al Fadl had a lot to gain from doing a good job as a witness. He pled guilty to acting against the United States in 1993 by using an al Qaeda boat to smuggle weapons into Yemen, where he thought they would be deployed against U.S. troops. The U.S. government was quick to point out that the weapons had never been used for this purpose, but that al Fadl *thought* they might be allowed him to plead to working against the United States (p. 335). It appeared that this charge had been carefully crafted so that it could easily be dismissed. At the trial al Fadl expressed his hope that he would not go to jail at all (p. 530).

14. The sentencing judge would make his decision after al Fadl's appearance in the embassy bombings trial.

15. The transcript was posted each day on www.cryptome.org. The website describes its mission: "Cryptome welcomes documents for publication that are prohibited by governments worldwide, in particular material on freedom of expression, privacy, cryptology, dual-use technologies, national security, intelligence, and secret governance—open, secret and classified documents—but not limited to those" (accessed July 22, 2004).

16. The following answer was offered early on when al Fadl was asked about activities at the Farouq Mosque in New York, where he had studied before his first trip to Afghanistan: "At that time they got office help for Afghani leave during the war against Russia, and we tried to help them bring money from the Muslim brother in New York and take some papers from the Sudan—from the mosque to give to them about jihad." Prosecutor Pat Fitzgerald's follow-up—"Why don't we go through that a little bit more slowly. Can you tell the jury who you raised money from and who the money was for?"—was only the first of many times that the lead prosecutor patiently rephrased or repeated questions in an effort to tease out more responsive answers (p. 165).

17. In a law review article written after the trial, attorneys for Wadih el Hage asserted that at least one prosecution witness may have been using his lack of fluency in English to avoid giving a direct answer to a difficult question (Sam A. Schmidt and Joshua L. Dratel, "Turning the Tables: Using the Government's Secrecy and Security Arsenal for the Benefit of the Client in Terrorism Prosecutions," *New York Law School Law Review* 48 [2003/2004]).

18. Sam Schmidt and Joshua Dratel, attorneys for Wadih el Hage, decried the Protective Orders and other aspects of the government's "secrecy and security arsenal" (ibid., p. 76). They point out, however, that although the ability of the defense counsel was greatly compromised by these procedures, certain opportunities arose to "turn the tables" on the restrictions and, for example, gain more time to prepare or receive greater leniency from the judge in questioning or constructing the defense. They also concluded that the "bureaucratic imperatives" to conceal the information in many sensitive documents "forced the prosecutor to forego inculpatory evidence that was classified. This occurred because the classifying agency objected to revealing it or because declassification of such evidence would have necessitated the declassification of other, exculpatory classified material that was even more sensitive" (Schmidt and Dratel, "Turning the Tables," p. 88).

19. Schmidt and Dratel sum up the issues at stake in the overt act relating to the attack on U.S. troops in Somalia. The prosecution had claimed that al

Qaeda members trained Somali fighters who were thus part of the conspiracy and who committed the overt act of attacking American soldiers in Somalia. The defense countered by claiming that the Somali fighters were entirely independent of al Qaeda. Schmidt and Dratel make the point that the overt act was eventually dropped in part because their defense team planned to call an expert familiar with the attack. From their perspective, the inaccessibility of much material, because of its security classification, influenced Judge Sand to allow them to call the witness, who might not otherwise have been considered appropriate. The threat of that witness's testimony likely led the prosecution to drop the overt act relating to Somalia from the list of charges.

20. Judge Sand agreed and ordered him to describe when and where he had seen documents, heard conversations, and attended meetings before he spoke about their contents. Asking for the foundation of al Fadl's knowledge made his reliability a persistent issue and reminded everyone in court that sometimes people make declarations they cannot back up.

21. As Carl Herman pushed him to confirm a point that would help build Odeh's defense case later on, these effects leaked out disturbingly:

Herman: Did you tell American agents that Bin Laden misinterprets certain portions of the Koran to justify violent action?
Al Fadl: I really, I don't remember exactly like this.
Herman: Does it sound like something that you said?
Al Fadl: It's similar like when we talk about who's scholar in our group.
Herman: Do you understand my question?
Al Fadl: Yes.
Herman: Did you say that?
Al Fadl: If they [the government] wrote it, yes. (p. 489)

22. El Ridi was an Egyptian who grew up in Kuwait. After he met Abdallah Azzam, one of the early leaders of the mujaheddin, he went to Afghanistan out of a commitment to jihad. He developed ideological differences with the organization once bin Laden became involved. As he testified, "One of the main sticking issue was I was totally opposing the fact that any rich individual who comes to Afghanistan would control the decision making." El Ridi moved back to the United States, where he had previously attended flight school and obtained a pilot's license. In the early 1990s he had intermittent contact with al Qaeda supporters in Sudan and helped the group to obtain a plane, which he flew from Dallas to Khartoum in 1993. He delivered the keys to Osama bin Laden at a dinner also attended by Wadih el Hage.

23. Kherchtou described how he was interviewed at the airport by intelligence officers from a country other than Kenya or the United States. After talking with them for four days, and realizing that they knew a good deal about al Qaeda, he agreed to work with them against the group. Kherchtou failed to keep his side of the bargain and ended up in Morocco working for yet another country's intelligence agency. In September 2000 he came to the United States and entered into a plea agreement (pp. 1307–16).

24. Membership in al Qaeda did not automatically make one a co-conspirator. Being a co-conspirator rested on whether an individual had agreed to participate in conspiring toward an illegal goal.

25. Precht, *Defending Mohammad*, 35.

26. As Precht writes, "Conspiracy law is the closest that Anglo-American jurisprudence comes to creating a crime of guilt by association. It encourages juries to look at a defendant not as an individual but as a representative of a larger group" (ibid., p. 34). Although admitting that "the line between associational freedom and conspiracy is not always crisp and certain," legal scholar Cass Sunstein worries about potential civil liberties violations, especially when religion is among the group's reference points. Yet he defends the use of conspiracy charges, especially in response to terrorist violence. As "the dark side of freedom of association," a conspiracy pushes those who join it into adopting extreme positions, a point Sunstein makes using psychological studies. Conspiracy is bad in and of itself, and should be charged separately from the crimes it facilitates (e.g., bombings, murder, etc.) because the "act of conspiracy has an independent effect, that of moving people in more extreme directions" (Cass Sunstein, "Why They Hate Us: The Role of Social Dynamics," *Harvard Journal of Law and Public Policy* 25 [2002]: p. 430).

27. Schmidt and Dratel point out that the protection of foreign governments is among the principles most rigidly followed as the U.S. government vets which information should be made public.

28. Haroun Fazul was a Comorian who appeared to have fled East Africa just before the embassy bombings. Authorities suspect that he returned to East Africa in the years just after the bombings and probably planned the 2002 attack on a tourist hotel outside Mombasa and on an Israeli jet taking off from the airport in Mombasa.

29. During the interview, bin Laden stated: "We declared jihad against the U.S. government because the U.S. government is unjust, criminal, and tyrannical. It has committed acts that are extremely unjust, hideous, and criminal, whether directly or through its support of the Israeli occupation of Palestine."

30. Precht, *Defending Mohammad*, p. 34.

CHAPTER 5

1. Each al Qaeda cell pursued activities in a different geographical area and consisted of four parts, including intelligence, administration, planning and preparation, and execution.

2. The primary job of these interpreters was to ensure that the defendants understood everything that was said in court. They translated the testimony of witnesses and facilitated conversations between each defendant and his attorneys. They also interpreted for East African observers who listened through headsets.

3. Investigators traced the package and then used DNA from Ahmed's family members to identify the driver's remains.

4. Writing in an editorial about the reforms needed to protect criminal defendants, especially those facing capital offenses, Thomas Sullivan and Scott Turow, who served together on the board charged with examining the Illinois death penalty law, argue that police interrogations should routinely be videotaped, a finding the board also endorsed. See Thomas Sullivan and Scott

Turow, "Taping Interrogations a Much-Needed Reform," *Chicago Tribune*, May 6, 2003, p. 23.

5. In further exploring the puzzling question of why K.K. would confess to so much, Stern asked Abby, "Did he ask you what benefit that would be to him?" Her reply, "We told him we could promise him no benefit, so no, he didn't ask" (p. 143).

6. Roger Shuy makes the point that some people confess even to crimes they have not committed in order to create a certain image of themselves: "Such confessors are more concerned with their macho image and tough guy reputation than with the punishment that is bound to accrue. Criminologists claim that some people commit crimes more out of a perverted need to take great risks, to walk on the edge. The thrill of risk taking is well known in the psychological literature, and concealment of the risk just taken deprives the person of the recognition of this admired characteristic. Secretive crimes offer only a very narrow spectrum of potential admirers because crimes are, by definition, covert" (*The Language of Confession, Interrogation, and Deception*, ed. William A. Kretzschmar, *Empirical Linguistics Series* [Thousand Oaks, Calif.: SAGE, 1998], p. 6).

7. Before cooperating, al-'Owhali insisted that the American investigators guarantee that he would be taken to the United States. They consulted with their superiors and created a document indicating that they would attempt to do so, with the Kenyan government's cooperation, but could not guarantee it. Al-'Owhali signed two versions of this document. During the course of these discussions, his rights, including a Miranda warning, were explained to him more fully. Judge Sand admitted into evidence the statements made after those discussions.

8. The exact term would be "non-resident alien suspects."

9. Frank Tuerkheimer notes that this is a "hard-line" departure from some previous case law and yet sees a trend toward this position in intervening cases; see idem, "Globalization of U.S. Law Enforcement: Does the Constitution Come Along?" *Houston Law Review* 39 (2002): 350. See *USA v. Osama bin Laden et al.*, 132 F. Supp. 2d 168, 30 (2001).

10. As Tuerkheimer notes, "What is perhaps most uplifting about Judge Sand's decision in *bin Laden* is his refusal to be cowed by the government's apocalyptic claims that its efforts at effectively prosecuting transnational crime would be hamstrung if the rule were otherwise. Certainly, where hundreds of deaths are involved, as was the case in *bin Laden*, the temptation to assent to aggressive law enforcement techniques might be tempting. . . . The end result buttresses the trial court's wisdom in remaining unmoved by the government's dire predictions, and may undermine the government's credibility when it makes similar assertions in a future setting where it may have more basis to do so" ("Globalization of U.S. Law Enforcement," p. 350).

11. This ruling has sparked considerable debate on issues that are much contested in the post–9/11 context. See Tuerkheimer, "Globalization of U.S. Law Enforcement." Contra Sand's ruling, M.K.B. Darmer proposes a foreign interrogation exception to *Miranda*, which would relieve agents acting abroad from informing suspects of their rights prior to questioning ("Beyond bin Laden and Lindh: Confessions Law in an Age of Terrorism," *Cornell Journal of Law and*

Public Policy 12 [2003]: 353–54). Other legal scholars have argued that U.S. protections of rights need not travel abroad. See, for example, Mark A. Godsey, "Miranda's Final Frontier—the International Arena: A Critical Analysis of United States v. bin Laden, and a Proposal for a New Miranda Exception Abroad," *Duke Law Journal* 51 (2002).

12. Daniel arap Moi followed Kenya's first president Jomo Kenyatta. Under Moi's leadership, Kenya's ruling party, the Kenya African National Union (KANU) consolidated power, banned the formation of opposition parties, and punished (often through detention) those who spoke out against the government.

13. One call in 1997 linked Wadih el Hage to Mohamed Atef, bin Laden's military commander.

14. The content of some phone calls indicated that cell members realized the lines were tapped. In al Qaeda code, one member asked cell member Haroun, "How is your telephone? Do I get a headache if I use it?" (from Gov. Exhibit 223A-T).

CHAPTER 6

1. Executions were becoming less frequent throughout the 1960s in the United States. In 1972 the Supreme Court decision in *Furman v. Georgia*, 408 U.S. 238 (1972), struck down all existing death penalty statutes. The decision in *Gregg v. Georgia*, 428 U.S. 153 (1976), reversed *Furman* and executions began again in many jurisdictions.

2. Prosecutors had hoped to charge Odeh with capital crimes but, presumably, lacked the evidence to do so.

3. Trying the cases separately would have meant mounting two or more trials using much of the same evidence at considerably more government expense. Dilemmas regarding, for example, which case to try first and how to avoid publicity would likely have delayed the trial. Moreover, prosecutors were presumably unwilling to reveal evidence in an initial trial that would help the remaining defendants prepare for later prosecutions.

4. As a colleague on another defense team admitted, "We trusted Ruhnke." Yet Schmidt and Dratel make the point that the voir dire process was very difficult for the non-capital defendants (Sam A. Schmidt and Joshua L. Dratel, "Turning the Tables: Using the Government's Secrecy and Security Arsenal for the Benefit of the Client in Terrorism Prosecutions," *New York Law School Law Review* 48 [2003/2004].)

5. The Supreme Court decision in 1991 in *Payne v. Tennessee*, 501 U.S. 808 (1991) affirmed the constitutionality of victim impact statements in penalty phases. The *Payne* decision is a startling example of the expansion of the victims' rights movement into all areas of a murder trial, and of the volatility of the Court which had, only a few years before, stood firm against impact evidence in capital cases. In the large literature in this area, see, for example, Susan A. Bandes, "Empathy, Narrative, and Victim Impact Statements," *University of Chicago Law Review* 63 (1996); Vivian Berger, "*Payne* and Suffering—a Personal Reflection and a Victim-Centered Critique," *Florida State University*

Law Review 20 (1992); Jennifer Culbert, "The Sacred Name of Pain: The Role of Victim Impact Evidence in Death Penalty Sentencing Decisions," in *Pain, Death, and the Law*, ed. Austin Sarat (Ann Arbor: University of Michigan Press, 2001); Paul Gewirtz, "Victims and Voyeurs: Two Narrative Problems at the Criminal Trial," in *Law's Stories: Narrative and Rhetoric in the Law*, ed. Paul Gewirtz and Peter Brooks (New Haven: Yale University Press, 1996); Angela Harris, "The Jurisprudence of Victimhood," *Supreme Court Review* 77 (1991); Lynne Henderson, "The Wrongs of Victims' Rights," *Stanford Law Review* 37, no. 937 (1985); Robert Jay Lifton and Greg Mitchell, *Who Owns Death? Capital Punishment, the American Conscience, and the End of Executions* (New York: Morrow, 2000); Wayne A. Logan, "Through the Past Darkly: A Survey of the Uses and Abuses of Victim Impact Evidence in Capital Trials," *Arizona Law Review* 41 (1999); Martha Minow, "Surviving Victim Talk," *UCLA Law Review* 40 (1993); Austin Sarat, *Pain, Death, and the Law*, Law, Meaning, and Violence series, ed. Martha Minow, Elaine Scarry, and Austin Sarat (Ann Arbor: University of Michigan Press, 2001); and Austin Sarat, *When the State Kills: Capital Punishment and the American Condition* (Princeton, N.J.: Princeton University Press, 2001).

6. See, generally, Scott Turow, *Ultimate Punishment: A Lawyer's Reflections on Dealing with the Death Penalty* (New York: Farrar, Straus, and Giroux, 2003).

7. El Hage still faced five counts of terrorist conspiracy and more than twenty counts of perjury and false statements.

8. For more details, see Benjamin Weiser, "Reporter's Notebook: Finding Time for Pet Pictures at the Bombings Trial," *New York Times*, April 30, 2001, p. B5.

9. A. J. Arberry, *The Koran: Interpreted* (New York: MacMillan, 1955).

10. Abou el Fadl, *Rebellion and Violence in Islamic Law* (Cambridge: Cambridge University Press, 2001), p. 22.

11. The Koran also mentions other possible punishments including exile and denial of inheritance rights. See M. Bassiouni, "Quesas Crimes," in *The Islamic Criminal Justice System*, ed. M. Bassiouni (London: Oceana, 1982), p. 204.

12. Some scholars note that it is important for the individual giving the punishment to be trained to cause only an appropriate degree of pain to the condemned.

13. Compensation for a female is less than that for a male. See Bassiouni, "Quesas Crimes," p. 209.

14. "It was by some mercy of God that thou wast gentle to them; hadst thou been harsh and hard of heart, they would have scattered from about thee. So pardon them, and pray forgiveness for them, and take counsel with them in the affair; and when thou art resolved, put thy trust in god; surely God loves those who put their trust" (III: 159) (Arberry, *The Koran: Interpreted*, p. 93).

15. The application of these measures against women, including pregnant women who were allowed to deliver before facing lashes or death, came in for especially ardent condemnation.

16. Aharon Layish and Gabriel R. Warburg, *The Reinstatement of Islamic Law in Sudan under Numayri*, Studies in Islamic Law and Society series, ed. Ruud Peters and Bernard Weiss (Leiden: Brill, 2002).

17. Postcolonial Kenya has a death penalty, and, since the early 1960s, thousands of individuals convicted of murder and armed robbery have been sen-

tenced to die. A very small number have been executed, the last in 1987 when two convicted coup plotters were hanged.

18. Wadih el Hage had also made a similar statement to FBI agent Robert Miranda when interrogated about his views on killing civilians.

19. Odeh borrowed money from his father to pay for further schooling. Then, on the advice of a sheikh, he decided to use the money to travel to Pakistan to join the struggles in that region.

20. The many achievements of Imam Siraj Wahaj are noted online at http://onlineislamicstore.com/sirajwahhaj.html.

21. As the anthropologist Lawrence Rosen describes, many Muslim societies treat individuals as "situated persons in a variety of particular encounters" rather than as abstractions (*The Justice of Islam* [Oxford: Oxford University Press, 2000]).

22. In his statement Odeh distinguished between better and worse bombings, calling the Nairobi bombing a "blunder" and, by comparison, the Khobar Towers a "hundred times better."

23. Numerous scholars have written about the concept of war in Islam. See, for example, Jean Elshtain, *Just War against Terror: The Burden of American Power in a Violent World* (New York: Basic Books, 2003); Abdulaziz A. Sachedina, "The Development of *Jihad* in Islamic Revelation and History," in *Cross, Crescent, and Sword: The Justification and Limitation of War in Western and Islamic Tradition*, ed. James Turner Johnson and John Kelsay, *Contributions to the Study of Religion* (New York: Greenwood, 1990); Abdulaziz A. Sachedina, "From Defensive to Offensive Warfare: The Use and Abuse of *Jihad* in the Muslim World," in *Religion, Law, and the Role of Force: A Study of Their Influence on Conflict and on Conflict Resolution*, ed. J. I. Coffey and Charles T. Mathewes (Ardsley, N.Y.: Transnational, 2002).

24. A number of victims who are opposed to the death penalty say that they would rather seek vengeance as an individual than have the state do the job for them. They also admit that this kind of private violence is not possible or prudent.

CHAPTER 7

1. *Payne v. Tennessee*, 501 U.S. 808 (1991).

2. Supreme Court decisions in *Payne v. Tennessee* and several other cases broadened the concept of "victim," allowing family members not present at the crime scene to testify as to the impact on them of a loved one's death.

3. *Booth v. Maryland*, 482 U.S. 496 (1987).

4. See, for example, Susan Brison, *Aftermath: Violence and the Remaking of the Self* (Princeton, N.J.: Princeton University Press, 2002).

5. See Jennifer Culbert, "The Sacred Name of Pain: The Role of Victim Impact Evidence in Death Penalty Sentencing Decisions," in *Pain, Death, and the Law*, ed. Austin Sarat (Ann Arbor: University of Michigan Press, 2001).

6. The Supreme Court decision in *Payne v. Tennessee* established that the sensibilities of surviving victims are an important and relevant impact of the crime. Prosecutor Garcia argued as follows: "Especially the photograph of the body lying outside the embassy, this is not a government photograph. This is what the scene looked like as other victims were walking out of the embassy. This is what happened in Dar es Salaam and this is an impact on the survivors, as well as the individual who was killed in this manner depicted in the photograph. There were 11 people killed in Dar es Salaam. These photographs show that and they also show the impact. . . . Sometimes it is seen in light of the Nairobi bombing but it is still a case of mass murder. I think these photos are relevant and restrained and that the jury should see them" (p. 6353).

7. For discussions of emotion in relation to narrating trauma, see Susan A. Bandes, "Empathy, Narrative, and Victim Impact Statements," *University of Chicago Law Review* 63 (1996); idem, ed., *The Passions of Law*, Critical America series, ed. Richard Delgado and Jean Stefanic (New York and London: New York University Press, 1999); Vivian Berger, "*Payne* and Suffering—a Personal Reflection and a Victim-Centered Critique," *Florida State University Law Review* 20 (1992); Brison, *Aftermath*; Culbert, "The Sacred Name of Pain."

8. Garcia phrased the gateway factors as follows: "1. That the defendant intentionally killed the victim or victims. 2. That the defendant intentionally inflicted serious bodily injury that resulted in death. 3. [That the] defendant intentionally participated in an act contemplating that the life of a person would be taken or that lethal force would be used, and the victim or victims of a particular count died as a result of the act, or the defendant engaged in violent conduct, knowing that the acts created grave risks of death to a person such that the act constituted a reckless disregard for human life, and the victims died as a result of the act" (p. 7150). "The statutory aggravating factors were: Death during the commission of another crime, substantial planning and premeditation, grave risk of death to other persons, and multiple killings and attempted killings" (p. 7157).

9. See Berger, "*Payne* and Suffering."

10. Ashraf Rushdy, "Exquisite Corpse," in *Best American Essays, 2001*, ed. Kathleen Norris (Boston and New York: Houghton Mifflin, 2001), p. 261–69; quote at 269.

11. "All Things Considered," National Public Radio broadcast, June 19, 2001.

CHAPTER 8

1. Salim had behaved erratically in his early court appearances. He balled up paper and put it in his ears; he insulted his attorneys and spoke out of turn. Testimony indicated that he was angry and demoralized after his request for new counsel was denied.

2. Each correction guard in the MCC wears a body alarm that sends a distress signal if he or she falls.

3. When I interviewed him months after the trial ended, defense attorney David Ruhnke said that at first his team was denied access to K.K. after the attack. Then, for a very long time, K.K. refused to speak about what had happened. His behavior reminded Ruhnke of the kind of jailhouse solidarity seen in the 1960s among political activists who refused to inform on one another.

4. Salim's attorneys had each testified that they were surprised to see that Salim's eye did not appear badly injured when they saw him just a few days after the incident.

5. The prosecution showed videotapes of prisoners attacking guards at maximum security prisons; some attacks took place in the highly secure Supermax facilities that would most certainly house the convicted embassy bombers. As a counter, the defense argued that, if properly implemented, Supermax security procedures would guard against such incidents, which are rare.

6. Dr. Jerrold Post had a long career of studying terrorists. In his written statement and testimony, he distinguished three different types: those fighting for their homeland in the names of their forebears (e.g., the IRA); those fighting against the old ways (e.g., younger generation Marxist groups); and religious terrorists that emerged in the 1970s. Although the latter could be any religion, he had focused on Islamic groups.

7. When I later interviewed him, Post said that after his training K.K. had been offered a position in the Kashmir conflict between India and Pakistan. Understanding it as a guerilla-type military operation, he refused, because he wanted a more conventionally military mission that would involve defending innocent Muslims.

8. When I interviewed Post, he said that K.K. had burst into tears when David Ruhnke showed him pictures of the victims.

9. Established in 1947, the extradition treaty between the United States and South Africa did not compel the South African government to secure a guarantee that the U.S. would not seek the death penalty. However, just prior to K.K.'s arrest, the two nations had signed a new treaty that would have allowed South Africa to refuse extradition unless it received assurances that the death penalty would not be sought or imposed. Although signed, the treaty had not yet been ratified at the time of K.K.'s deportation.

10. Many months later Salim was sentenced to thirty-two years in prison for his role in the assault on Officer Pepe.

11. Hannah Arendt, *Eichman in Jerusalem: A Report on the Banality of Evil* (New York: Penguin, 1963), p. 5.

12. David Parkin, "Blank Banners and Islamic Consciousness in Zanzibar," in *Questions of Consciousness*, ed. Anthony Cohen and N. Rapport (London: Routledge, 1995), p. 203.

13. Aryeh Oded discusses several incidents in Kenya, including those associated with the rise of the Islamic Party of Kenya (IPK) in the early 1990s (*Islam and Politics in Kenya* [Boulder: Lynne Rienner, 2000]). In 1997 I witnessed a parade in which young boys and teens from a religious school carried signs with anti-U.S. and anti-Israel slogans. When my husband questioned their teacher about the signs, he was told that a foreign donor to the school had asked that they be carried and that the young people did not know their meaning.

CHAPTER 9

1. Had the date for sentencing not been changed in early August—moved from mid-September to early October—the attacks of 9/11 would have appeared to be a direct response to the trial's outcome.

2. The debate over whether sensitive information had been leaked through the trial or another means raged on for years. See Glenn Kessler, "File the Bin Laden Phone Leak under 'Urban Myth,' " *Washington Post*, December 22, 2005, P. A2.

3. Many of former President Clinton's advisors counter that they made extraordinary attempts to eliminate bin Laden and other al Qaeda members, and to reduce the network's ability to operate. See, for example, Madeleine Albright and Bill Woodward, *Madam Secretary* (New York: Miramax Books, 2003); Daniel Benjamin and Stephen Simon, *The Age of Sacred Terror* (New York: Random House, 2002); Richard A. Clarke, *Against All Enemies: Inside America's War on Terror* (New York: Free Press, 2004).

4. Kenyan families were already bracing for the shock that would come once the U.S. government's commitment to fund three years of school fees for victims' children ended. Some later staged protests.

5. In the months after the trial, the *New York Times* journalist Ben Weiser conducted extensive interviews with the jurors and found that they had split on several issues. One juror felt that Jews had been al Qaeda's target along with Americans. As a Jewish American, the juror was afraid for what might transpire were the defendants to be executed. Weiser's articles revealed that one juror had sought information about legal terms on the Internet, and another had received counseling from her pastor on the issue of the death penalty. Defendants el Hage, al-'Owhali, and Odeh have cited jury misconduct as grounds for appeal of the trial court's decision. See Benjamin Weiser, "Jury Behavior Raises Issues in Terror Case," *New York Times*, January 16, 2003; and idem, "A Jury Torn and Fearful in 2001 Terrorism Trial," *New York Times*, January 5, 2003.

6. Austin Sarat, *When the State Kills: Capital Punishment and the American Condition* (Princeton, N.J.: Princeton University Press, 2001), p. 24.

7. Abdullah Saleh Abdullah, apprehended in East Africa, was alleged to have been instrumental in the embassy bombings. The Kenyan press reported his capture and handover to U.S. authorities, but the U.S. government has had no comment on his whereabouts.

8. For instance, the trial of Zacharias Moussaoui, the only individual facing trial in the United States for the 9/11 attacks, has been delayed over these very issues.

9. Prosecutors claim that it was not until 2002 that they learned of the existence of the videotapes of the interviews with al Fadl. Counter to standard procedures for handling an individual in witness protection, federal marshalls, apparently acting without the knowledge of prosecutors, had taped the interviews.

10. Jean Bethke Elshtain, *Just War against Terror: The Burden of American Power in a Violent World* (New York: Basic Books, 2003).

11. As political scientist Joel Barkan argues, when asked by the U.S. to play a major role in the war on terror, Kenya's fragile leadership was ill-prepared for the task given a history of ethnic conflict and enormous economic and security problems. Nevertheless, over the past few years, Kenyan police have come to the U.S. for training, the U.S. military has used Kenya's ports and airfields, and FBI agents have worked closely with Kenya's new U.S.-funded anti-terrorism squad. See Joel D. Barkan, "Kenya after Moi," *Foreign Affairs* 83, no. 1 (2004), p. 97.

12. Giovanna Borradori, *Philosophy in a Time of Terror: Dialogues with Jurgen Habermas and Jacques Derrida* (Chicago: University of Chicago Press, 2004), 97.

13. Feisal Abdul Rauf, *What's Right with Islam: A New Vision for Muslims and the West* (San Francisco: Harper-San Francisco, 2004), p. 9.

Glossary

bayat — oath
buibui — black cloak and veil worn by Swahili women
dhikri — ceremony that invoke's God's name
edda — legal waiting period for widows and divorcees
fatwa — edict by a religious authority
hadith — story, especially from Prophet Mohamed's life
heshima — respect, honor, modesty
imam — religious leader
jihad — struggle
kadhi — Muslim judge
khalifa — Muslim political authority
madrasa — religious school
marehemu — the blessed, euphemism for "the deceased"
matanga — post-funeral gathering
mujaheddin — Muslims fighters against the Soviet occupation
mwalimu — teacher, learned elder
ndugu — sibling or cousin
sheikh — learned elder
shura — advice, as in an advice council
subira — be patient
sufism — sect of Islam
waqf — charitable foundation

Index

Better
BUY B

W

**Indianapolis
Marion County
Public Library**

**Renew by Phone
269-5222**

Renew on the Web
www.imcpl.org

For General Library Information
please call 269-1700